Ali Crockett

THE WOMEN
WHO WENT ROUND
THE WORLD

THE WOMEN WHO WENT ROUND THE WORLD

EXTRAORDINARY STORIES OF TRUE PIONEERS IN GLOBAL CIRCUMNAVIGATION

SALLY SMITH

Front cover: A nineteenth-century Thomas Cook travel poster. (Pictorial Press / Alamy Stock Photo)

First published 2024

The History Press
97 St George's Place, Cheltenham,
Gloucestershire, GL50 3QB
www.thehistorypress.co.uk

© Sally Smith, 2024

The right of Sally Smith to be identified as the Author of this work has been asserted in accordance with the Copyright, Designs and Patents Act 1988.

All rights reserved. No part of this book may be reprinted or reproduced or utilised in any form or by any electronic, mechanical or other means, now known or hereafter invented, including photocopying and recording, or in any information storage or retrieval system, without the permission in writing from the Publishers.

British Library Cataloguing in Publication Data.
A catalogue record for this book is available from the British Library.

ISBN 978 1 80399 468 0

Typesetting and origination by The History Press
Printed and bound in Great Britain by TJ Books Limited, Padstow, Cornwall.

Trees for LYfe

CONTENTS

Introduction and Acknowledgements   7

1 **1767** Jeanne Baret: the first woman to go round the world. *Discovering the Bougainvillea plant and avoiding arrest*   11

2 **1791** Mary Ann Parker: the first woman to travel east round the world. *Shocking society by welcoming an Aboriginal Australian into her home*   36

3 **1846** Ida Pfeiffer: the first woman to go round the world both ways. *Sleeping next to freshly cut heads in Sarawak*   53

4 **1889** Nellie Bly and Elizabeth Bisland: the first women to race round the world. *Taking full advantage of the new steam-powered passenger liners*   86

5 **1895** Hattie McIlrath: the first woman round the world by bicycle. *Using her gun to restrain jeering hoards in rural China*   107

6 **1900** Annette Meakin: the first woman round the world by train. *Escaping from Russia to avoid the Boxer rebellion*   129

7 **1909** Harriet White Fisher: the first woman to drive round the world. *Unable to turn when the track ended in a precipice high up in Japan*   151

8 **1929** Lady Grace Drummond-Hay: the first woman round the world by air. *Meeting luxury, intrigue and danger on a giant airship*   176

9 **1963** Valentina Tereshkova: the first woman round the
world in space. *Working in a Soviet textile factory before
beginning an extraordinary journey*   209

10 **1986** Jeana Lee Yeager and Kay Cottee: the first women
  −88 round the world non-stop. *Nine days in a tiny cockpit
and 189 days tossing about in a small yacht*   229

Bibliography   249
Index   253

INTRODUCTION AND ACKNOWLEDGEMENTS

Humans have been great travellers for thousands of years but, until surprisingly modern times, some people and societies still believed that a flat Earth meant you could fall right off the edge. It was only thanks to more recent explorers, such as the crew of Ferdinand Magellan's expedition in 1519 and those on Francis Drake's westward trip in 1577, that witnesses became available to state that, following the horizon continually in one direction, they had actually ended up back where they started. The world was indeed round!

Since then, numerous other men have made a full global circumnavigation, with many of them, such as James Cook, becoming household names. For women, with their traditional roles of looking after the house and children, there were far fewer opportunities to take part in exciting expeditions.

Some, however, did manage it. According to handed-down stories, it seems that Gudrid Thorbjarnardóttir, born on an Icelandic farm in around 985 CE, visited Newfoundland and the Americas as well as heading south to visit Rome – amazing journeys for a woman in those days.

In more recent times, other women have undertaken exceptional travels and have been involved in extraordinary adventures. Many of these, women such as Lady Hester Stanhope, Marianne North,

Isabella Bird and Gertrude Bell, are well recognised in history, and their writings, stories and pictures continue to enthral us.

However, there is one group of women who have somehow been omitted from most of the history books and historical records, women who were true explorers and pioneers yet whose names are unrecognised and their stories virtually unknown.

These are the women who were the very first to go right around the world, to experience the extraordinary variety of different lives, languages and scenery across the entire globe, and then to return home with a wealth of fascinating stories and incredible tales that they could use to entertain their friends for the rest of their lives.

This book was written to finally record and properly set down the remarkable journeys made by these women; the very first women to achieve a full circumnavigation by sea and land and, more recently, in the air and in space. Some of their stories are breathtaking, others are simply hugely entertaining, but they all deserve a proper place in the history books.

Today, many women as well as men are still achieving records in various fields and, with new vehicles and breakthrough technology and equipment, there will be many fresh ways to go around the world. The fastest on foot, going solo by various means, using exciting new styles of engines and vehicles ... records will continue to be broken; but nothing can take away the achievements of the women in this book who travelled the world in such different times to become true pioneers.

Most of these women were not looking for fame or glory, so finding out the details of their journeys was in some cases very challenging indeed. Numerous people and organisations have assisted in uncovering the real events and indeed have provided evidence to ensure the information in this book is as accurate as possible. It would be impossible to thank all of them fully without writing another book! However, I would specifically like to acknowledge the wonderful and patient experts at various universities and illustrious bodies around the world, including the notable British historian and classicist Dr Christopher Stray, Honorary Research Fellow, Department of History and Classics, Swansea University, and Senior Research Fellow at the Institute of Classical Studies, University of London; Ellen Heath, Director of Research at Chicago History Museum; and Karen Pymble at the Australian National Maritime Museum, all of whom gave so much time and made so much effort to help me with my research.

When researching names and events from a long time ago, it is ridiculously exciting when one suddenly establishes contact with a direct descendant and I would seriously like to thank Jess Mortimer for all her assistance in confirming some details of her great aunt Annette Meakin, who made an extraordinary trip around the world by train in 1900, and also Rebecca Urban, whose ancestor was so involved in Harriet White Fisher's global journey by car in 1910.

Many people, including author and writer Frank Comstock, Dominique Taylor of the Canadian Museum of History and Judith Cetina, County Archivist in Cuhahoga, Ohio, were extremely generous in sharing their research across the Atlantic. I also owe thanks to my agent Andrew Lownie and to Amy Rigg and Jezz Palmer of The History Press, without whose professional advice and assistance this book would never have been completed.

Really the list is endless. All I can do is sincerely thank everyone who has been willing to give their time to help ensure that the achievements of these true women pioneers have, at last, been properly recorded for posterity.

Sally Smith
Somerset, 2024

1

1767 JEANNE BARET
THE FIRST WOMAN TO GO ROUND THE WORLD

Two hundred and fifty years ago, plants provided a major area of exciting new study. There were so many strange and unrecognised plants around the world, and wealthy people sought prestige by creating beautiful gardens and obtaining unusual and rare flora. To be a botanist was to occupy a very respected position. Expedition leaders took experienced botanists with them, and when new plants were found, they were often named after someone connected with the expedition – a huge honour indeed.

It was in an attempt to try and hush up a scandal that the beautiful and colourful Bougainvillea plant acquired its name instead of it being called the Commerson or, even more appropriately, the Jeanne Baret.

Sometimes the biggest adventures in life are had by the least likely people.

If, in the mid-1700s, someone had pointed to a poor, illiterate French peasant girl and suggested she would one day be noted in the annals of international history, there would have been few believers. How could anyone have possibly dreamed that this simple country girl, born in a remote area and brought up in abject poverty with no schooling and very limited knowledge of the wider world, would become the very first woman ever to travel right around the world?

It was certainly not the future young Jeanne Baret dreamed of in her youth. A good meal and a warm bed would probably have been her biggest desire, for when she came into this world in 1740, her family was destitute. The family home, in La Commelle, an isolated French village around 200 miles south-east of Paris, was just a small, poorly thatched wooden house with an earthen floor. Her father exhausted himself every day, working in the nearby fields, mainly for the benefit of the landowner, a local uncaring seigneur. Her mother spent her time desperately trying to keep her family fed and warm with tiny amounts of grain, worn-out clothing and often damp wood for the fire.

In such conditions, life was precarious, and before Jeanne was 7 years old, in her small home she had experienced the death of her mother, the death of a stepmother and the death of a new baby brother.

There would have been some moments of happiness, even joy perhaps, as the summer months brought light and warmth into the little community and Jeanne could join other local children collecting wood, picking fruit and searching for herbs in the calm and peaceful countryside surrounding her small home. When winter returned, however, icy winds tore into the village, forcing their stinging chill through the gaping gaps in the roughly constructed wooden house, and once again life became a cold, miserable challenge.

Things began to change when Jeanne's older sister married and left the village to set up home with her new husband in Toulon-sur-Arroux, a small town about 15 miles south of La Commelle. The following year, Jeanne's father died and her older brother brought a wife into the family and into the little house. Jeanne was still working hard to keep the family fires and food going, but she no longer felt the house was really her home. As she reached her late teens, she started thinking of a different future. Maybe her sister mentioned that there were employment opportunities in the town. In any case, on one big day in her life, Jeanne packed up her few clothes and other belongings, waved goodbye to the only home she had ever known and walked down the gravelly track heading south out of the village to join her sister in Toulon-sur-Arroux.

Catholicism was the only religion allowed in France at this time, and once Jeanne arrived in Toulon, from the very first Sunday, along with her sister and all the local people, she made her way up to the big, old church in the centre of the town. It was through the local priest, Father Beau, that Jeanne found a job that was to alter her life forever.

Father Beau's sister had recently died giving birth to a little boy. His brother-in-law, Philibert Commerson, desperately needed help in his house and also help with the motherless baby. Jeanne had found a job.

Jeanne's life had already been one of relentless hard work. Fitting into Philibert's household was not difficult; in fact it was made far easier because not only was Philibert a trained doctor with good earning potential, but he had inherited a lot of money from his dead wife. For the first time in her life, Jeanne was suddenly in a home not driven by grinding poverty. There was money for food; money for fuel, furniture and clothes. Suddenly Jeanne's life changed out of all recognition. With a huge work ethic, a gentle maternal instinct for a little motherless baby and a fascination for life in general, Jeanne soon established herself as an essential part of the household.

Initially Philibert was aloof and distant; with the death of his beloved wife, he had no time for small talk and Jeanne was just a simple servant girl employed to keep the house running. Quietly getting on with her chores, though, Jeanne couldn't help but also be drawn into Philibert's obsession with botany and natural history. In the mid-eighteenth century, medicine and botany were close partners. It is likely Jeanne already had some knowledge of local plants, as herbal remedies would have played a strong role in her youth. Philibert had carefully created a beautiful botanical garden around his house, and strolling outside with the baby, Jeanne slowly became fascinated by the huge range of unusual and beautiful plants.

It would only have needed a small question to fire up Philibert's enthusiasm. More than passionate about plants, insects and the wider natural world, he was slowly casting aside his medical career as he spent more and more time and became more and more absorbed in a total fascination in all aspects of the natural world. His name and knowledge were already becoming recognised nationally, and while he was generally a quiet, self-absorbed man, he could become almost chatty on his favourite subject.

One day, Philibert asked Jeanne to help sort out his vast collection of plant species and Jeanne was more than willing, showing a real interest in some of the new plants he had collected. Philibert started explaining to Jeanne the basics of different species, and how to organise them properly. When he found she couldn't read or write, he started teaching her the basics so that she could start cataloguing the items under the correct names.

For the first time, Jeanne was having an education, and she absorbed new facts easily and quickly. Her childhood years were disappearing into a hazy memory as she happily immersed herself in her brand-new life. Neglecting his medical practice, Philibert would often disappear for days, searching for new plant specimens and new variations. When he returned, Jeanne was there, ready to help sort and organise the new plants as well as looking after his baby and the house.

The inevitable happened. Although Philibert was older and still very reserved except when talking about plants, and although he was always very clear that Jeanne was just a servant, not an equal, their living together in such close proximity ended up in the most predictable conclusion. Jeanne, one month after she turned 24, became pregnant.

One can only assume it was Philibert's child, although this was never officially stated. But once he learned of the pregnancy, there was a lot to think about. Philibert could have simply thrown Jeanne out; he certainly had no interest in the coming child. But by now perhaps he had learned to really value the constant support from a quiet, dedicated woman who was proving increasingly useful in helping to sort and categorise his extensive collections. While Philibert still dearly missed his beloved wife, Jeanne offered a level of support and comfort that he clearly appreciated. It was never a love match – plants were now the only love in Philibert's life. But he made a decision. He would keep Jeanne on as his servant and helper. This didn't go as far as keeping the child; once the baby was born, it would have to be adopted or put in a home. But Jeanne could stay.

For Jeanne, there were few options. While she had food and a secure roof over her head, she had no savings; where could she go to raise an illegitimate child? It is likely Jeanne was also becoming attached to her employer. Either way, Philibert's option sounded the only way forward.

Once the decision had been made, Philibert felt the time had come for radical change. It was two years since his wife had died. He was now 36; he had no real interest in a career as a doctor; all he wanted to do was to pursue his absorbing fascination in all areas of botany. To really become acclaimed, to make a serious name for himself, he needed to leave this small country town. Philibert then acted fast. First, he visited his brother-in-law, the local priest Father Beau, and arranged for him to take on his first child.

He sent Jeanne to a nearby town to register her pregnancy – something that was decreed by French law – but interestingly he made sure his name was not included as the father on the official declaration.

Then he made arrangements that he hoped would really help him create a name for himself. He would move to Paris, the modern, vibrant French capital, where morality was not so ingrained and where he had good contacts.

For Jeanne, the idea of travelling to Paris must have been enthralling. As she helped pack up the household, sort out Philibert's botanical collection and get ready for the four-day coach ride, she must have been in a daze. Paris, with its mass of people, exotic buildings, huge markets and elegant women; it was to be an astonishing eye opener into a new world for Jeanne.

Philibert had rented a second-floor apartment in central Paris, just south of the river and Notre-Dame Cathedral, and not far from the Jardin des Plantes. This was already one of the world's leading botanical gardens, and as soon as they arrived, Philibert energetically pursued his acquaintances and connections.

Jeanne, in the meantime, settled in and got on with her work, learning where best to buy fresh food, keeping house and also helping Philibert with his biological records. The excitement of being in such a lively city for the first time must have been muted as Jeanne's pregnancy progressed, and it is likely her happiness ebbed further as it became clear that Philibert definitely wanted nothing to do with the baby.

As the birth of her baby approached, arrangements were made for the child to be taken into a home and then hopefully adopted. Illegitimate children were common in Paris at the time, and organising things was fairly straightforward. Nevertheless, for a gentle, caring woman like Jeanne, it must have been a dreadfully sad time. With no family to offer support, she had her little boy in a special facility for single women and then immediately handed him over to strangers. Philibert offered no support or care either; his only love was his plants.

Jeanne showed enormous resilience and, hiding her desperate sadness, returned to Philibert's flat to resume her chores. A few weeks later, Jeanne received news that her baby had died. Death in those days was far more common among babies and young children; nevertheless, Jeanne must have spent some restless, painful, tear-filled nights as she tried to recover emotionally and physically. The energy of Paris life may have helped her move forward.

A few months later, in the summer of 1765, Philibert suddenly became seriously ill, suffering chest pains and lying in bed sweating as he breathed. Along with her household duties, Jeanne now took on the role of nurse. For the rest of 1765, she simply spent her days shopping, looking after the house and looking after Philibert. Maybe this was the time when he at last began to grow fond of Jeanne, or at least value her properly for all the support and help she was giving him. Every day she would ensure his plant collection was well looked after; every day she brought him food, helped him wash, told him what was happening around the house and outside. Philibert was now relying almost totally on Jeanne's support, and it was a comfort for him to know that she now knew enough about his precious plants and collections to look after them properly.

For Jeanne, this time may well have brought about another change. From being the quiet servant running around after an educated employer, she was beginning to take a lot more control and also making most of the day-to-day decisions. She was proving to be very capable, responsible and astute. The balance between the two was changing.

Philibert was very sick, but he didn't die, and as he slowly recovered, some of his youthful energy returned. Lying in bed, he had kept up correspondence with his colleagues and other leading biologists of the day; he was also visited by some of the contacts he had already made in Paris. As his health improved, once again he pursued his ambition to be fully recognised as a biologist of real note and esteem.

The middle of the eighteenth century was still very much the age of discovery, and in Europe major powers, especially the ambitious Spanish, Portuguese, French and British with their substantial navies, were desperately trying to outdo each other in finding and then claiming new lands. It was also an era when countries everywhere were involved in intensive research in both philosophical and scientific areas.

Philibert heard through his many colleagues of an exciting new maritime voyage being organised. Commissioned by the French government and led by the renowned military man and navigator Louis-Antoine de Bougainville, it was to be a voyage of scientific discovery, with two ships sailing together to make France's first official trip right around the world. From the first, the plan attracted interest from the highest level, including from King Louis XV. It was ambitious and generously funded, for its success would ensure France was right up there helping to lead the world in global exploration and scientific discovery.

As the plans for the voyage took shape, thanks to his network of friends, his experience and his enthusiasm, Philibert's name was raised as a possible nomination for the important position of scientific botanist on the trip. Exploring and preparing reports on the flora of new lands, plus discovering and bringing back samples of exciting new plants, were vital aspects of the voyage; and with Philibert's background, he seemed a good potential candidate. He stood to receive an excellent salary as the official botanist and naturalist for the voyage. On return, he would more than likely receive huge recognition, a medal and a big bonus. It would set him up for the rest of his life.

By December 1765, Philibert had been officially asked to go on the voyage. By now it seems that Jeanne may well have been pregnant again, with a baby due the following March. This did not deter Philibert, who accepted the offer with enthusiasm and started making detailed plans immediately. They would be covering huge oceans in small ships. It would be quite a risky voyage: in the mid-eighteenth century, many ships foundered in the wild oceans, while disease and lack of provisions also accounted for many on-board deaths. Philibert was advised he should make a will. Jeanne was growing in confidence and it is likely that she now raised the issue of her future. After nursing him back to health and caring for his plant collection so well, and with the obvious close relationship between them, Jeanne was now far more than just a domestic assistant; she was beginning to show signs of being as astute and self-assured young woman. While Philibert left his main effects to his brother and his plant collections to the Royal Collection, in the will he agreed to give formal recognition to Jeanne. He named her as his housekeeper, stating that he wanted to leave her a small yearly allowance and his furniture, plus the use of the apartment he was renting for up to a year, so that she could look after and finally sort all his plants before giving them to the Royal Collection.

Having written his will, Philibert's life was then dominated by plans for the voyage. The more he learned about the trip, the more enthusiastic he became. It was to be a big expedition with two ships: the *Boudeuse* and the *Etoile*. Philibert, holding the prestigious position of official botanist, would be paid more than either of the two captains. He would sail on the smaller of the two ships, the *Etoile*, and could take an assistant/valet with him, also paid for by the expedition organisers. Philibert's job was to discover and make collections from all the countries they visited, keeping detailed records, and prepare a full account on his return of the plants he had encountered.

During the early months of 1766, preparations for the trip began in earnest, but they didn't affect Jeanne a great deal. It seems likely she gave birth to a second son in March, and again the baby was put out for immediate adoption. After that, she continued with her work as Philibert's housekeeper and assistant, spending a lot of time helping to carefully sort and categorise all the plants in his vast collection. Her writing was improving and her knowledge was growing daily: the official botanical names of plants were becoming familiar and she was beginning to understand how plants could be classified into genus, family, order and class. Slowly Jeanne was herself becoming a very knowledgeable botanist.

The months passed steadily as Philibert finalised his plans, but the answer to one question – who could he take as his assistant – remained elusive. He would definitely need expert help in sorting and categorising all the exciting new plants he expected to find; but he also might need physical help, as his health was still far from perfect. At some point during the summer of 1766, it was suggested that possibly, just possibly, Jeanne could accompany Philibert as his assistant. Who came up with the idea is not known; but Jeanne by this time was 26, had matured and gained enormous confidence, and she may have thought the position on board with Philibert would be preferable to being left alone to look after the apartment. It is also likely that, despite the fact that he had refused to take any interest in her pregnancies, she had grown really fond of Philibert. He was without doubt the rock that, at this time, was holding her life together. Possibly, though, the suggestion came from Philibert himself; after all, he knew what an excellent assistant Jeanne was, plus she had already proved herself as a good nurse when he was sick. If his health deteriorated on the voyage, he would be able to rely on Jeanne to look after him and also to help collect new species. There must have been many discussions in the little flat in Paris as Jeanne and Philibert worked out a plan. Jeanne herself was no longer a poor, submissive domestic servant. It is more than likely she was fascinated by the idea of travelling right around the world with a man she knew so well, although her concept of what it would entail would have been very limited. However, there was one hugely important aspect that needed consideration: no women served in the navy, no women were allowed on official ships; the only way Jeanne could go on the voyage would be to disguise herself as a man.

Could it be done? As an assistant and valet, Jeanne wouldn't have to dress in similar clothes to those worn by the other sailors on the ship; she could choose loose garments that could work as a disguise. If she bandaged her breasts with strips of fabric, she could probably flatten them enough below a loose shirt. If she had short hair and kept herself to herself, could it work? Jeanne must have spent many hours pondering on whether she should really do this. If she were discovered, she would be sent home in disgrace to face trial – or worse. On a shipload of vigorous, uneducated men, there were many dangers to consider.

Finally the decision was made. Jeanne agreed to go on the trip as Philibert's male assistant and valet. Really it was an extraordinary and hugely courageous idea, but once Jeanne had made up her mind, she didn't hesitate. Immediately she became involved in the preparations, helping to pack equipment, containers and all the other items Philibert felt vital to carry out his commission. Jeanne's ethics of hard work and quiet dedication now came into play; she was going to do all she could to help her employer and make the voyage a success.

When all was ready, early in 1767, Jeanne Baret said goodbye to her past and became a man. She flattened her chest with fabric wrapping, donned loose clothes and stepped up from the position of domestic servant into the role of assistant and valet to a recognised, respected and well-paid botanist. From the moment she clambered up into the carriage in Paris for the 300-mile journey to Rochefort, on the west coast of France, Jeanne carefully took on her new role. Jeanne's childhood had taught her to live by the day, live in the present. Nevertheless, Jeanne was more than aware there would be many challenges and surprises in the weeks and months ahead.

She had never seen the sea; arriving at the naval town at the estuary of the Charente river, she would have seen a million new sights as ships of all sizes crowded the waterway and sailors and tradesmen rushed to and fro, carrying big bundles and loads. The ship they were to sail on, the *Etoile*, was 100 years old and was just 110ft long by 30ft wide. However, the ship was well appointed and Philibert had been allocated a cabin in the stern of the ship, an area reserved for officers and passengers. The room was small, the headroom low, but at least it offered some privacy. Many officers brought servants with them on a voyage, often boys as young as 13, and sleeping arrangements were haphazard. Sharing cabins was common, and some of the ship's boys didn't have allocated spaces and just slept where they could. For Jeanne to share the cabin space with Philibert was not an issue of major comment.

When Philibert arrived with a mass of equipment, plans were changed at the last minute. He was offered a slightly larger cabin so that he could successfully store all the plants he expected to collect. This extra space would have been a blessing for Jeanne, as she stayed quietly in the cabin sorting things, away from the endless noise and frantic activity that accompanies any ship preparing for a long voyage.

Philibert was happy in his important role; he met the officers and was treated with respect and dignity. While the ship was towed to Ile d'Aix, an island just off the coast, for final preparations, Philibert and Jeanne experienced their first days of living on water. Both seemed unaffected by the gentle roll of the ship and Philibert stated to friends that he was clearly a good sailor and everything was going well.

Jeanne, meanwhile, was keeping herself below deck, speaking to as few as people as possible, as she looked after the cabin and Philibert. She had to collect food, which she ate in the cabin, but she said little and attracted little comment. She was just the botanist's assistant who kept herself to herself ... or, as the sailors assumed, himself to himself.

Finally, all was ready, and on 1 February 1767, the sailors started work in earnest. The huge sails were hauled up and started filling out with the wind. Slowly and creakily, the *Etoile* edged forward through the water, rocking gently and then steadily gaining speed. She was on her way, first stop South America. The expedition's leader, Louis-Antoine de Bougainville, was on the sister ship of the voyage, the *Boudeuse*. They had sailed earlier, leaving France in December 1766, and planned to rendezvous with Jeanne's ship in the southern Atlantic.

So far, Jeanne had shown an indomitable spirit, quietly weathering all obstacles as she steadfastly got on with life. She had developed a very pragmatic character and lived life quietly by the day; thoughts of rough seas and huge storms ahead didn't bother her too much as she went about her daily chores. Soon, however, her resolve was going to be tested yet again. As the ship sailed west into the notoriously rough seas of the Bay of Biscay, both Philibert and Jeanne went down with very bad seasickness. For Philibert, able to sit openly in the fresh air on deck and discuss his symptoms with fellow gentlemen, things were bad enough. For Jeanne, though, keeping herself hidden in the dark, stuffy, enclosed cabin, it was a time of real endurance. For days on end, she stayed below, feeling truly dreadful. However, after ten days, as the *Etoile* reached steadier seas far out in the Atlantic, both Philibert and Jeanne improved and got over their seasickness.

Jeanne did go up on deck occasionally, carefully keeping herself distant from the crew. However, it didn't take long for the other 100-plus sailors, who lived and worked so closely together, to start talking about this aloof young assistant who kept so hidden. As the days went by, all sorts of rumours started spreading and finally someone suggested she could even be a woman. Eventually all this came to the ears of the captain, François Chenard de la Giraudais.

It was a prestigious appointment to be captain of one of the ships in this important expedition. François didn't want trouble. If Philibert's assistant did turn out to be a woman, what was he to do? It would cause an enormous scandal; he would have to remove her from the ship as soon as possible, and that might upset Philibert, a key player in the voyage. Nevertheless, he had to do something. He summoned Philibert and Jeanne to his cabin. Their response must have originated from Philibert; despite Jeanne's growing experience in life, it is unlikely she would have been aware of eunuchs. This, however, was the solution decided upon. When Jeanne was asked about her reluctance to join in as part of the crew, Jeanne stood steadfast before the captain and stated that she was similar to the feminised men kept by the Ottoman emperor: she was a eunuch. It was a subject no man wanted to discuss, as the fear of being captured and made a slave in the Ottoman empire terrified many sailors. All François wanted was a successful voyage. This admission, whether François believed it or not, was the perfect solution.

With the very strict discipline on any sailing ship of the time, the crew had to accept the captain's decision and any talk about the strange assistant soon stopped.

The traditional celebration when crossing the Equator was another problem Jeanne had to cope with ... if celebration is the right word. Crossing the line, as it was called, was a major event on every ship at the time, with those who had never crossed the Equator before subjected to a range of quite brutal 'baptism' rites to appease Neptune, a god of the sea. Paired with senior officers, Philibert could escape fairly lightly, but there was no way out for Jeanne.

As the ship neared the Equator, Jeanne must have dreaded the coming events; how could she possibly maintain her disguise when everyone else was stripping off and being submersed in a specially constructed pool of filthy water? It seems the celebrations on the *Etoile* were especially vigorous, but Jeanne stood her ground and quietly refused to strip off. Heeding the earlier comments from their captain, the crew did not insist on Jeanne's full participation, and although she was still subjected to a horrible dousing in foul sewage-filled water, she escaped fairly lightly and gave no conclusive proof that she was a woman. However, it was all very unpleasant and this must have been another tough time for Jeanne.

As the weather improved, and as Jeanne spent a little more time on deck without the continual pestering of the ship's men, her confidence returned. Bad ulcers had started appearing on Philibert's legs and Jeanne's days were now busy looking after him as he rested on his bed. Life in some ways was monotonous and repetitive, and with only

Philibert as someone she could talk to freely, Jeanne was leading a very solitary existence. But she liked the sea and was very happy when she had a quiet moment, just to sit on a secluded part of the deck and watch the water rushing past.

Finally, after weeks steadily sailing to the south-west, the *Etoile* dropped anchor in the waters off Rio de Janeiro to meet up with the *Boudeuse*, the other ship in the voyage. Jeanne must have been staggered by the beauty of the harbour, with Sugarloaf Mountain rising high on the southern shore. It would be another 150 years before the giant Statue of Christ was built overlooking the town, but the harbour was still hugely impressive. While expedition leader Louis-Antoine de Bougainville and the two ships' captains sorted out their provisions and plans, Philibert and Jeanne quickly went ashore.

Yet again, Jeanne was on a steep learning curve. The town was busy: a mix of wealthy Portuguese and local poverty. Sugarcane was already well established as a thriving industry, and African slaves had been brought in to work on the plantations. But there was no time to stop and stare; there was exciting work ahead. The couple quickly headed out of the town onto the narrow tracks winding up and down the steep hillsides that surrounded the town, and almost immediately they spotted a wealth of fascinating new species to collect and take back to the ship. It was exciting work, spotting and collecting so many plants they had never seen before, but after a couple of tiring days Philibert realised he was not really up to the task; his legs were still causing him pain. From then on, while he sat on the lower slopes, Jeanne scurried up and down the hills, looking for new plants that offered something different. When she came across the deep-red leaves of what we now know as the Bougainvillea plant, she was impressed. This was a plant unlike anything she had seen before and she knew immediately it was something worth examining. Jeanne picked some samples to take back to Philibert and the ship.

Louis-Antoine de Bougainville, the expedition leader, although based on the other ship, had already met Philibert and Jeanne and had heard the rumours that Jeanne was not a man. Philibert thought perhaps that naming this new plant after him would help smooth out any problems, and this proved to be the case. Louis-Antoine was delighted to learn that a dramatic new plant find would be named in his honour. He also realised that, with Philibert clearly unable to undertake strenuous exploration because of his leg problems, Jeanne's help was essential to ensure the expedition returned with a good variety of exciting new plants; so he kept any thoughts about Jeanne to himself. Jeanne was safe for a while.

Once the ships were stocked and ready, the little fleet headed off south, calling in at Montevideo and then at various anchorages as they steadily sailed down towards the southern tip of the Americas. At each stop, Philibert was eager to collect as many samples as possible, but his legs were now covered in ulcers and he was finding every movement challenging. So Philibert stayed near the shore while directing Jeanne on where to go. On her own, Jeanne headed inland and started exploring new lands. She walked through forests, climbed steep hills and scrambled up rocky headlands, searching relentlessly for interesting plants. Her knowledge was enough to help her decide what sort of plants might be useful, might be worth investigating. Time after time, she struggled back down to the coast laden with armfuls of plant samples that then needed to be carried back to the ship for sorting, labelling and drying. It was backbreaking, exhausting and relentless work, but she kept going. It would be nice to think that sometimes, at the top of a hill with a magnificent view of the land and far ocean, Jeanne found the time to stop for a moment, to sit down and wonder at the new scenery, to think about what she was doing and seeing.

As the ships headed south, Jeanne would have noted and probably discussed with Philibert the different soils, the different landscapes, the new animals and changing insects and birdlife as they left the tropics for cooler climates. When the ships reached the southern latitudes, the weather deteriorated fast. Storms became more frequent; at one point a ferocious gale tore off the large middle topsail on the *Etoile*. Along with the violent motion and noise, Jeanne and Philibert, hanging on in their small, dark cabin, would have been very aware of the drama taking place on the deck above as the sailors frantically rushed around, trying to save the sails and get the ship back under control. With the roaring water and winds pounding the rolling vessel, there must have been some truly terrifying moments.

The ships survived, though, and finally, in early December 1767, they reached the Straits of Magellan on the southern tip of the American continent. After the close heat of the tropics, the ships were now trying to sail in furious icy winds in very restricted passageways. Nights were often spent in dire anxiety, as the crew looked out for signs the creaking vessels were dragging their anchors and heading for the steep, rocky shorelines. At one point, despite it being midsummer, snow fell on the decks. For Jeanne, life was again becoming a serious struggle, but there were compensations. At each stop Jeanne headed onto the land, often fighting against bitterly cold winds, as she sought new plants and tried to pull up samples from the hard and sometimes frozen soil. She found ferns and lichen, different grasses and sometimes more colourful plants, including daisies, blooming lilies and a type of bilberry bush that would later prove effective in the world of medicine. At one point, the ships were met by a group of hardy Patagonians, who had horses and somehow survived in this barren southern landscape. When they saw what Jeanne was doing, they helped by collecting and bringing her plants. The collection on board was growing fast, the number of boxes was taking up increasing space in the small cabin and the work continued relentlessly as each specimen was carefully examined, described and labelled.

At the end of January 1768, a year after they had left France, the *Etoile* finally entered the Pacific Ocean and headed north-west, aiming for the far-distant spice islands of Indonesia. At last there was some respite for Jeanne; she could spend days in the cabin with Philibert, sorting out and itemising their vast collection of plant samples, seed pods and other vegetation. For the next two months the little ship sailed steadily into warmer waters, passing no visible land and with only the sights of new fish and occasional dolphins to break the monotony of endless horizons.

Then, eventually, land appeared. On 5 April, amid much excitement, the voyage reached Tahiti in French Polynesia. Jeanne and Philibert rushed ashore, keen to explore the wonderful tropical vegetation. As soon as they stepped down from the little rowing boat, however, they hit a problem.

They were greeted by a crowd of Polynesian men who, in their traditional way, examined the visitors carefully, studying their faces and their clothes. It didn't take long for the cry to go out – *this one is a woman*. It was clear to the staring, examining Polynesians that Jeanne was not a man. Jeanne looked around as the men began to surge forward to examine this strange visitor, who dressed as a man but was not one of them. One of the men approached Jeanne and tried to pick her up. As Jeanne called out in fright, a nearby French officer drew his sword. Jeanne quickly escaped their clutches and fled back to the landing boat; she was rowed fast back to the *Etoile*.

Louis-Antoine de Bougainville, the leader of the expedition, was annoyed. Now it had been made pretty clear to everyone that Jeanne could really be a woman, he realised at some point he would have to deal with the situation. At that moment, though, there was too much going on. He had to keep the crew motivated to do the repairs and restocking rather than spending too much time ashore; he needed to work out navigation, and he had to sort out a dispute after a fight involving his crew left three Polynesians dead. Also, he had been impressed by Jeanne's sheer hard work and dedication in ensuring the botanic aims of the voyage were fulfilled. So, for the time being, Louis-Antoine put aside the subject of Jeanne's sex. While there was now much stronger talk among the sailors, they were still wary of saying too much against the expedition leader's instructions.

Jeanne did not risk going back ashore. Stuck in her cabin, she must have been upset and disturbed by the confrontation and frustrated that she was unable to go ashore to discover and collect some fabulous new flora. She was also becoming nervous. She had struggled under her disguise for so long, but it seemed now that everyone knew she was a woman. She had broken the law by going on the ship. What would happen to her?

After ten days moored safely in the beautiful bay at Papeete, the two ships raised their sails and headed out west across the South Pacific. Jeanne continued with her masculine style, dressing in large, loose clothing, although at last she felt she could remove the constant pressure of the bandages around her breasts.

As the ships slowly made their way across the large expanse of empty ocean, tempers began to get ragged. It was hot; the dried food didn't last well in the constant humid heat and the drinking water was tepid and unpalatable. Then Philibert's legs started playing up again, with one causing him immense pain. Jeanne went back to her old routine of nursing him, and looking after his food and the collections as he slowly recovered. The voyage was becoming highly dangerous, with uncharted islands appearing and minimal maps to help navigation. The ships sailed on west, but by the end of May supplies were becoming dangerously low.

On 6 June 1768, the crew spotted breaking waves above a coral reef, now known as the Bougainville Reef, part of the Great Barrier Reef off north-east Australia. It was clearly a dangerous area and so Louis-Antoine de Bougainville turned his ships sharply north. They totally missed Australia, but there were more pressing concerns. It had been two months since Jeanne or anyone else had had fresh water for washing; in the constant heat, the last remains of the fresh fruit had rotted away; the unpalatable food that was left, together with drinking water, had to be rationed. As Jeanne continued to look after Philibert, she herself began to suffer from various skin conditions brought on by a lack of proper nourishment. Life and morale on the ships were deteriorating fast.

They stopped off at one island and took on fresh water, but there was no food, and so the two ships upped anchor and sailed on, desperately collecting fish when they could to supplement their meagre rations.

The crew were still discussing Jeanne, and finally Louis-Antoine called Jeanne over to his ship to talk to her. After strong questioning, she confessed that the assumptions were true – she was indeed a woman. This annoyed Louis-Antoine intensely; it was a major problem he could do without. At that moment, though, his priority was survival and the life-threatening situation of being unable to find sufficient food. He would deal with Jeanne later.

With food and water running out, there were some desperate weeks to follow, but finally the ships reached Buru in the Moluccan islands. Here they were given a warm welcome by the Dutch, and an abundance of fresh meat and fruit was available. Jeanne's situation, much to her relief, was now being ignored by the captain, and with better food, she found her health quickly returning. Together with Philibert, she must have relished going ashore and seeing the wonderful tropical wildlife and amazing plants. Along with new flora, they also collected some extraordinarily coloured birds.

With more provisions, life on board soon returned to normal. Sailing west, the ships stopped for a short time at what is now Jakarta. Few new plants were collected here, but with repairs and restocking completed the little fleet then headed west out into the Indian Ocean. So far, Louis-Antoine felt the voyage had gone well: they had charted and even claimed some new land and made many observations. The botanical aspects, thanks to Philibert and Jeanne, also looked very good indeed. Now he was anxious to complete the trip back to France. He once again put the problem of Jeanne being a woman at the back of his mind.

Day after day, the ships continued steadily on their westerly passage, heading towards Mauritius. Jeanne spent the time carefully going through all the plant – and now some bird, shell and insect – samples; labelling them; checking the descriptions; ensuring their careful preservation and storage; plus once again looking after Philibert who was once more suffering badly from leg problems. It was repetitive work and life on board was now becoming tedious, not just for Philibert and Jeanne, but for all the crew. They had been on their constantly rolling and moving ship for over a year and a half, and the novelty had long worn off for everyone.

In early November 1768, land was spotted far ahead. The ships had reached Mauritius. Despite the distance from France, it must have felt like arriving home. Following rule by the French East India Company for many years, the French government had recently taken control of the island and the French language was widely spoken. Even better, there was a friend of Philibert's waiting to greet him. Pierre Poivre was a French administrator on the island who had known Philibert in France. For Jeanne, despite the joy of stepping onto dry land, there must have been some real anxiety. Would she be arrested for her impersonation; what would happen to her now?

On French soil, Louis-Antoine de Bougainville could have officially declared that a woman had smuggled herself onto his expedition, but he chose not to. After all, it would bring some discredit to the voyage and to him. If this became an official report, there would probably have to be a court hearing and who knows where that could lead? Instead, Louis-Antoine brushed the problem aside and concentrated on repairing and restocking the ships for the final voyage back to France. However, it seems likely it was Louis-Antoine who was behind the idea that Philibert and Jeanne should stay behind on the island to help examine the medicinal plants there. If they were left in Mauritius, he could then arrive back in France as the leader of a hugely successful voyage, the country's first ever fleet to sail around the world, with no threat of scandal to dent his achievement.

The deal was done quickly. Philibert was enthusiastic about staying on Mauritius; true to his nature, he could already see the potential for some additional plant discoveries that would make him even more famous when he eventually arrived back in France. Also, because of the ulcers still causing serious problems on his legs, he was very happy not to be stepping immediately back onto a ship. His collection was roughly sorted: some to go back to Paris with Louis-Antoine, some to stay with Philibert in Mauritius for further examination and classification.

Despite all she had done for him, despite her total loyalty and dedication, Philibert still treated Jeanne as his domestic servant, albeit one he deeply respected, valued dearly and perhaps even loved in his own way. Now Jeanne could revert to dressing as a woman, but if she had ever had any idea that their relationship might at last be formalised, that dream was now firmly put to bed.

While comfortable accommodation was sorted out for Philibert in the centre of the capital Port Louis, Jeanne was allocated poor servant accommodation nearby. It must have been hurtful for Jeanne that Philibert did nothing to intervene. Moreover, while she continued to help, Philibert increasingly spent his time with capable local assistants. Jeanne's knowledge and support no longer seemed important.

While she continued to remain loyal and as close as she could to Philibert, after eighteen months she started to think seriously about what was going on and about her future.

She was approaching 30 and it was time to take more control of her life. While the plan was for them both eventually to return to France, her relationship with Philibert was clearly going nowhere. She may also have been concerned about his health because, although he was not a well man, he continued to push himself to extremes as he explored new areas in his fanatical devotion to finding new plants and species. Jeanne had earned – and saved – some money from her voyage; the salary that the government had offered to Philibert to cover an assistant had been given to Jeanne. It was a start.

While it would be nice to think that Philibert now stepped in to help sort out a new future for Jeanne, it seems more likely that it was her idea to apply for her own land concession in the middle of Port Louis. Either way, in August 1770, a small stone building on a piece of land in the middle of town was assigned to Jeanne. While she didn't own the house, she could live in it as her own or rent it out. It is not clear how much time she spent there, but it was certainly a small move towards independence. Jeanne's life, however, continued in the same pattern, helping Philibert with his vast collections.

Four and a half years after their arrival on the island, Philibert, on a collecting trip in the mountains just outside Port Louis, suddenly fell seriously ill. He was in poor health anyway and this time he did not recover. Philibert collapsed into bed and, on 13 May 1773, at the age of 45, he died.

Jeanne might have slowly been moving away from Philibert, but nevertheless this would have been a dreadful shock. After all, Philibert had been her mentor, companion, teacher and lover for nearly seventeen years. They had been through storm and tempest together, climbed rugged mountains and descended deep ravines; they had examined the natural world, searching for plants, insects, birds and shells together. Jeanne had nursed him through various illnesses; she had borne his children.

Suddenly the rock that had supported Jeanne for so many years had gone. There was little help or condolence from the local officials and their families. Philibert's friend Pierre Poivre had been replaced by a new official who had already stated he had no time for botanists. Philibert's collections would be sent back to Paris.

Suddenly Jeanne was completely on her own. All the plants and items she had so carefully sorted and catalogued in detail over the years were now being packed up and shipped out; she was not consulted and she had no part to play at all. On Philibert's death, his official papers indicated very little savings and no will was discovered. It must have been a very sad time for Jeanne, but at least she had her little house in the town to move into. At one point, to earn some money, she took a job in a local tavern and would have coped with this well; after spending so long at sea herself, rowdy sailors would not have been a problem for her.

However, perhaps things weren't quite as they seemed. The job might have been just to tide her over and perhaps the future was not looking so bleak after all. Despite her still-quiet demeanour, Jeanne was now proving she had grown into a shrewd, independent woman, and she may have known a little more than she let on to the authorities. For while Philibert had spent so much of his money on trips collecting various species, it seems he may well have had some wealth hidden away from the long arms of the French government. Not long after his death, Jeanne suddenly became quite wealthy. There is no record of where this money came from, but it is almost certain either that Philibert had already given Jeanne something valuable as a safeguard for the future; or that on his death Jeanne was able to retrieve some savings. Either way, it was something that would dramatically help her cope with the loss of Philibert and was a fitting finale to her years of devoted hard work and this major chapter in her life.

Now, in just a few weeks, everything changed. Jeanne suddenly had money … and was totally free. The girl from a poverty-stricken childhood had transformed into a hugely experienced woman of the world with her own independent means. The days of dressing up in shabby men's clothes were gone; now she could celebrate being a woman. It was an extraordinary transformation for Jeanne. She could furnish her small house properly; she could even afford to dress like elegant French ladies. But extravagance had never been an option in Jeanne's life and her new wealth didn't change her habits. She may have enjoyed visiting the few shops that existed in Port Louis, but it wasn't in her nature to splash out on expensive, elegant items. Perhaps also she didn't want to draw attention to her newfound wealth; whatever the reason, the frugal habits of a lifetime remained. Living quietly while she planned her future, it didn't take long for a new man to come into Jeanne's life, a much more suitable partner. Jean Dubernat was four years older than Jeanne, a drum major in the French army. A year after Philibert's death, in May 1774, they were married. After so many adventures, Jeanne was still only 34 and a new life was beginning.

Interestingly, and also very unusual at that time, in the marriage contract Jeanne stipulated that much of her money was to remain hers alone. Jeanne had learned a lot; she was never going to be subservient to another again. Now married, Jean Dubernat decided to leave the army, and six months after their marriage the couple returned to France as passengers on a small merchant ship. This must have been a happy experience for Jeanne, travelling on a ship as a woman, being herself as she watched the sails and the seas, talking openly to the other passengers and perhaps to the sailors, too. But Jeanne had had enough of the sea; what she wanted was to be back in France. When, in August 1775, Jeanne finally saw the coastline of her beloved France appear on the horizon, it must have been quite emotional for her. She had been away for eight years and had travelled right around the world. At the time, the fact that she had done a circumnavigation probably didn't occur to Jeanne. Her extraordinary trip, the sights she had seen, the terrible times and the moments of joy – it was all blurred into a long history as she and her husband moved forward to start their new life together in France.

There was no big welcome as the couple stepped ashore. They made their way quietly down to Jean Dubernat's hometown of Sainte-Foy-la-Grande, on the Dordogne river just east of Bordeaux, and moved into their own unpretentious four-roomed house. They also bought another larger property nearby, with buildings and 40 acres of land. Jeanne contributed a lot towards the purchase and she also made sure her name was included on all the legal documents. She was going to ensure her money was invested well; after such a poor beginning in life, she wasn't going to let it slip through her fingers. She even went up to Paris to ensure she received the furniture and other items left to her in Philibert Commerson's original will and, showing a huge level of confidence, she also contacted the navy about her trip and any money still due. The navy conveniently forgot about the rule-breaking and instead finally recognised that she had actually circumnavigated the globe, paying reference to her great courage and exemplary behaviour. She was granted a small naval pension, and when it didn't arrive, Jeanne employed a lawyer to chase it up. Now a strong woman of wealth and some standing, Jeanne wasn't going to be trodden on by anyone.

While it seems there were no children, Jean and Jeanne's marriage appeared to work well. Looking after their properties and land, and enjoying time with her husband's family, Jeanne's later years were busy in a happy way. It's possible that she returned to the region of her childhood, but there is no record of this and it seems likely that Jeanne was content to put the past well behind her. She had money, respect, a husband and a good life; she didn't need to bring up ghosts from a darker era.

In 1807, at the age of 67, Jeanne died at home. She was buried at the church in Saint-Aulaye, on the bank of the Dordogne river, remaining quietly spoken and modest to the end. Amid the background sounds of the gently flowing water, it was a fitting resting place for a woman who had spent so long at sea, becoming the first woman ever to travel right around the world.

2

1791 MARY ANN PARKER
THE FIRST WOMAN TO TRAVEL EAST ROUND THE WORLD

When James Cook landed at Botany Bay in Australia, in April 1770, he encountered the local Gweagal people. Eighteen years later, when Britain's first fleet of eleven ships arrived in Australia and established a settlement, once again the British came into contact with the indigenous Aboriginal people.

Violence started almost as soon as the colony was set up and there were many fights, mainly over food and land. As the incomers gradually took control and established their way of life, among most of them there was little understanding that the local people, even if they didn't write or dress in the British style, still had a lot to offer.

One captain's wife, who had arrived with the third fleet, shared this disdainful attitude until she met and came to really know a local Aboriginal person. It made her rethink her views to such an extent that she finally welcomed him into her London home, much to the horror of neighbours and friends.

It was a happy moment when, on New Year's Day in 1791, Mary Ann Parker learned that her husband had been appointed as commander of HMS *Gorgon*. Busy in their London house, with her mother helping to look after her two young children, 24-year-old Mary Ann must have been pleased her husband's career was going so well.

There was a downside, though. In the 1700s the world was being opened up by the tall-masted sailing ships that were plying across the world, bringing home news of fascinating lands and exciting new products as well as being involved in gunship wars and support for land conquests. Being commander of a large 900-ton ship meant Mary Ann's husband would be away for months at a time. But that was a career she had married into and travel was in her blood. Her grandfather, a London apothecary trading in medicinal remedies for the sick, had travelled to Jamaica and her ambitious father had also travelled as part of his job as a personal medical adviser to wealthy patients. He didn't actually have any formal medical qualifications, but he was happy to gloss over this aspect in the same way he tended to ignore his continual debt problems. In fact, it was to stay one step ahead of his creditors that, when Mary Ann was around 9 years old, he moved his little family to Cartegena in southern Spain, where he worked for a while as a medical adviser to the British consul. Mary Ann picked up the Spanish language quickly during the years she spent as a child in Spain.

Mary Ann may have first met her husband during her time in Europe; he was certainly in the navy when they were married in London in January 1783. Her mother would have been delighted at this good marriage for her only child; the years of constant financial battles had been wearing, but now the prospects for her daughter were looking really good.

There was a slight embarrassment when, not long after their wedding, Mary Ann's father was officially declared bankrupt. There was no hiding the situation and, with no money and nowhere to live, Mary Ann's parents moved in with the young, newly married couple.

The day after Mary Ann's husband was appointed as commander of the *Gorgon*, on 2 January 1791, she learned more details. The ship had been commissioned to head off for an extended voyage to Port Jackson, now known as Sydney, on the other side of the world. The First Fleet had arrived there just three years before, in January 1788, and the settlement was struggling to survive. The *Gorgon* had been urgently commissioned to take desperately needed goods and livestock out to Port Jackson along with some convicts. It would be a long trip and Mary Ann wouldn't see her husband for fifteen months or more.

However, a month later, as the ship made its final preparations to leave Portsmouth, Mary Ann had some unexpected news. She was invited to join her husband on the trip. She was given two weeks to make up her mind, as there were many things to consider. Conditions on the multi-masted wooden sailing ships of the day were neither comfortable nor safe. Regular stories of ships foundering in storms or hitting rocks, disease taking hold on board, even food and other supplies running out, were not unusual. No one went on long journeys unless there was a real purpose. For Mary Ann, though, there were two good reasons. One, she had already travelled a little and a journey to the other side of the world would certainly be interesting. Secondly, she loved her husband and may also have thought it a very good idea to keep him close; he offered the financial security her own family had never known. It would mean a heart-wrenching separation from her children, who would be left with her mother, and there could well be danger, but she didn't hesitate. She would go.

Thankfully, she wouldn't be the only woman passenger on board. Navy captain Gidley King was travelling out on the *Gorgon* to take up his new position as governor of Norfolk Island, and he was also taking his wife with him, so there would be company for Mary Ann on the voyage.

Once the goodbyes had been said, it was a reasonably cheery party that sailed away from Portsmouth on 15 March 1791. The ship was only 140ft long and 38ft wide, but Mary Ann's cabin was comfortable, albeit small, low-roofed and a little dark. After a couple of weeks of seasickness, Mary Ann soon became adapted to the ever-rolling life at sea. Her husband was always busy, but she was there to offer support when she could, and there was a small group of other congenial passengers to talk to, to enjoy meals with and to play cards with in the evening.

Four weeks later, as the weather became warmer, the *Gorgon* anchored up in Tenerife. As the wife of the commander of the ship, Mary Ann was greeted with the greatest respect, taken to the best sights and given the top place at dinner parties. She enjoyed the attention very much and also the acclaim she received after demonstrating her near-fluent Spanish. It was a very happy ten-day visit. On 25 April 1791, under a fresh and favourable breeze, the *Gorgon* set sail to continue its journey south.

On board, it seems Mary Ann gave no thought at all to the convicts carried below deck. There were only around thirty on board, all men, compared with up to 700 or more that had been transported on earlier ships in the First Fleet. Nevertheless, she must have been aware of the situation; how the convicts locked away below were just part of a huge number being transported to the other side of the world. By keeping away from the subject, perhaps she could ignore the fact that they had mostly been sentenced for very minor crimes and sent off in awful conditions for seven years, or even life, to a far-off land they knew little about. Almost like the goods packed tightly below decks, the convicts were held below and simply not talked about.

After four weeks of steady progress south, towards the end of May, the weather took a turn for the worse and, for the first time, Mary Ann experienced a really rough sea. It meant boards were fixed over the window in her cabin, which made it dark and dismal, and meals had to be eaten there as well. But the cook on board somehow coped with the conditions and managed to continue to provide excellent food for the officer-class passengers, including surprisingly roast pig and plum puddings; a dramatic contrast to the minimal fare supplied to the convicts below decks. Finally the winds subsided, but as a precaution the ship sailed on past Cape Town and down round the Cape of Good Hope to anchor up safely in the well-protected Simon's Bay to the east.

Their arrival was greeted with a fifteen-gun salute, and while her husband was busy with formalities, Mary Ann was whisked ashore to be met by the local dignitaries. Ushered into a carriage drawn by eight horses, she was shown great respect as she was invited into local homes to meet and dine with the most influential people in the Dutch colony. Mary Ann thought it all wonderful; she loved the attention she was being given and began to enjoy being considered an important person. She was sometimes a guest of honour at a luncheon and the first to be served, often by enslaved Africans. These were the first she had met, but she was careful neither to comment on them nor to note their role. She merely continued her polite conversation with the charming and attentive Dutch women around her.

In this elegant society, Mary Ann was more than aware that her position was solely due to her husband's role as a navy captain, and so she took care to remain the epitome of sensibility and politeness. She could not risk saying anything that would bring him into disrepute. One day, however, her guard failed when she was invited to stay at the home of a Dutch woman and, talking about her visit later, she compared the size of her hostess to that of a Dutch man-of-war. It was a slightly humorous but unusually negative comment from someone so careful in ensuring she behaved correctly.

Mary Ann was also quite happy to meet the captain of the notorious *Neptune*. This ship had been part of the Second Fleet sent out to Australia, subsequently nicknamed the Death Fleet because of the number of deaths on board. Over 1,000 convicts were being transported, but during the voyage over a quarter died. Of the survivors who managed to make the colony, around 40 per cent arrived in such poor condition that they died within six months. The *Neptune* had been the ship with the highest number of deaths.

Yet Mary Ann, who would have been aware of these numbers, greeted the *Neptune*'s captain with friendliness. With her concentration on polite, dignified behaviour, suitable for her new position in life, she wouldn't have considered discussing anything controversial. If, at this stage, she had had any thoughts at all about the treatment of the transported convicts, she put it to the back of her mind. While the convicts on her ship remained below, Mary Ann continued to enjoy the social life in Cape Town.

At the end of July, having refuelled and full of new supplies, the *Gorgon* set off again and for a month Mary Ann had a pleasant time. She was finding her companion, Mrs King, easy to pass pleasantries with and, apart from the pitching of the ship, all was going well. Early in September, though, a carpenter and another crew member fell overboard and were lost. Then the midshipman, the young son of a lieutenant in the navy with a great future ahead of him, fell ill and died, and this was quickly followed by the death of yet another seaman. Mary Ann attended the services as the bodies were committed to the deep; the dangers of long ocean voyages were becoming very real.

Nearly seven weeks after leaving Cape Town, on 19 September, land appeared, but any excitement about reaching the shore quickly abated as the ship sailed into a ferocious thunderstorm. Lightning struck the pole of the main topgallant mast and it split down two-thirds of its length. Lightning then struck another mast, and some of the crew on the deck were knocked down. Luckily there was no more damage and the *Gorgon*, after being driven well past Port Jackson, finally managed to turn round. On 21 September 1791, they sailed into what is now the beautiful Sydney harbour and dropped anchor. After a journey of just over six months, they had arrived at the other end of the world.

It didn't take long for Mary Ann to learn some real facts about the fledgling colony. Looking around, it was astonishing to think that just three years before there had been no big boats, no buildings, no sign of cultivation at the water's edge. Now the area was a hive of activity and she was impressed by the progress on everything from buildings to cultivation to the organised order of the community. Mary Ann usually stayed on board overnight, but then went ashore after breakfast, often to the home of the governor and his wife. She also met some of the wives of the marines who had come over with the First Fleet and learned the problems they were encountering with food and water rationing and also about their fears for the future. She learned about the poor soil and the failure of early crops; how for the first year everyone in the colony had been on tight food rations; and how, at one point, when the supply boats didn't arrive, they thought they had been forgotten and might simply die like the early colonists on America's Roanoke Island.

Mary Ann travelled inland, usually with Mrs King and other ladies who lived in the colony, and she loved the peaceful creeks and beautiful inlets that bordered the large harbour area. The little group often stopped to admire the vegetation, and Mary Ann was delighted with the beauty of the flowering shrubs and the sweet perfumes from some of the blossom.

In contrast, though, Mary Ann was totally disgusted by the appearance of the local Aboriginal people. She thought the men rather short and didn't approve of the decorations in their hair or the fish bones in their noses, which she found frightening. The other British wives Mary Ann was mixing with talked distastefully about the local people – their dingy copper colour, how they went without clothing. Even worse, the local inhabitants covered themselves with fish oil, which gave off a dreadful smell. At this stage, the thought that they had been in the area before the First Fleet was of no interest to any of the ladies Mary Ann was mixing with, and Mary Ann took her cue from them. She really wanted nothing to do with these awful local people.

One day, Mary Ann was ashore with her husband and they were sitting down having a picnic when some Aboriginal people came up to them. One man particularly showed a real interest in what they were eating and sat down beside them. Instead of gesturing to him to go away, Captain Parker showed immediate friendliness and they exchanged names. Following the action of her husband, Mary Ann also showed friendliness, and when the man became interested in the travelling knife and fork that Mary Ann was using, she found him very gentle and not in the least threatening. He seemed to have deep, sensitive eyes and he smiled sweetly at her. Mary Ann decided to give her knife and fork to the man and he was delighted.

This was a dramatic turning point for Mary Ann. When she had really only noticed the local Aboriginal people from a distance, it had been easy to behave like many of the other women, remaining aloof and scathing. Now, close and talking to a smiling, friendly man, her initial fears and prejudices began to disappear. Her husband was friendly towards them and Mary Ann was happy to follow his lead. She was also impressed when the same man who had sat down with them visited the ship the next day to politely show that he had not lost his gift of the knife and fork. Again Mary Ann was watching when, under her husband's direction, he was welcomed on board with kindliness and given food to eat. Mary Ann also greeted him kindly and demonstrated again how to use a knife and fork.

The official policy of the early British settlers had been to live in peace with the native inhabitants, and as Mary Ann got more familiar with the Aboriginal people of the region, especially the local Eora people, her views began steadily to change. She started to mix a little more and realised that, despite people's very different appearances, she never, ever felt fear; in fact, she was surprised by their openness and their exceptional honesty. In groups, they could appear intimidating, but meeting individuals, she found they seemed genuinely kind people and Mary Ann reflected on what seemed a natural goodness in their hearts. Suddenly, the lack of clothing didn't seem quite so offensive; after all, the climate was a lot warmer than in England.

Through her husband, who went to great efforts to befriend the Aboriginal people, Mary Ann became more familiar with their lifestyles and began to appreciate their skills – skills that were so very different from anything of value in her home country, yet were vital for survival in this strange and rugged land. One local man named Woollarawarre Bennelong, after some initial problems, had accepted the Europeans far more than most in his community, and had even learned to speak some English. He became a friend of Captain Parker and they even went on a trip together inland; Mary Ann also came to know him and they became friends. She went for a walk with him and began to appreciate Woollarawarre's knowledge of plants and the land. His values were so different; he drew his happiness from different sources. It really made Mary Ann think. She realised that the women she was mixing with weren't so impressed by the locals and that, in her position as a captain's wife, it wouldn't be correct for her to make controversial remarks. But she didn't laugh so naturally now when disparaging comments and jokes were made about the locals and their lifestyles.

It was Mary Ann's husband who also awakened in her a real awareness of the convicts. Mary Ann had already heard about the dreadful mortality among the convicts. When talking about this to others in the settlement, she often heard the convicts referred to not as people but simply as poor miserable objects.

Then, one evening, her husband came back with graphic descriptions of the misery and suffering of the convicts in Port Jackson's hospital; how he had been surrounded by mere skeletons of men and how he was furious at the methods of transportation. He railed against a system that paid ship owners per person transported, whether the convicts survived and arrived at the colony or not. He shuddered at the exhibition of human misery – and Mary Ann listened. When she travelled west on a trip with other wives inland to Parramatta, she noted with surprise the industrious efforts of over 1,000 convicts who were working so hard to help build the new community.

This all made Mary Ann reflect. She had been and, despite the separation, still was an emotional and loving mother; now she was beginning to have new, softer thoughts not just about the Aboriginal people but also about the convicts. They were real people, like any others. She was also aware her father had once been badly in debt; perhaps if it had all gone a little further, he too might have ended up a convict.

While she could think about these things, and even talk to her husband, in public she knew she had to remain the dutiful wife of a captain, offering no real opinions but behaving with polite reticence as she passed the time while the *Gorgon* was repaired and reloaded. They were taking on board a strange mix of items including kangaroos, possums, shrubs, plants and birds, plus a party of First Fleet marines and their twenty-six wives who had served their time in the new colony and were now very anxious to get back to England.

Finally, all was ready; goodbyes were said and the *Gorgon* sailed out of the large harbour on 18 December 1791. They had been in Port Jackson just under three months.

Many of the ships that left Port Jackson, having unloaded their cargo or people, went up to China or other Asian areas to collect produce to take back to England. The majority then sailed west across the Indian Ocean, often via Batavia (now Jakarta), to Cape Town and then north to Europe. However, there was an alternative route back from Australia, and that was to travel east across the southern Pacific and round Cape Horn. This offered the potential of a faster trip because of the strong westerly winds in the far southern latitudes, but it was a region notorious for its huge seas and violent weather; many early ships and sailors has been lost in these violent southern seas. Because of this, sailors tended to avoid this route; any voyages around Cape Horn were usually approached with trepidation and often real fear.

When Mary Ann learned this was the route her husband was planning, suddenly she felt afraid. While she had not entertained too many fears in her voyage out to Australia, now the idea of the trip home began to really frighten her. She was not happy about the thought of heading down to an area where there could be icebergs. Just the day after leaving Port Jackson, the *Gorgon* ran into heavy weather with torrential rain and violent squalls of wind. Mary Ann, trapped in her small, dark cabin and listening to the ferocious noise of the rolling, creaking ship and roaring wind, once again suffered from bad seasickness. This probably wasn't helped by her sense of panic; for the first time, as the storm reached its height, Mary Ann started to imagine that the violently rocking, groaning ship was beginning to founder. It was a miserable four days for Mary Ann, but slowly the weather improved.

After that it was a steady run down across the Pacific, although the ship continued to head through a series of gales and squalls that made shipboard life damp and uncomfortable. The only positive aspect was, when Mary Ann could get up to the deck, the number of curious porpoises, whales and other species, which she found fascinating. By early February, having suffered split sails and other expected damage in these wilder regions, the *Gorgon* finally reached the vicinity of Cape Horn. There were huge swells and frequent squalls, visibility was poor, and Captain Parker was keeping his ship well south to avoid the risk of sailing into one of the many islands and rocky areas of this treacherous coast. Early on 8 February, they could just make out land on the far horizon, which was thought to be the Diego Ramirez islands. Cape Horn, the renowned rocky headland on Hornos Island, lay a little further to the north-east. There were fresh breezes, but the weather at last turned kind and there were no ferocious storms as the *Gorgon* steadily churned its way east. Late in the afternoon the distant smudge on the horizon, thought to be Cape Horn, was finally to the north-west. They had passed the notorious Cape.

Two days later, they were almost becalmed and Mary Ann could once again enjoy being on deck, watching the penguins, seals, albatrosses and other birdlife of the wild southern oceans. But just as she thought the worst might be over, in a surprisingly short time, the sea started building into giant rollers and the ship sailed into a full-on gale that struck with a startling, shattering violence.

It was another challenging time, and then worse was to come. Early on 17 February, the crew spotted several icebergs to the north of them. This was not good news, as it meant they were now between icebergs to the north and the ice of Antarctica to the south. It was summer in these southern latitudes, so they had the blessing of longer daylight hours, but it was still cold and frightening. Mary Ann went down to her cabin to collect herself, but she couldn't get out of her mind the disasters that had already occurred to ships in these icy waters. She finally summoned up her courage and went back on deck to look at the spectacle. The view was certainly beautiful; by 7 p.m. there were fifteen tremendous icebergs in sight; the ship had to constantly change sails and direction to clear them. It was a very hectic, challenging time for the sailors; the weather was rough and the icebergs were huge, and as they sailed clear of some, more started appearing on the horizon. Detailed attention was given to the ship's log, the winds, the directions, the possible currents and the distance run. Isolated in these frightening southern waters, lookouts and navigation were key to safety. At night, in the short hours of darkness, along with maximum lookouts, the ship sometimes lay-to, arranging its sails to counteract each other so that movement was minimal.

For five days the steadfast *Gorgon* battled its way through great swells and surging, turbulent waves, sudden dreadful gusts and ferocious rain squalls. For Captain Parker and the crew, it was a totally exhausting time. For the returning marine wives and Mary Ann, it was a terrifying period as they held on in their small, damp cabins uncertain of their fate.

Finally, on 27 February, the heavy seas and furious gales started to subside. Fishing lines were often hung out from the ship, for fresh fish were always welcome to supplement supplies, but one day the crew pulled on board a large shark and on opening it up they found an old prayer book inside. It caused a lot of talk and speculation.

At last, in the early days of March, the weather greatly improved. Once more Mary Ann could meet fellow passengers in the salon; they could eat together, chat and play cards. The trip had finally become tolerable, even enjoyable.

On 12 March, the *Gorgon* once again reached Table Bay at Cape Town and Mary Ann renewed her acquaintances from her visit on the way out. Then, a week later, a Dutch sailing ship arrived from Batavia and on board were some interesting passengers who were transferred onto the *Gorgon*. These included Captain Edwards and a small group of mutineers from the *Bounty* with an extraordinary story.

Captain Edwards had been sent out on a ship from England to round up the mutineers from the *Bounty* after they took over the ship and sent the harsh Captain Bligh and his supporters off in small boats. Captain Edwards had managed to collect a lot of the mutineers, mainly from Tahiti, and was returning with them when he hit rocks in the Great Barrier Reef off Australia and the ship foundered. The survivors managed to reach land, were eventually rescued, and finally had arrived at Cape Town via a Dutch ship. They transferred to the *Gorgon* for the final trip to England. While Mary Ann wouldn't have spoken to the captured mutineers, she would have heard the story of the terrible conditions on the *Bounty* that made them rebel. She was learning so much. In a shielded life right up until she had left England on the *Gorgon*, she had had little conception of real life outside her sphere; initially her sympathies would immediately have been with the authorities. Now the inequalities and unfairness of life were being thrust on her with first-hand reports. It was all very disturbing.

Also arriving into Cape Town on the same Dutch ship was the first woman convict ever to escape from Australia, an attractive young Cornishwoman named Mary Bryant who had been sentenced to transportation on the First Fleet for robbery. In Australia, she married another convict and after secreting away food and supplies, on 28 March 1791, along with her children and seven others, she escaped the colony in a small open boat. Heading north up the coast, they caught fresh rainwater and fish and, after an impossible journey of sixty-nine days and 3,000 miles, they reached the island of Timor. Here, there was no escape. The Dutch captured them and handed them over to Captain Edwards. They too had arrived in Cape Town to be transferred to the *Gorgon* and taken back to England for trial.

As prisoners, they weren't allowed to mix with Mary Ann or the other passengers, but the story would certainly have created interest among the residents in Cape Town. The voyage of escaped convict Mary Bryant would go down in history and certainly would have made Mary Ann think; Bryant had lost her husband and one of her two children on the voyage across to Cape Town. Mary Ann could hardly imagine what this feisty young Cornish girl had been through: conviction; being a prisoner; having children; the courage of escaping and a long ocean voyage; being recaptured and then seeing her child die. It made Mary Ann's separation from her own children seem almost trivial.

During this second stay in the Dutch colony, Mary Ann's changing attitudes became very clear. Unlike on her trip out to Port Jackson, now she started taking a serious interest in the enslaved people kept by many of the Dutch families. From complete indifference, Mary Ann now showed real concern about their welfare. She made enquiries and found that they were generally treated with humanity; although, as a token of their servile condition, they went barefoot and without a hat. Mary Ann noted down other details, from how they stood behind chairs at meals ready to drive away flies, to how they dressed. Mary Ann was changing fast and dramatically; she even noted down how she was struck by the natural beauty of one of the enslaved girls, not just the lovely symmetry of her features but also her fine, dark hair and the elegant way she carried herself.

This was a very different woman from the one who had arrived excitedly at the Cape just eight months before. There was also now another factor in her life to be considered and which perhaps was heightening her emotional state and concern for others: Mary Ann was heavily pregnant; she was desperately hoping they would get back to England in time for her to have the baby.

Leaving Cape Town, they had an uneventful journey back up the Atlantic, with Captain Parker watching the wind, the sails and the crew, and now concerned for his nearly nine months' pregnant wife as well. It was all a huge responsibility, but the *Gorgon* finally arrived in Spithead off the Isle of Wight in the middle of June 1792. Neither Mary Ann, nor any of the marine wives on board, realised that whoever was first among them to step ashore would be the first woman ever to have travelled east right around the world, and it was only thanks to her position and pregnancy that Mary Ann was in fact the first ashore. Once the ship had anchored up, and despite the wind and tide being against them, Mary Ann stepped carefully into a small landing craft. It took four hours of arduous rowing to make Portsmouth and when, damp and cold, she finally stepped on land, the fact that she could lay claim to the record of being the first ever woman to sail east around Cape Horn was certainly not on her mind. Instead, after a night in the local Fountain Inn hotel, she headed for London, where the joy of meeting her mother and little daughter was offset by news that her son had died while she had been away.

Just a few days later, Mary Ann had a little boy. With all being well – and with her husband, having discharged the ship, also back with them – it was a happy interlude in Mary Ann's life. Captain Parker's career continued well and Mary Ann went on to have a third baby – another girl. With two daughters, a son and a busy husband, life was good. Then, two years later, in 1794, when Captain Parker was commanding the HMS *Woolwich* in Martinique, he caught yellow fever and quickly died. This was devastating news for Mary Ann.

After her husband's death, Mary Ann tried to organise her life and her finances, but life would never be quite so secure again. Then, one day and unexpectedly, Mary Ann received a visit that astonished and indeed disgusted many of her neighbours and friends. Woollarawarre Bennelong from the Wangal people, whom she had met in Australia, had been brought to England for a visit when the governor, Arthur Phillips, returned. Before Woollarawarre went back home, he called on Mary Ann.

In these days, in 1795, this would have created quite a stir and, indeed, generated much comment and criticism in this very class-conscious era of British life. Mary Ann, however, was very happy to welcome him. When Mary Ann's daughter showed him a picture of Captain Parker, and explained that he had died, Woollarawarre could not help tears running down his face. This meeting had an enormous impact on Mary Ann. Woollarawarre, an Aboriginal person with so much going on in his life, had taken the trouble to look her up and then be so supportive and kind when he learned of Captain Parker's death. The visit brought back happy memories and also consolidated her realisation that the indigenous people of Australia were caring people with real emotions, just like her.

Bringing up three children, Mary Ann struggled on her navy widow's pension and wrote a short memoir of her trip to try and bring in more money. This was the first published account by a woman of life in the new Australian colony and it attracted some interest. Here, it was clear that Mary Ann's slight arrogance and superiority of youth had completely disappeared. Instead, in her book, her newfound tolerance of different people became quite evident. She made a point of including comments about the natural goodness of the Australian Aboriginal people; how she hoped that the time would come when they would no longer be considered strange savages and how, whatever colour the skin, underneath people are all the same. She even wrote a poem, which she included in her book:

Fleecy locks, and black complexion
Cannot forfeit nature's claim.
Skins may differ, but affection
Dwells in white and black the same.

Not only was this an exceptional turnaround for Mary Ann, but also it was incredibly brave of her to publicly air these views, which went right against the mainstream beliefs of western society at the time. While, in 1795, there were undoubtedly movements against the slave trade, Charles Darwin's book *Origin of Species* and his theories of evolution wouldn't be published for another sixty-four years and many firmly believed that white-skinned people had been created as a completely separate, superior group.

Mary Ann's views at this time weren't generally popular and the money that came in from her book wasn't enough. Her change in status from being the respected wife of a ship's captain to a poor, single woman with apparently strange attitudes was difficult to cope with, although it seems she kept some friends who at least gave her moral support during this difficult time. Mary Ann moved away from her critics to cheap lodgings in Drury Lane, central London, but she still couldn't cover her expenditure and finally her funds ran out. In society at that time, her views on race were radical and among many officials she wasn't going to attract much sympathy. She ended up in the Fleet debtors' prison. Somehow life had gone full circle and there she was, like her father, struggling against debt. Having seen how the convicts in Australia had survived and flourished after dreadful treatment, and how the Australian Aboriginal peoples lived without the trimmings of European life, Mary Ann, now 37 and with every reason to despair at the situation, nevertheless seems to have coped with her short spell in prison surprisingly well.

While in the prison, she may also have thought of Mary Bryant, the escaped convict who survived such an incredible journey in a small boat up the coast of Queensland before being recaptured and joining the *Gorgon* in Cape Town. For Bryant, it was a happy ending as, while escaped prisoners were usually sentenced to death, when Bryant reached London her case was taken up by the writer James Boswell and she was fully pardoned.

Someone also took up Mary Ann's case; possibly an ex-naval colleague of Captain Parker or a relation. Either way, the payment required by the court was finally received and a grateful and relieved Mary Ann was discharged.

Again, repeating history, Mary Ann's daughter married well and Mary Ann's new son-in-law, Robert Vincent, was a successful solicitor; Mary Ann moved in with them. Living in the comfortable Vincent family home in London's Connaught Terrace, Mary Ann Parker spent her last years in relative peace, helping out with the house and watching her little grandchildren grow up. She lived into her eighties and died in 1842, the same year and just a few months after two indigenous Australians, Tunnerminnerwait and Maulboyheenner, had been publicly executed in Melbourne. For Mary Ann, who had seen and learned so much on her journey west to east around the world, this event is likely to have saddened her a lot, but she probably wasn't surprised.

3

1846 IDA PFEIFFER
THE FIRST WOMAN TO GO ROUND THE WORLD BOTH WAYS

In the early nineteenth century, the whole world seemed to be at war. It wasn't just France's Napoleon wreaking havoc across Europe. Russians were fighting in Alaska and Iran, the British were fighting in India and Africa, the Dutch were fighting the Javanese, the United States was fighting in north Africa, Burma was fighting Thailand, Maori tribes were battling it out in New Zealand; it seemed that hardly a nation was untouched by war in this troubled time.

Astonishingly, it was against this backdrop that middle-aged mother of two Ida Pfeiffer decided she would travel around the world on her own. After numerous adventures, once she had arrived back in her hometown of Vienna, Ida then decided to set off again to go around the world the other way. Unlike most voyages of the time, it was not as a missionary or for a scientific endeavour that Ida undertook these extraordinary trips – she journeyed around the world simply because she loved travelling!

It took a lot to upset Ida Pfeiffer. Perhaps it was her age. At 49 years old, with marriage and motherhood behind her, she had long outgrown the passions of youth. Small, mature and with a quiet determination to see the world, in her travels Ida had already faced many dramatic moments with stoicism and calmness.

It was an event in Canton (now Guangzhou) that finally floored her. When Ida arrived, in 1846, China was no longer a closed, isolated country. After the First Opium War and the Treaty of Nanking four years earlier in 1842, ports had begun to be opened to foreign trade. Missionaries too had been granted the right to live and work in five Chinese towns, and news of life in China had begun to filter out. So Ida, before she arrived, had already heard about chopsticks, about the shaven heads and pigtails of the Chinese men, the stoning of defenceless visitors and the tiny, bound feet of Chinese women. This knowledge, however, was not enough to prepare her for the sight of so many women tottering and waddling around on feet that were no more than 4in long.

Ida saw for herself the agony of the little Chinese girls having their toes bent right back under the sole of the foot, and then held permanently like this with strong, tight bandages; she witnessed how the compressed foot then grew to develop into a small ball that could be put into a tiny decorative shoe and how even the women accepted this procedure as normal, even desirable. Having witnessed all this, Ida found it hard to hide her emotions. She described it as a mutilation and she found it shocking.

This distress caught her by surprise, for she felt she was independent and resilient – characteristics she had developed during her childhood in central Vienna. When she was born, in October 1797, the whole of Europe was in turmoil as Napoleon stomped his way around the continent. In her comfortable central Viennese home, provided by her wealthy merchant father, the background adult conversations in Ida's young life were not about business or local Viennese social gossip. More often than not, they were about battles and fights, about which army was winning and who had been defeated.

Once, soon after she was 8 years old, she watched quietly out of the living-room window as column after column of smartly dressed French soldiers marched steadily and rhythmically down the street in front of her home after Vienna had fallen. Instead of dressing up in the pretty dresses laid out by her mother, Ida would put on her big brothers' clothes and march behind them in the garden with a little stick over her shoulder; when she grew up, she wasn't going to take any nonsense from Napoleon and his blue-coated troops!

As Ida grew, her dreams of battle turned into dreams of travel: the idea of seeing foreign lands excited her from a young age. However, as with so many dreams, life got in the way. In her teens, she fell desperately in love with her private tutor, but her parents thought him unsuitable. The tutor was sent away and Ida was banned from having any further contact with him. What sort of life might Ida have had if the couple had been allowed to marry? Ida never fell in love again; she ended up marrying a 'suitable' older man and did her duty as a loyal wife and then mother. At one point, her husband ran out of money and, instead of asking her mother for help, Ida resorted to giving drawing and music lessons to keep food on the table. But the marriage was never a real partnership and finally Ida and her two boys went back to live in her Viennese family home. When her mother died, Ida received a reasonable inheritance, so she could give her beloved sons a good education. Only after the boys grew and then left home did those early thoughts of travel come flooding back.

Sitting alone by the fire in her comfortable lounge on snowy winter evenings, Ida started once again to dream about seeing new countries and new people. The more she read about foreign countries, the more her excitement grew. Now middle aged, and envisaging a future filled with coffee mornings and music recitals with friends and relations, she was beginning to sense a void, a lack of purpose, in her life. She began to research travel seriously.

Finally, feeling quietly excited, she made a decision. She would arrange a trip to the Middle East, to the Holy Land. It was a path well travelled and shouldn't be too difficult to organise. When she mentioned the idea to her family and friends, though, opposition came flooding in. She was told firmly that no respectable woman would travel without a chaperone; that the dirt and foreign climes would make her ill; that she would expose herself to terrible dangers. Hearing all this made her think carefully, but it didn't put Ida off. Men were travelling all over the place. Sometimes wives were taken on trips. Why shouldn't a single woman see some of the world? Ida altered her story and started saying she was going to make a religious pilgrimage; that was a much more acceptable story for her family and friends.

Nevertheless, when, in 1842, Ida finally packed her bag and clambered aboard the boat that was to take her down the Danube river and then on to Istanbul, concerned friends and family were still voicing their firm disapproval. If they had had any idea what Ida would eventually get up to, this disapproval would have turned to total horror.

In those days, even the journey from Vienna down the Danube could be hazardous. On Ida's trip, it took her over a month and several changes of boats just to reach the Black Sea. She knew her inheritance wouldn't afford luxurious travel, so when she could, she went second or sometimes even third class rather than choose the best accommodation.

Right from the start of the journey, Ida took on the role that would eventually see her successfully navigate robbers in Brazil and a kidnapping in Armenia. Wrapped in a long cloak and skirt, or sometimes in wide, flowing Turkish trousers in warmer weather, as she strode along, Ida gave out a strong message of high morality and firm confidence. Her age and her determined no-nonsense attitude, her genuine interest in people rich or poor, and her willingness to ask for assistance whenever it was needed gave her a ring of protection that was, perhaps surprisingly, rarely dented.

Ida also had another trick. On her journey, as she travelled through the Holy Land and Egypt, she took the trouble to make the acquaintance of other European travellers, or at least educated people, and then stick with them for as long as it was useful for her. Occasionally, this could cause some inconvenience to her fellow travellers, but Ida wasn't oversensitive; she was an exceedingly practical woman and latching on to a good companion not only helped with travel arrangements but also gave her additional protection.

This first trip – by sea down to Istanbul and Beirut, by land around the Holy Land and then by more boat and land trips to Egypt and the pyramids, before returning via Italy – all went surprisingly smoothly. Ida encountered few really dangerous moments and was fascinated by what she saw, the different lifestyles, the amazing monuments and the surprising scenery.

Shortly after she started the trip, Ida began to write a detailed diary so that she could relive her journey once she got home. Every day, she would note down in long detail where she had been and what she had seen, all carefully handwritten in a flat, informative style that was without humour but without judgement either.

After a journey of over eight months, Ida arrived back at her home in Vienna to find nothing really had changed. Her friends all welcomed her and praised her for undertaking such a journey. News of her trip reached local publisher Jakob Dirnböck, and soon he and Ida were in discussion about publishing her notes as a book. She had written over 100,000 words of detailed description and Dirnböck recognised a commercial opportunity. He offered a substantial payment and Ida quickly accepted. When *A Visit to the Holy Land* was published in 1844, it was an immediate success and Ida was delighted. It also got her thinking: with money coming in from the book, why not consider another trip?

This time Ida decided to head north. With minimal preparation, in spring 1845, she booked a berth on a ship to Iceland followed by journeys to Denmark, Sweden and Germany. Her style of travel was the same: seeking out affordable accommodation, latching onto fellow travellers for assistance and company, and every day making copious factual notes of what she had seen. She now became more open with her descriptions, adding opinions and even criticism – she commented that Icelanders were as dirty as their houses and were remarkable for their laziness.

Ida was unexpectedly becoming a travel writer and, after a trip of six months, she had more than enough copy to publish a second book:

A *Visit to Iceland and the Scandinavian North*. This met with modest success, but again brought in a useful amount of money.

Ida, though, had returned home with growing confidence; it seemed that travel really was possible for a single woman. She had loved travelling. Seeing new sights, meeting foreign people, finding out about how they lived had all become intoxicating for Ida. The alternative — sitting at home, visiting friends, attending various recitals and social functions as she grew older and older — had little appeal. As she shopped in the elegant centre of Vienna and as she organised the domestic duties in her house, all she could really think of was the idea of visiting distant lands. She had already negotiated thousands of miles in strange countries; why not negotiate a few more thousand miles and go right around the world? America, Brazil … what about China! In a moment of sudden, real excitement, it occurred to Ida that she could really see these unfamiliar, far-off lands.

Once the idea took hold, Ida couldn't get it out of her mind. She worked out her money and decided that, by living really frugally, she would have enough to survive for at least a year and possibly more.

Ida's recent trips had boosted her determination and confidence, and she decided a much more ambitious trip was quite feasible. She had a limited idea of the wider world and the real hazards ahead, yet did little research. She would simply take each day as it came. Again she kept her plans quiet, just mentioning to a few close friends and family that she was hoping to get across to the Americas, possibly to see some acquaintances.

Sorting out a minimal number of long skirts and clothes for all climates and ensuring hiding places for her money, in May 1846 Ida once again waved goodbye to Vienna. She had no real idea of what she would see or experience, but she was going to go as far as she could. She would start with Brazil. It sounded exotic and had been explored by geographer and scientist Alexander von Humboldt, someone Ida had read about and admired.

Arranging travel from central Europe was not easy. Instead, Ida travelled up to the bustling port of Hamburg. After asking around, she found a berth on a two-masted, square-rigged sailing ship laden with cargo and bound for Rio de Janeiro. She was one of eight passengers, and before sailing, she stocked up with dried biscuits and eggs and also took on board her own mattress and bedding to help make her small, basic accommodation as comfortable as possible. For a woman used to fairly luxurious Viennese living, it was a huge contrast. Ida knew she was in for a challenging two-month journey tossing about on the ocean, but she had no hesitation. Her extraordinary and ambitious journey was about to begin.

The ship set sail on 29 June 1846, and headed out, via the English Channel, into the vast Atlantic Ocean. For Ida, time soon began to lose its meaning as the days blurred into a regular pattern of simple shipboard life, accompanied by bouncing horizons and the ever-present sounds of creaking and straining as the giant sails filled to push the ship onwards. Day after day, Ida would sit on a small chair on deck, or huddled in her little cabin when it was too windy or wet, making copious notes on every aspect of the trip. She wrote about the quantities of flying fish she saw, lifting themselves up to 15ft above the water; she described in detail the large shoals of tunny fish tumbling about the ship and other weird sea creatures the sailors pulled on board. As the ship approached the tropics and warmer weather, Ida increasingly spent her days on deck, sitting reading a book or chatting to her fellow passengers who, after their initial surprise and questioning, had accepted this unusual woman who was travelling without a chaperone or company.

After weeks of distant horizons and heaving water, suddenly land was in sight. On the morning of 16 September 1846, Ida could pick out the dramatic pointed outline of Sugarloaf Mountain, and in the early afternoon they entered the bay and port of Rio de Janeiro.

Even placid, controlled Ida must have been thrilled: this was the start of her big dream, the first time visiting somewhere she knew so little about, somewhere really different.

After so much anticipation, it was unfortunate that Ida's first impressions of the town were hugely disappointing. As Ida left the port area and walked into the centre of Rio de Janeiro, looking at the buildings and the people, watching street life and observing all she could, she steadily became appalled at most aspects of Brazilian life. She couldn't find any attractive squares in the town; instead she found sewage-filled streets, putrid dogs and cats lying around, and dirty, disgusting people squatting on the ground in front of a shabby selection of poor fruits they had laid out to sell. She also found most of the locals ugly and generally, as she described them, half naked with only a few miserable rags on their backs. Overall, Ida found the whole town and its people slightly horrifying. It had all been a massive learning curve for disappointed Ida, but when she got back to the ship, she dutifully noted down the details of her new sights and experiences. She had arranged with the captain to keep her cabin on for a few days, so at least she didn't have to worry immediately about getting accommodation in this unappealing town.

On the following days, Ida persevered with her sightseeing. She had struck up a friendship with Count Berchtold, an Austrian who had travelled over on the same boat. He also wanted to do some sightseeing and Ida had no hesitation in suggesting they look around together. With someone to talk to, it didn't take too long for Ida's early revulsion of the town to turn into interest. She became accustomed to the high number of black people and discovered some young black women whom she found very pretty. She noted that the importation of enslaved people had been banned, although thousands were clearly being smuggled in, and gradually her stance against the country softened.

It was when Ida attended a service and festival held to celebrate the emperor's birthday that she finally started to be impressed by Brazil. The service was held in a chapel near the Imperial Palace and was attended by the Imperial family, officials of state and military men, all in full uniform. Ida said it was impossible to describe the richness and profusion of the gold embroidery and the splendour of the occasion, and she had to admit that it was as good as anything she had seen in European courts. Ida also managed to befriend the Austrian consul and his wife, who had a comfortable home in the town. Soon Ida had organised to move in there; she was becoming very good at making useful friends.

Once she had seen Rio, Ida started travelling out of the town. Climbing the Corcovado mountain, she was stunned by the wonderful tropical vegetation, the fabulous orchids, coffee trees, huge mimosas and startlingly brilliant birdlife. Wandering in her sandals on the gravelly paths, stopping to touch plants and leaves, the abundance of new sights and smells was overwhelming. The details were too much even for Ida to put down in her diary. There was one place Ida particularly wanted to see: Petropolis, a town founded by Germans about 40 miles inland. She talked to Count Berchtold, who agreed to accompany her, and with small overnight bags, they set off together out of Rio, first by boat and then along a long gravel path up to the settlement, a route they had been told was perfectly safe.

They met several mule wagons and other pedestrians along the way and felt quite at ease, looking at and examining the lovely plants and trees surrounding the path as they walked along – until they noticed a large man steadily following them. Suddenly, with no one in sight, he rushed up to them, holding a long knife in one hand. Ida felt at once that it was a fight to the death. The only weapon the couple had was a small clasp knife that Ida had kept for general purposes. She quickly drew it out of her pocket and started to open it as the man attacked. He violently knocked the knife out of Ida's hand and started hitting and slashing out at them. Both the count and Ida struggled vigorously, and at one point the man dropped his long knife. Showing amazingly quick reactions, Ida pounced on it, but the attacker was stronger, kicking her out of the way to grab the knife and then slashing at her, causing deep cuts in her upper arm. The count sprang forward and tried to seize the man, who then cut viciously at the count's hand.

Suddenly, two horsemen appeared on the road coming towards them. As soon as the attacker spotted them, he let go and started to run away. It had been a close call. While the count and Ida shakily sat down on the road and tried to staunch their deep, bleeding wounds with material from their clothes, the two horsemen ran into the forest and captured the man, dealing him such blows that Ida feared his skull would be broken. It was a sorry scene in the midst of such beauty. The whole party then made their way to a nearby house, where the owner helped Ida and the count wash and dress their wounds and recover. The attacker was soon taken away.

This had been the very first stop on Ida's planned voyage and the realities of potential dangers now became very clear. Ida must have been badly shaken from this very frightening experience, but instead of scuttling back to the safety of the Austrian consul's home in Rio, this determined middle-aged woman from Vienna said she wanted to continue with her trip inland. She had come to see the world and that was what she was going to do. One unsuccessful attack wasn't going to put her off. The count, nursing his wounds too, wanted to head back to Rio, but he felt he couldn't abandon determined Ida. After thanking everyone as best they could, they both proceeded once more on their journey inland.

When they reached Petropolis, Ida had an enjoyable time, speaking her native language to the many German immigrants there and admiring the magnificent palace under construction for the emperor of Brazil. After a few enjoyable days, they returned safely to Rio without incident, but as Ida talked confidently about seeing more of inland Brazil, the count realised their friendship had gone as far as it could. He felt he had seen enough of Brazil and definitely didn't want to be dragged into any more danger by this extraordinary woman.

Ida, though, with her deep cuts healing well, started on another trip a few days later, hiring two mules and a local guide to take her inland again. In a land filled with coffee plantations and other agriculture ventures, initially finding hospitality with European managers was not too difficult. However, as she reached the edge of the European settlements, things became more challenging. Continuing with her walk, now on small paths through uncleared, vibrant tropical growth, in one small village a priest welcomed her into his home, and Ida was surprised and indeed delighted to witness the interesting event of a wedding and a funeral being held together in the same ceremony. Ida was still making copious notes, and she jotted down every aspect.

It is astonishing that this traditionally brought-up woman decided that she now wanted to venture even further into the more remote, thicker-forested areas of Brazil. What was she thinking? She had left her European contacts behind; communication was now by sign language. After the attack just a few days earlier on a well-populated route, she must have been more than aware that heading further inland would greatly increase the danger for an unprotected woman. There were very real dangers from insects and animals too. What drove Ida to ignore all the dangers and continue with her plans to see all she could? Did she lack imagination and just feel the attack she had already suffered was an unfortunate, one-off occurrence? She certainly seems to have had an almost complete faith that she would be able to find help among local people and that no real harm would come to her.

She managed to hire a local woman to help guide her and, in her flowing long skirt and carrying a small fabric bag, off she strode along winding narrow paths through dense undergrowth until she finally made it to a remote native village. The village she had found belonged to the Puri people, now thought to be extinct. The first thing that struck Ida about the group was that they were all heavily tattooed in red and blue, and they smoked all the time. She called them 'savages' as a generic term, for despite their nomadic life they were fairly well organised and the tribe welcomed Ida without showing any aggression or fear. Perhaps the vision of this middle-aged white woman suddenly arriving in their little village surprised them so much they didn't even think about robbing her; she didn't look wealthy and she had little they needed anyway.

As soon as Ida arrived, she immediately started showing an interest in the people and their lives. The tribe's houses were temporary structures made from poles covered in leaves. Ida noted carefully that they were around 18ft long by 12ft across, open on three sides with one side again covered in leaves. Hammocks hung from the roof, and food was cooked over a central fire. After a couple of hours of looking around and trying to talk to the people, using hand signs to ask questions, Ida became fully accepted by the people. She went on a local hunt with them and admired their excellent skills with a bow and arrow, shooting parrots and monkeys for food. The Puris offered Ida a space in their very best hut for the night, and after a meal and a demonstration of dancing, she fell into a fitful sleep, now at last rightly concerned about all the wild animals, snakes and spiders that were without doubt in the vicinity.

The following day, Ida began the journey back to Rio. It had been a two-week trip and she had been invigorated by all she had seen, so different from anything in Europe. Instead of her experiences putting her off, she was now exhilarated, looking forward to continuing her trip to exciting new places.

Making arrangements for onward travel took her longer than she hoped, but through contacts she had made in Rio and steady persistence, she finally managed to secure a passage on the *John Renwick*, a three-masted English ship that was taking coal to Santos down the coast before picking up a cargo of sugar to take around the southernmost point of South America and up to Valparaiso in Chile. That was perfect for Ida and, despite the limited room and very basic accommodation, she was happy to be on board. This time there were nine passengers on the ship – five Frenchmen, a Belgian and two Italians along with Ida herself – and she soon made friends with all of them.

As the year turned into 1847, the ship headed south to encounter a fearful storm, the worst Ida had ever experienced. White foaming billows of water crashed over the deck, thunder drowned out the roar of the ocean, and flash after flash of lightning gave instant glimpses of raging turmoil outside the small cabin windows. Ida and the other passengers held on as best they could, as the ship rose and rolled at dramatic angles while the storm crashed around. Ida, in her very controlled way, said she did not feel really alarmed or panicked. There was nothing she could do, so instead she resigned herself to whatever fate had in store. It was a frightening time, though.

Finally it abated and, in a sudden peace after the storm, the ship was then becalmed. Under a glorious display of all sails, the creaking ship eventually found enough wind to continue its journey south. There were more periods of violent storm and calm, but eventually, on 3 February, the little ship made its way through the Straits of Magellan to leave the Atlantic and reach the Pacific Ocean.

Now, at last, Ida felt she really was travelling. Brazil was just about within reach of Europe … but the Pacific! What would her friends at home say now? What would her sons say when they finally heard what she was up to? But Ida wasn't doing this to impress people; her intense interest in the world and its people had only increased since she started her journey. She keenly anticipated what might lie ahead.

When she arrived in Valparaiso in March 1847, Ida set the pattern of travel that she would follow for the rest of her life. She looked around, made contact with a German-speaking resident, took copious notes, and then began asking about a boat so she could continue her travels. There was a Dutch barque in port, about to head off for China via Tahiti. Perfect! Ida secured a place on board and then immediately went down with an attack of cholera. There wouldn't be another boat doing this route for months or more; Ida treated herself with a series of cold baths and struggled on board. She couldn't miss this opportunity.

As she recovered, Ida found she liked the ship she was on; it was surprisingly clean and had good food, apart from too many onions. For nearly a month they sailed steadily westwards, and while the weather was hot, Ida found the trade winds helped to make the heat bearable. As the ship reached the Society Islands, things became more dangerous. In those days of early mapping, the area was dotted with unmarked hidden reefs and low islands. On a wet, windy, moonless night it was a time of real worry. At one point the captain climbed up to the shrouds and the rest of the crew and passengers, including Ida, peered out into the intense darkness, trying desperately to spot any dangers as they ploughed on through the water.

On 26 April 1847, they reached the sheltered waters at Papeete in Tahiti. As the large, heavy anchor rattled and splashed down from the bow, Ida looked at the lovely tropical surroundings and was delighted. Here was somewhere totally different. Those plans in her lounge in

Vienna had come to fruition. Her hometown now seemed a very, very long way away; she really had reached the other side of the world.

When Ida left the ship and was rowed ashore to the town, she found it heaving with French troops. Using her knowledge of French, she was soon making herself known to the soldiers and also to the local people. With no hesitation in asking for assistance, she managed to find local accommodation and even meet members of the Tahitian royal family. Ida then decided to travel around the island. Always accompanied by her latest friend, maybe a French officer, perhaps a paid local, she sometimes walked as far as 20 miles a day to visit different areas. All the time, Ida was making notes on every aspect of life, on one occasion recording her surprise on finding that the more lovers a Tahitian girl had, the more she was respected. Ida, though, who had only known one man in her life, never moralised; she simply noted down what she found in a totally factual, unemotional way.

Ida enjoyed her three weeks in Tahiti, and when she learned that her ship was ready to sail, she was reluctant to leave. But her money wouldn't last for ever and anyway the ship was now heading to China, a place Ida simply had to visit. On 17 May 1847, once again this intrepid woman from Vienna set off to see more of the world.

After two months of relentless rolling up and down over the ocean, with its never-ending bouncing horizons, the ship finally sailed into Victoria (now Central) in Hong Kong.

After the end of the First Opium War and the Treaty of Nanking, the English had obtained Hong Kong from the Chinese in 1842, and when Ida arrived five years later there were around 200–300 Europeans in the town. Ida, however, felt that Victoria wasn't the real China and she decided to visit the inland town of Canton (now Guangzhou).

She was strongly advised not to go. Just a few months earlier, the British had mounted a punitive expedition to Canton after local Chinese had attacked foreigners who had arrived to set up trading posts. This had not improved general relations and the town was now an especially dangerous place for Europeans. Ida, though, with perhaps more obstinacy than bravery, was not going to change her plans.

However, at last she might have begun to understand the reality of what she was doing, for she did acquire two pistols to carry with her before she left.

Ida managed to find a slot on a small Chinese junk heading inland up the Pearl river. When she went aboard the little boat, she found her cabin mates were two Chinese women, busy smoking out of pipes with bowls the size of thimbles. While the effects of the opium drug on Chinese men were well recognised, women smokers were generally hidden from society. Passive and in their own world, her cabin mates caused no problems at all. It wasn't the most comfortable voyage, but Ida passed the time observing her fellow travellers.

Before she had left Hong Kong, Ida had managed to procure a letter of introduction to a European, a Mr Agassiz, who lived in Canton. Once they reached the town, the captain of the boat organised a Chinese man to take Ida to Mr Agassiz's home. On the way, a large crowd of noisy Chinese started to build up around her, hooting and pointing. Clutching her little bag, Ida ignored the commotion and strode on confidently and with an air of authority, a tactic that was to prove useful in all her travels. When she knocked on the door, Mr Agassiz was shocked and quickly ushered Ida inside, saying he was appalled at the thought of the dangers that could have befallen her. He told her she could easily have been stoned, something that was a common occurrence in the very fragile peace then existing between the Chinese and British.

Ida didn't like her time in Canton, but she couldn't help but be fascinated by the different lifestyles. Eating dogs, cats and rats; the lack of washing and the sheer filth of the poorer Chinese; the men's shaved heads, apart from the small patch of hair left long to coil into a single plait – Ida noted that this style was common among nearly all the Chinese men she encountered. One day she happened to go through a place of execution and saw a long row of bleeding heads stuck on high poles. This was not an unusual sight: in the year before Ida arrived, 4,000 people in Canton had been beheaded. Seeing the heads was quite shocking to Ida, but she took it in her stride and simply made more notes.

It was only when Ida studied the small bound feet of the Chinese women, sometimes no longer than 4in long, bound in silk and stuffed into pretty little shoes, that she felt some real emotion. Her distress continued when she learned that these women had had their feet tightly bound as little girls, enduring months and years of pain as their feet were prevented from growing, and that this was common practice over much of the country. Despite their tiny feet, these women were surprisingly agile, and Ida watched them in surprise as they waddled about like geese. Most evenings, Ida would retire to her room at Mr Agassiz's house to write down her thoughts and experiences in her neat and tidy handwriting. In Canton she certainly had enough to write about.

All in all, China was even more different than Ida had expected, and while she had several bad experiences, she also saw a happier side of life. She was impressed by the creation of deep lacquered ornaments and she loved the fine gardens of the wealthy with their ponds and beautiful lotus flowers. At one point, Ida even visited a tea factory. In the five weeks Ida spent in Canton, using her persuasive skills to the maximum, she certainly saw more of the country than even many long-term visitors. There was so much more to see, but Ida had limited funds and she was by now also becoming addicted to travel and seeing new places; she was set on moving on.

Travelling via Singapore and Ceylon, Ida arrived in India in October 1847. She had just turned 50 and had now been travelling for eighteen months. She was living from day to day and her money was just holding out, helped by her willingness to take the cheapest accommodation and food that was available. From high-powered governors to poverty-stricken locals, Ida was happy spending time with anyone and everyone. This long-skirted mother from Vienna was showing a side of her that no one could ever have anticipated.

In India, as well as on boats, Ida travelled on horses, carts and even man-carrying palanquins as she wandered on a roundabout route to Benares (now Varanasi), Delhi and Bombay (now Mumbai). In many cases, she was passed from one resident, usually English, to another, with notes of introduction and offers of friendship and hospitality in many towns. The arrival of an extraordinary middle-aged Austrian woman, travelling on her own with amazing tales, created a pleasant diversion for many stuck in hot and tedious officialdom, and Ida was always interested in what they had to say. With her notebooks filling up, she never failed to record her new sights, including elephants, wonderful old temples and forts, sacred apes and the Taj Mahal as well as people's lifestyles and habits.

There were frightening moments, of course. In March 1848, when Ida was travelling alone in a horse-drawn waggon down a quiet stretch of road, the driver suddenly stopped and picked up a hatchet from the floor beside him. Ida showed no fear but just quietly sat there, and after staring at her for a while, the driver put the hatchet back and continued on with the journey. Ida realised it had been dangerous and she planned that in future she would try not to travel entirely on her own.

Once Ida reached Bombay, the German Federation consul took her under his wing and she could relax again as she enjoyed excellent hospitality while she saw the sights and chatted happily in German.

At the end of April 1848, two years after she had left Vienna to start her journey, Ida embarked on a small passenger boat to Muscat. She had to sleep on the deck surrounded by other passengers, but her main concern was the presence of smallpox on the boat. Three people died during the voyage. After Muscat, Ida continued north. Arriving at Basra, for once Ida's contact system failed, and while she had procured a letter of introduction to a local businessman, he refused to assist Ida. There was a British military steamer in port, so Ida decided to head on and secured a passage up to Baghdad.

In Baghdad her adventures really began. Dressing in what she described as a large linen wrapper, she decided to clothe herself as much as she could like a local to avoid comment. She made visits to the ruins of Babylon and other landmarks by horseback; on one journey she was invited into the tent of a local prince; she met famous archaeologist Henry Rawlinson, who helped her visit various sites and also happened to mention the revolution that had just occurred in Austria, resulting in the resignation of Prince von Metternich. Ida was astounded, but she had no urgent desire to get back home to find out what was really going on. After two years away, it was hard for Ida to think clearly about her friends or family or about normal town life in Vienna; it all seemed so distant. Concentrating on the immediate challenges and new experiences of continuous travel took up all her thoughts. Deciding to visit Mosul, after some determined discussions with astounded and rather reluctant Arabs, she joined their local caravan and started out on a two-week trek north across dry, open desert land. No shelter, no fresh food or water; for several days, Ida lived on bread and cucumber.

At Mosul, under the patronage of the British vice consul, she toured the town and visited the ruins of Nineveh. Then on she went, finally making it all the way to Tabriz, now in Iran, where an English-speaking man showed total astonishment that she should have reached the town on her own. Getting nearer to Europe, her adventures were still not over. Collecting the right papers to cross borders, she headed on north, with a guide ahead of her, to Nakchivan, now in Azerbaijan but at that time controlled by Russia, and then joined a group of Tartars heading north for Tbilisi in Georgia.

One evening, when the group had stopped for the night, a carriage drove past and suddenly a man jumped down, seized Ida and violently pulled her back up into the carriage. Though fighting as hard as she could, the man was a lot stronger and she was powerless. She was driven off to a small cell with no facilities, locked in and left. It was a worrying night for Ida and finally she may have thought that, if she survived, it might be time to think of going home. When morning finally came, she tried to talk to her captors. Ida's age, her air of authority and her quiet, determined manner impressed them. Once she showed them her papers and spoke to them firmly, albeit in a language they didn't understand, they let her go. Determined as ever, Ida continued and reached Tbilisi, then made her way to the Black Sea, taking a boat across to Odessa.

Travelling via Athens and still writing copious notes, Ida finally made it back to Vienna on 31 October 1848, two and a half years after she had left.

When she arrived back home, she was delighted to see her family and friends and also delighted to find that she had become quite well known. Reports of her travels and exploits had gone ahead of her. With just under 200,000 words in her notebooks, it took a while to sort them out into a readable fashion, but in 1850 her book, *A Woman's Journey Round the World*, was published in three volumes. It brought much acclaim and also some useful money, although perhaps not as much as Ida had hoped.

Back in her home in Vienna, Ida soon felt restless and bored. While Ida had found it easy to chat to people on her travels, she had established no close relationships. Now, reconnecting with her friends in Vienna, while she tried to be friendly, she found there was a barrier. She had no real interest in what she saw as their monotonous lives. They, in return, had little understanding of where Ida had been and the sights she had seen. Fully self-contained, she did not feel any need for close or loving support. For Ida, travelling had become her only real love, her way of life. She started planning yet another trip.

On her previous voyage, she had collected and brought back some interesting species of insects that she had sold successfully to the Royal Museum of Vienna. Perhaps she felt it was indulgent just to go travelling again, so this time she decided that collecting unusual species would become a key objective in her travels. She knew museums were also paying well for new species and all money was useful to help cover her costs.

But where to go? When Ida set off again, in March 1851, she had only a vague idea of where her next journey would take her. Travelling first through Europe, she arrived in London and had a good look around, visiting the Bethlem hospital for the insane and also the Great Exhibition in its magnificent Crystal Palace in Hyde Park. Visiting and talking to as many influential and interesting people as possible, at some point Ida heard about Lake Ngami in what is now Botswana and how David Livingstone had first seen it a year and a half before, in August 1849. The news intrigued Ida and she put it top of her list. It was somewhere that sounded different and exciting to visit.

Taking a ship to Cape Town, Ida soon learned however that, with the money and resources she had to hand, to reach Lake Ngami would be impossible. The logistics of travelling over 1,000 miles into the interior of Africa were simply too difficult and too expensive even for Ida. She then considered visiting Australia. Learning that a boat was about to leave for Singapore, she made a quick decision. The success of her previous travels and her books had given her already strong confidence a boost. Now, with her forceful personality, Ida had no difficulty in persuading the captain to give her a special discount and soon she was heading east across the Indian Ocean.

Back in Singapore on her second visit, Ida quickly renewed old acquaintances and this time she explained that she was really keen on collecting butterflies and other insects. Underneath, though, she was also very pleased at the prospect of being paid by museums for unusual species. Despite the money from the books, Ida was still travelling on a very tight budget, and when she investigated, travelling down to Australia sounded expensive. Instead, she decided to make a cheaper voyage to Sarawak, a lot nearer and by all accounts still a fascinating place. It had been in the news thanks to its British white rajah Sir James Brooke, but it was public knowledge that the interior was dominated by headhunting Dyaks. In her usual style, Ida managed to arrange a very cheap passage with the captain of a barque and soon she was off on the twelve-day trip down to the capital, Kuching. After some pleasant days with the European community there, it was time for Ida to head off to see the real Sarawak.

It is extraordinary that after reasonable success, and now well into her fifties, Ida still had the energy and desire to trek into seriously remote regions. She listened to the warnings: how she could easily be caught up among different warring tribes; how headhunting was a key part of the tribes' culture because heads were thought to hold special supernatural powers; how the areas were so remote that there was no hope of calling assistance; but Ida decided to head on regardless. She made a vague plan of where she wanted to visit, heading inland by river, crossing the Klingkang mountains to Sambas, and then continuing by river down to Pontianak on the east coast.

When it was clear Ida was determined to set off, the nephew of Sir James Brooke organised and paid for a Malay guide and eight boatmen to go with her, and soon a voyage up the long Batang Lupar river was organised. Ida hoped she might be able to stay at Dyak villages, otherwise she could bed down in the boat. As before, when on an interesting trip, comfort meant little to Ida. At least, in her long flowing clothes, the worst of the biting insects were kept away.

The little party set off on 11 January 1852, paddling up the slow-flowing, muddy-brown river enclosed on both sides by luxurious tropical vegetation. To begin with, all was well: the Dyaks were near enough to European settlements not to be overwhelmed by the sudden appearance of a white woman; indeed, most were quite welcoming. The Dyaks' dress comprised simple strips of brown bark hanging from the waist down; the women were topless. Their homes were huge longhouses built high on stilts, with rubbish and sewage drying out on the ground below. At one longhouse, Ida came across her first human heads, hanging out to dry. She stared at the half-dried flesh, the shrivelled lips and ears, and the terrifying open eyes, but she accepted the experience calmly, well aware that the Dyaks weren't the only group of people in history to inflict horror on other humans.

But as the days went by and Ida sat in her little boat, being paddled further and further into the remote jungle, she reflected that she really was now on her own, well away from European help.

One night they pulled ashore and the Dyaks again appeared friendly, offering a bed in their longhouse. However, on the side of the sleeping area allocated to Ida were three fresh human heads, hanging there as they dried out. For once, as Ida lay there, she became truly afraid. What might happen to her in the night? There was no chance of sleep; the smell alone from the nearby heads was disgusting.

Even worse, next morning the little team of Malay boatmen that had been accompanying Ida wanted to leave and head back. Despite their being promised good payment by the family of the English rajah back in Kuching, the journey was becoming frightening. Ida persuaded them to continue upriver, but soon their fears seemed justified. As they paddled up the calm, muddy water, they could hear drums and gongs and chanting. Rounding a bend in the river, suddenly they saw perhaps a hundred Dyak men, armed with spears and shields, on the shore. When the Dyaks saw the little boat party, their chanting turned to screams and they raised their weapons, making threatening gestures.

Ida sat quietly, not quite sure what to do. The recent sight of the freshly cut heads by her bed had disturbed her; now she was seriously fearful. Was this, finally, the end of her travels? It was thanks to one of the Malay boatmen that the situation was saved. He could communicate with the Dyaks; perhaps he explained that they were not offering any threat but had an old woman on board who simply wanted to collect butterflies. Either way, the Dyaks suddenly took to the river, surging out to the boat. Ida sat there, quite still. Not having understood the conversation, she still thought this was probably the end.

In fact, the Dyaks had decided to welcome the little group, and soon everyone was ashore sharing in a basic meal of unappetising rice flour. Ida was grateful and also quite excited. For some reason, she suddenly felt confident about the rest of the trip, and she was right.

By the end of the month, Ida had reached the foot of the mountains. Here the boat was left and the small group prepared themselves for a long trek through the mountain range. It took three days of eight-hour marches along small tracks and sometimes across streams on thin bamboo poles before they finally reached the next river.

From then on, the trip was more straightforward and the fast-flowing river took them down to Pontianak, arriving on 6 February. It had been a remarkable trip and once more being a single, older, confident woman had been the key. Sensing no threat, the Dyaks, despite their fearsome reputation, had only offered friendship and support.

Once in the Dutch settlement, Ida reverted to her usual mode of travel. Making friends and obtaining letters of introduction, she visited local sites and places of interest, including an opium den, where she criticised both the Dutch and English for continuing to trade in the harmful drug. She also made a point of collecting small wildlife and insects and then headed on. Jakarta was her next stop, and from mid-May 1852 until July 1853 Ida wandered around the islands of Indonesia. Conserving her precious funds as much as possible, she almost always found hospitable local people to offer help and accommodation, and she discovered new sites and new ideas to write about everywhere she went.

Finally, by July 1853, she arrived back in Jakarta to find a three-masted ship anchored offshore, about to depart for San Francisco. She was ready to leave. With her well-polished negotiating skills, Ida persuaded the captain to take her on board free of charge. Once in the United States, Ida continued with her adventures, visiting native American villages, travelling down to Panama and Peru, and finally taking various paddle steamers up the Mississippi and then Missouri rivers to finally reach St Paul.

From there, on her travels via Montreal down to New York, accommodation became difficult. No longer was Ida an unusual white woman in a strange area; she actually became quite offended when she found many people had not heard of her and her travels, and she was asked to pay a full price for a hotel room. She finally left the United States in November 1854 on a steamer for Europe.

Even then, she didn't rush straight home but took six months to visit one of her sons, who was now living in the Azores, before finally arriving back in Vienna in July 1855. She had spent four years travelling around the world from west to east and had become the first woman ever to travel around the world in both directions. They had both been truly extraordinary journeys, and Ida had experienced so much that there was little chance of her settling down again to a quiet life in the sophisticated Austrian capital. While she enjoyed the level of fame and applause now given to her after her remarkable travels, and despite being 58 years old, Ida couldn't give up her addiction.

On 21 May 1856, Ida left Vienna again, this time with a free ticket to Mauritius and a hope to visit Madagascar. Her collection of insects, butterflies and plants had been praised, and she knew she would find some unusual species in Madagascar. But more than anything, she would see more new places and meet more new people.

Again the trip was full of drama and fascinating moments, but her travels were at last having an effect. Ida had suffered many bouts of fever and sickness, which she had done her best to ignore. Now, however, she was in her sixties and her resilience was weakening. She made it to Madagascar, but everything was becoming difficult, and early in March 1858, Ida left Mauritius to return to Europe. Travelling via Hamburg on her way back, she was admitted to hospital. She rallied enough to be taken back to the home of her brother in Vienna, but she died on 27 October 1858.

With the legacy of a fascinating collection of insects and plants, and her diaries and books from her travels, Ida Pfeiffer certainly made her mark, even without the additional accolade of being the very first woman to travel around the world in both directions.

Philibert Commerson, a French expert in botany and natural history.

Mary Bryant was one of the first convicts to escape from Port Jackson (Sydney), but after sailing up to Timor she was recaptured and transferred onto Mary Ann Parker's ship.
(Chronicle / Alamy Stock Photo)

Mary Ann Parker spent time in London's notorious Fleet debtors' prison.
(Chronicle / Alamy Stock Photo)

Ida Pfeiffer had to wait until she was middle aged before she could follow her dreams and start travelling the world.
(Universal Art Archive / Alamy Stock Photo)

Ida Pfeiffer soon became accepted by local tribesmen.
(Biblio Asia, National Library, Singapore)

It was thanks to the *World* newspaper that Nellie Bly could start travelling right around the world.
(The Granger Collection / Alamy Stock Photo)

Nellie Bly sailed on the SS *Augusta Victoria*. The new luxury ocean liner still carried sailing masts, but thanks to its new steam power, it was the fastest ship to cross the Atlantic at the time.
(DeGolyer Library, Southern Methodist University, via WikimediaCommons)

Sophisticated Elizabeth Bisland hadn't really wanted to sail west around the world.
(The Wallach Division, New York Public Library)

Arriving in Hong Kong, Nellie Bly was aghast to learn that Elizabeth Bisland had got there first. However, she still took time to admire the view from the Peak.
(Chronicle / Alamy Stock Photo)

Hattie McIlrath and her husband set off with minimal luggage and a big ambition … to cycle right around the world.
(Chicago Inter Ocean newspaper)

As the McIlraths headed north towards Tehran, the snow just got deeper and deeper until Hattie, with frozen legs, could go no further.
(Wide World Magazine / George Newnes Ltd)

With delightful manners and elegant clothing, Annette Meakin appeared totally unsuitable to brave the rugged conditions in Siberia.

Annette Meakin set off with her mother on a basic tarantass carriage to drive 50 miles out to a remote Russian prison.

Visiting a remote Kazakh yurt, Annette Meakin learned that *beshbarmak*, a specially flavoured horse-meat stew, was particularly popular.
(Engraving by Vasiliy Vereshchagin, via ilbusca/iStockPhoto)

Annette Meakin travelled on the very earliest trains across Siberia.
(clu/iStockPhoto)

Still elegantly dressed, Annette and her mother at Otaru, in northern Japan.
(Annette M.B. Meakin / Forgotten Books)

4

1889 NELLIE BLY AND ELIZABETH BISLAND
THE FIRST WOMEN TO RACE ROUND THE WORLD

In the late nineteenth century, Nellie Bly and Elizabeth Bisland were fortunate to be travelling at a time when ships had undergone a transformation and travel generally was becoming safer and more reliable, thanks to the power of steam.

Use of this innovative source of energy had progressed steadily since 1838, when the first passenger ships, the *Sirius* and the SS *Great Western*, crossed the Atlantic by steam power alone. It had been a close contest between the two ships and the *Sirius* had beaten the SS *Great Western* by just one day. Both ships had had remarkable journeys. The crew of the *Sirius* had been concerned they were running out of coal and resorted to burning barrels of resin while the SS *Great Western* had been delayed when a fire broke out in the engine room.

Over the following years, steam power continued to develop, but there were still many difficulties to be overcome – plus wind was free. This resulted in an overall general reluctance for ships to give up sail entirely. By the 1880s, at the time when Nellie and Elizabeth were rushing around on the new 'steamers', many of the ships still carried two or three masts as well as funnels, although the masts were used more often for lights and flags than for sails.

For a small-town girl from rural Pennsylvania, it was difficult enough to gain entry into the New York offices of the biggest newspaper of the time. To actually navigate through the warren of corridors and get past numerous employees unchallenged to reach the door of the editor-in-chief was really remarkable.

But 23-year-old Elizabeth Cochrane was desperate. After quitting her job on the *Pittsburgh Despatch*, and using her new, catchier name of Nellie Bly, in 1887 she had come to New York full of dreams, ambition and real hope of at last escaping the dreadful struggle for money her family had endured during the last few years. It hadn't worked out. After renting a small, shabby apartment on the wrong side of Manhattan, her many letters and calls had got her nowhere. She had run out of money, yet admitting failure and going back to her widowed mother's meagre home was unthinkable.

Now, on a final desperate call, she was within striking distance of a big editor. She smiled sweetly and confidently at the clerk, explaining that she was an experienced reporter who had a groundbreaking story. She was going to offer it to the *New York World* newspaper first before going to the other newspapers.

Somehow, amazingly, Nellie gained admittance to the most important room in the building. The renowned editor, Colonel Cockerill, looked up from behind his desk, but there was no welcoming smile. He had been called the best news editor in the country, but he was not known for his tolerance ... he had once shot dead a man who had burst unexpectedly into his office.

Nellie knew this was her moment. Standing upright, she presented her idea clearly and with as much confidence as she could muster: she wanted to go to Europe and travel back across the Atlantic, reporting on the poor women immigrants who were said to be suffering truly dreadful conditions on the voyage.

Colonel Cockerill listened to Nellie carefully. It wasn't a bad idea, and this girl reporter was clearly very determined and passionate about the situation of these women. He told her he would discuss the idea and she should come back in a few days.

When she returned, full of hope, she was told her idea didn't stand up. As Nellie absorbed this huge disappointment, she went on listening as she was told about another idea. Evidently, there was already a story running about the dreadful conditions for women in New York's Asylum for the Insane on Blackwell Island. The paper was looking for someone who would be willing to pretend they were insane in order to get admitted into the asylum, so they could write a genuine report. Nellie didn't think twice; she would do this.

At last, she had a foot in the door. Could this be the big break she was looking for?

At home in her little flat that evening, the excitement gave way to serious thought. To get admitted to a lunatic asylum meant she would have to pretend to be actually insane; and what would it really be like inside? It was a very frightening thought, but Nellie was determined. First, with an advance from the paper, she rented a cheap room. One day later she sat on the stairs, refusing to move and saying she was frightened; then she started demanding fictional luggage. When she was finally arrested for her erratic behaviour and taken to court, she feigned blankness; in a hospital she talked to doctors about faces on a wall. All the time, she was worried she would be discovered, but after three days she was at last taken to Blackwell Island. It had been an Oscar-level performance, but she had done it.

Nellie spent ten horrific days in the asylum, enduring icy baths and inadequate clothing, bedding and food, and sitting on benches without being allowed to talk or stand up for sometimes twelve hours at a time. She was just beginning to get seriously worried when a lawyer from the *World* newspaper finally came to her rescue. Her first story for the *World*, called 'Behind Asylum Bars', created a sensation. Her follow-up, 'Inside a Madhouse', instantly established Nellie as a well-reputed reporter. It had all been worth it. The prestigious *World* newspaper took her on as a full-time investigative journalist, and she found she was good in the role, continuing to uncover stories from the darker side of New York life.

Now, with a secure job and regular money coming in, Nellie could afford to be a little pleased with herself. She had done it! She took a new flat in a better part of town, brought her mother up from Pittsburgh to live with her, and continued uncovering scandals and horrors for the *World* newspaper.

Living just a few blocks away from Nellie in central New York was another woman journalist of the time, Elizabeth Bisland. Elizabeth couldn't have been more different from Nellie. She had been born, in 1861, on the successful Fairfax Plantation just west of New Orleans, in the far south of America. Fairfax House, with its wide, sweeping terraces overlooking glorious lawns and oak trees, was a place of beauty. Her father, a doctor by profession, had decided to become a full-time planter and had become very successful. The year after Elizabeth's birth, thanks to the help of over 100 enslaved workers, he produced over half a million pounds of sugar from the flat sugarcane fields surrounding the property.

When Elizabeth was aged 2, though, everything changed dramatically and the family fled the homestead as the area became a base for Confederate troops in the American Civil War. When the family returned, two years later, there were no enslaved workers and no money. Her parents tried to sort out life as best they could, but even when they finally abandoned Fairfax and went to live in Elizabeth's father's old home further north, a lack of money was still making life very challenging.

One thing the family took with them from their old home was a bound collection of works by British poets. As she grew up, Elizabeth buried herself in these books and became especially enchanted by the works of John Keats, Thomas Gray and Alexander Pope. She started writing poetry and one day she thought she would send one of her poems to the *Times Democrat* paper in New Orleans.

Her poem, about the fierce wild wind, immediately caught the attention of the editors, who thought it was outstanding, and they subsequently published several of Elizabeth's poems. This encouraged Elizabeth and, aware of the family's great need for money, she decided to see if she could get a paid job. The *Times Democrat* agreed to take her on as a women's writer, and in 1882, when she was 21, she set off for New Orleans.

Elizabeth had grown into a very well-read and knowledgeable young woman, with refined and exquisite manners, and she did well in New Orleans, turning her hand to whatever stories the paper required. Her love of poetry continued and now she also started looking at serious literature. One of her favourite jobs was to write book reviews for the paper. It wasn't long before, like Nellie Bly, she decided that to further her writing career, she needed to move to New York. Armed with letters of introduction from her editors in New Orleans and renting a small apartment in central Manhattan, she was soon making a good living, writing freelance stories for several top magazines and doing book reviews, which she loved. One of her sisters joined her, sharing her apartment, and gradually Elizabeth became recognised and welcomed into the leading literature cliques of the city. Intellectual gatherings and afternoon tea parties became part of her life and, like Nellie Bly, she became happily settled into New York life.

For both women, their lives were about to be turned upside down, and it was due to French author Jules Verne. In 1872 he had written his best-selling book, *Around the World in Eighty Days*.

The *World* newspaper, who now employed Nellie Bly, were always looking for dramatic stories to boost circulation. One evening, as they discussed ideas for stories, the editors of the newspaper decided a race around the world to try and beat the fictional Phileas Fogg in Jules Verne's book would be a real circulation booster. The more they discussed it and the more they looked into the boats and trains required, the more feasible the idea became. In fact, from their early research, they thought the actual trip could be made in just seventy-five days. Initially they planned to send a male reporter, but then the obvious occurred to them ... Nellie Bly. She would be the perfect person for the job and would attract far more interest than a man.

Nellie leapt at the idea. Right around the world! She had no hesitation at all; it would be a fabulous adventure. Immediately she started working out the practicalities. Rushing from train to boat to make the fastest time, she could not be hampered by too much luggage. She purchased a small hard-wearing carry bag and went to a top dressmaker in town to order a dress that would stand constant wear for three months. Along with three veils, a pair of slippers, a dressing gown, a drinking cup, pens and paper, and a jar of cold face cream, Nellie quickly filled her small carry bag. She obtained temporary passport papers, the newspaper gave her money, and suddenly she was ready to go.

The paper had worked out a possible itinerary but had only booked the first journey for her across to England. After that, it would be down to Nellie to confirm her passages on the fastest possible transport available.

At 9.40 a.m. on Thursday, 14 November 1889, Nellie stood on the deck of the ocean liner *Augusta Victoria*, waving goodbye to the United States. Next time she saw New York, she would, hopefully, be approaching it from the opposite direction and would have been right around the world.

The *World* newspaper was determined to make as much as possible of the trip to lift circulation and had announced the start of the journey as major news that morning.

On his way to work, John Walker, editor of New York's popular monthly general interest magazine *Cosmopolitan*, picked up the first edition of the *World* newspaper and read about Nellie's journey. Instantly he became excited; he recognised immediately that this was a great story, something that would attract readers everywhere. Racing into the office, he urgently called a meeting and announced to his startled colleagues that this was an opportunity too good to miss. *Cosmopolitan* would also send a woman to race around the world; and even better, she would beat Nellie. Surely, if she travelled from east to west across the Pacific, instead of first crossing the Atlantic as Nellie was doing, they would gain a time advantage because of the seasonal easterly winds in the China Sea.

Who to send? Elizabeth Bisland was the obvious answer; she was working regularly as a freelance writer for the paper. They knew she was unmarried and had no home ties. She was also very pretty, which would be useful for gaining extra readers.

The decision was made. John Walker urgently sent a man to the Thomas Cook travel agency to get travel details and book the necessary tickets in the fastest possible time, and then sent a messenger to find Elizabeth Bisland and get her into his office at once.

Elizabeth was working happily in her apartment, planning a tea party she was organising for friends, when she got the message. She couldn't imagine why she had been summoned so urgently. When she reached Walker's office, she was greeted warmly and then listened carefully as she was told about the proposal.

Elizabeth was not impressed. She was a serious writer, a calm woman who mixed in sophisticated circles. She certainly had no interest in any gimmick; racing around the world for a dramatic story was definitely not for her.

She said no. It took Walker enormous effort to win Elizabeth over. Perhaps it was finally the offer of a large salary and the promise of a full-time job writing the sort of stories she wanted; or perhaps it dawned on her that if she annoyed this powerful man by refusing, her name could be blacklisted across all New York media. However, the *Cosmopolitan* editor did it: in less than an hour Elizabeth's total refusal had turned into a very reluctant agreement. She too would go around the world.

There was no time to be lost; Nellie was already on her way. Leaving her sister to sort out her tea party guests, Elizabeth packed frantically, including both cloth and silk dresses, a pair of rubber overshoes, a wool overcoat and a travel rug. In the end she managed to get her luggage down to a small trunk and a small valise. Late in the afternoon, a car arrived to take her to Grand Central station, where she found her booked berth on a train.

At six o'clock that evening, eight hours and twenty minutes after Nellie's ship had pulled out of New York Harbor heading east,

Elizabeth's train worked up steam and started off towards the west. The race had begun.

The trip across the Atlantic was not a success for Nellie. The *Augusta Victoria* had been chosen for speed; it had eight double-ended main coal-fired boilers and was one of the first liners with twin screws. Just six months earlier, the ship, on its maiden voyage to New York, had broken the record and done the crossing in just seven days. This emphasis on speed didn't make the ship the most comfortable and Nellie found she was prone to seasickness, which gave her concern about how she would manage the rest of the trip. But as she recovered, she became more optimistic, and certainly, when she arrived in Southampton and was met by the London representative of the *World* newspaper, everything seemed easier.

There was one hiccup. The *World* newspaper had organised a proper passport for Nellie to replace her temporary papers and she had to collect it from the secretary of the American Legation in London. Rushing on a train up to London, at the American offices she had to swear, on oath, that the details were true. Nellie had no hesitation, yet the age given on the passport was 22 years, three years younger than her real age. Perhaps Nellie thought the idea of a younger girl travelling the world would be more exciting; perhaps she thought trying to change the details might jeopardise her trip. Either way, she had no hesitation about lying under oath and her claim to be younger than she was continued for some years.

The *World* representative then accompanied Nellie across the Channel to France, but it wasn't until she had waved goodbye and clambered onto the train that was to speed her down to Brindisi on the southern tip of Italy that she felt her real journey was about to begin. Until then everything had been organised; now it was down to her to complete a journey around the world.

The train journey wasn't comfortable, with just a single toilet and washroom for over twenty passengers. Nellie managed to get some sleep, but once morning came things didn't really improve; breakfast was simply bread and coffee, and the view, as the train rattled through northern Italy, was one of dense fog.

Nellie had details of possible boats with her and realised that, if the train was on time, she might be able to catch the P&O steamship *Victoria* heading from Brindisi for Ceylon (now Sri Lanka). The train was not on time, and as the afternoon turned into night, Nellie sat anxiously on the edge of her berth. There would be a long delay if she missed the boat, and even at this stage of the journey Nellie really didn't want to fail. She realised that, if she took longer than the eighty days in Jules Verne's book, her story would end up being of little significance or interest. It was an agonising few final hours, but eventually the train chugged into Brindisi station over three hours late at the unwelcome time of 1.30 a.m. The boat was due to leave at 3 a.m.

There was time – just. With help from porters and a frantic rush through the dark streets of Brindisi, she made it to the docks and organised her passage. She hadn't had a good night's sleep since she left her previous ship in Southampton three long days before, and once on board and entering her small, dark cabin, she collapsed into bed. She woke up the next morning soaking wet. The porthole window above her berth had been left open and the vigorous washing of the deck above her cabin had sent a few bucketfuls of water sloshing in.

Nevertheless, Nellie was now feeling good. It was a comfortable ship and all she had to do was relax for the next two weeks as the ship made its way steadily east. She found she was sharing her cabin with a friendly Englishwoman, and soon Nellie had also made several friends among the other passengers as they sat on deck and chatted away. Sometimes she went to the stern just for the joy of standing on deck in wonderful warm sunshine, watching the sparkling water froth up behind. Going through the Suez Canal, stopping off at Aden, Nellie was enjoying so many wonderful new experiences that she almost forgot she was meant to be rushing around the world.

As the ship approached Colombo in Ceylon, Nellie checked the provisional itinerary the *World* newspaper had given her. They had suggested she could transfer onto another P&O ship, the *Oriental*, which was due to depart Colombo on 10 December. When the *Victoria* finally docked at Colombo on 8 December, Nellie breathed a big sigh of relief. It was perfect timing. She could book into a hotel for a night, see a little of the country, and be in good time to get on board for the next stage of her trip.

What Nellie didn't know was that her new ship, the *Oriental*, had been delayed in Calcutta (now Kolkata) and was running late. When Nellie was given the news that the *Oriental* would not now depart until 13 December, her whole planned schedule was thrown out. She went over to the official building of the Colombo Telegraph Office and sent, at quite an expense, an urgent telegram back to the *World* newspaper in New York. Then there was nothing to be done. Her hotel, the Grand Oriental, was the best hotel in town and all expenses were being paid by the *World*. Nellie might as well enjoy herself while she waited for her ship to depart.

The news wasn't greeted by too much dismay in New York, for the words 'Nellie delayed in Colombo' made good headlines and simply added to the drama that the newspaper was trying to build up about the trip. Their belief that the journey would attract interest had proven correct; circulation was already soaring and bets were being organised on whether Nellie would make it back in time.

In Colombo, word was beginning to get out about her round-the-world trip, and Nellie found no shortage of single young men, and some older men, willing to chat and help her see the sights.

Nellie was especially impressed by the lovely vegetation, the vividly bright flowers and the tall, magnificent trees stretching up towards the deep-blue sky. It was all so beautiful. One evening, she went to a Parsee theatre and, while she found it fascinating, she didn't like the long nasal solos; it made her want to blow her nose. Arriving back at her luxurious hotel, with its cool courtyards and excellent food and service, Nellie could relax in total comfort. If this was work, she didn't mind it at all!

Finally, the *Oriental* arrived from India. Nellie gathered her bags up quickly and rushed to get on board; she was very impatient to be on her way again. Once the ship sailed, Nellie realised she loved being back on the ocean. Any ideas of seasickness had long gone and she spent the time lazing on deck, watching the sparkling blue sea. Five days later, the ship stopped off at Penang and Nellie went ashore for a quick visit. When she returned to the quay to get the little tender back to the boat, she found the weather had turned. In what was becoming a really rough, turbulent sea, she had to hang on tightly as she made her way back to the ship, this time to head off to Singapore.

It wasn't an easy journey and Nellie's mood began to change. From the carefree trip across sparkling waters, she was now looking at rain-drenched, heaving grey water, and she was fast becoming aware that time was rushing past. When the rough sea slowed the ship down and they had to wait until daylight before they could enter Singapore harbour, for the first time on the journey Nellie started to fret. She had been travelling for thirty-three days and was around halfway on the journey; but she knew the crossing of the South China Sea would be slow because of headwinds, and connections via Japan might be tricky.

The *Oriental* was only making a quick refuelling stop in Singapore, but it gave Nellie a few hours to go ashore and have a look. A Welsh doctor accompanied Nellie, and despite his efforts, she couldn't be dissuaded from buying a sweet little monkey in a cage. Nellie was, underneath, still a shrewd journalist and was aware that bringing a monkey back with her from her trip around the world would make excellent extra copy.

With Nellie back on the ship, and her monkey safely stowed in the cabin, the *Oriental* headed off for Hong Kong and ran straight into a full-force monsoon. It was terrifying and magnificent all at once, but Nellie was most of all concerned about time. She needn't have been. Despite the storm, the *Oriental* had made record time, and by the time they arrived in Hong Kong, Nellie was now back on the initial schedule.

However, there was a big shock awaiting Nellie when, on disembarking, she rushed ashore to sort out the next step. In those days, in 1890, transport in Hong Kong included sedan chairs carried on two long poles by strong local men. But after the initial surprise at being hoisted into the air, she found travelling by sedan surprisingly comfortable. Arriving at the offices of the Occidental and Oriental

Steamship Company, Nellie stepped down and went in to find the next possible ship leaving for Japan and the United States.

When she said her name was Nellie Bly, she was met with the most extraordinary response. The man in the office started checking on boat schedules and then he looked up, commenting that it was such a shame she was going to be beaten.

Nellie didn't understand and explained that she was, at thirty-nine days out of New York, a little ahead of schedule and still very optimistic that she could do the whole journey in less than seventy-five days, the time the *World* had been boasting about to its readers. She couldn't conceal the shock on her face when the clerk explained that a woman called Elizabeth Bisland had been there just a little while before and was trying to beat Nellie's time of travelling around the world. Nellie was totally taken aback. Why hadn't she had a cable from the *World*? Why had no one mentioned it? A race? Nellie felt her whole world drop before her; it was not what she had envisaged at all. The huge celebratory arrival back that she had hoped for would now be muted with two of them doing it. Even worse, Nellie had evidently just passed Elizabeth going the other way in the China Sea, and Elizabeth was ahead on time. When Nellie also learned there was no boat leaving for Japan for five days, she was really upset. Had all her efforts been wasted; was another woman going to claim the glory?

Nellie had booked a room in a hotel and she returned there totally despondent. After all that effort, all that rushing from train to boat to boat, it seemed that it might all end in failure. Word had got out that Nellie was in a race around the world and the next day she was invited to attend several dinners and receptions in her honour. She refused them all, for she only had one dress and, more importantly, she simply wasn't in the mood to socialise.

Gradually, however, once she got over the shock, Nellie's mood improved and she became resolute; she would do what she could and simply see what evolved. Either way, she had been given a completely free trip around the world. It wasn't all bad news. After that, though, Nellie made a point of researching local areas for when she returned to New York; even if the trip didn't work out, she should be able to write some great stories about the places she was seeing.

In the three remaining days before her ship left, Nellie spent the time having a good look at Hong Kong life. She got used to travelling in a sedan; she loved the view of the peak and was saddened by the number of filthy beggars around the temples. She also managed to book a quick trip to Canton (now Guangzhou), and there, like Ida Pfeiffer before her, she was warned that she might be stoned. She wanted to see the execution ground and walked over ground spattered with blood from the beheading of eleven men the previous day. She also visited a jail to see the cruelty meted out to prisoners. It was horrific and, even worse for Nellie, she suddenly realised it was Christmas. Suddenly, Nellie felt homesick, sad and a little lost.

Back in Hong Kong there was no more delay and, on 28 December, Nellie was on board the *Oceanic* together with her monkey in a cage. This time it was good news: the *Oceanic* was sailing via a quick stop in Japan all the way to San Francisco. Even better, the ship was recognised for its speed and was due at San Francisco on 22 January. To ensure she managed to do the trip in the planned seventy-five days, this gave Nellie six days to get right across the United States. It was feasible.

Nellie's natural optimism suddenly returned. Forget Elizabeth; she would beat the record and return with a host of good stories. Hopefully that would be enough to preserve her job at the *World* and its good salary.

When Elizabeth Bisland finally agreed to go around the world, she was less than enthusiastic. She was very aware that it would be a tiring and frequently uncomfortable trip, and when she boarded the train in New York to start her journey west, the comfortable carriages and berths didn't help to calm her down. It had all been such a terrible rush.

On that very first segment of the long trip, she failed to sleep at all and, with 800 miles to cover to reach Chicago, the long hours passed slowly. *Cosmopolitan* magazine had told her there would be someone to meet her at Chicago, but when she arrived late at night at the huge, bustling station, no one came forward. Slowly the station emptied as Elizabeth hung around, becoming increasingly annoyed and also quite lonely. With the help of some friendly railway staff, she finally found her way to the platform of the next train she was due to catch and then simply sat there to wait. After a few uncomfortable hours and still cross and unhappy, Elizabeth was at last on her way again, this time heading west on the 2,000-mile journey to San Francisco.

The transcontinental railroad had only been completed twenty years before and it was a difficult route through mountains and across rivers and vast areas of what appeared to be totally empty land. The journey continued to be tiresome for Elizabeth; she could find nothing of intellectual interest and it wasn't easy to sleep in the rattling, swaying carriage.

In San Francisco, *Cosmopolitan* had honoured its promise and booked her into a luxurious hotel. At last, she could clean up and have a good night's sleep, but when she woke up again, Elizabeth still felt cross that she had let herself be persuaded to do the trip. She was a very private person and it didn't help her mood when she saw, splashed across the front page of the local newspaper, an article all about her and the race around the world. *Cosmopolitan*, like the *World* newspaper, was determined to get every bit of publicity it could from this trip.

Bets were now being taken all over the United States on the race: some in favour of the elegant, sophisticated Elizabeth, and others cheering for Nellie, the lively street girl who wrote for and supported working-class women. The contest was already hotting up.

When Elizabeth boarded the ship that was to take her west, she had already used up a full week of her travelling time, but she wasn't too concerned. It was the magazine's race, not hers, and her mood lifted a little when she saw the comfort of her stateroom. *Cosmopolitan* had certainly been generous here. Elizabeth settled into shipboard life quite quickly and for the two-week trip across the Pacific, apart from a few periods of rough weather, it was generally a pleasant journey. She was beginning to find interesting people to talk to; things were looking up.

The ship was only stopping for a day and a half in Japan before it continued westwards, but Elizabeth saw as much as she could and was fascinated by the different life and different people. She was impressed with the beautiful silks, crepes and delicate fabrics, and ordered a dress that was, to her surprise, ready for her in just a few hours. It was all very pleasant, but the *Oceanic* refuelled quickly and soon it was time to continue on the rush westwards. The ship made good time to Hong Kong, arriving on 15 December.

In Hong Kong, Elizabeth found that her planned ship was held up by a damaged screw and so she visited the helpful staff at the Occidental and Oriental Steamship Company, who booked her on a British ship, the *Thames*, heading via Singapore for Ceylon. These were the same people who just a few days later advised Nellie she was not only in a race but also going to lose.

As soon as Elizabeth boarded the *Thames*, she was happy. Like Nellie, she found she loved being at sea, especially in luxurious surroundings. She was also one of the very few women on the ship and she revelled in the attention of ultra-polite British gentlemen. Having read so much English literature in her childhood, her admiration for the English only increased when she saw the quiet confidence and authority of the well turned out men on board.

Unbeknown to her, somewhere out to sea around 20 December 1889, Elizabeth sailed past Nellie going the other way. The timing was close and this added drama to the story back in the United States. Newspapers right across the country were now following the trip with growing interest, and some worked out, from their comfortable office desks, that Elizabeth was one day ahead.

In Singapore, Elizabeth had a very short stopover, but in the time she saw all she could and found the botanical gardens charming. She wandered slowly down the pathways, admiring all the beautiful plants and flowers.

The *Thames* made good progress from Singapore to Ceylon. There Elizabeth transferred to the P&O *Britannia* and again she was delighted with the facilities, with good company and entertainments including elegant afternoon tea and dancing on deck. Sometimes she would take a quiet moment in her cabin, reflecting on the gentle words of one of her favourite poets, John Keats; from her original stance of not wanting to go, now Elizabeth was revelling in the beauty of this exciting new world.

As the ship arrived in Brindisi, after a short stop in Aden, the real enjoyment of the trip ended for Elizabeth. *Cosmopolitan* had booked her on a train straight up through Europe. It had been confirmed by a recent cable from the magazine and she had under an hour to leave the boat and get to the railway station. She packed up early and made sure she was absolutely ready to disembark.

When the boat docked, custom officials came on board to check the luggage of the passengers before they left. Elizabeth was annoyed with the slow checking of paperwork and became even crosser when they decided they wanted her to open her carefully packed trunk and remove all its items one by one. Then, when she finally got off the boat, she was greeted by chaos with people everywhere rushing in different directions amid a mass of noise and clutter. It was not an environment Elizabeth liked or knew how to cope with.

She finally managed to find a porter and, despite having no Italian, somehow conveyed the urgency of her trip. In a panic, she heard the train hoot as she rushed into the station. In the nick of time, she clambered aboard just before the train steamed off. After such an alarm, Elizabeth was upset once again, and to begin with, staring out of the window, she disliked everything she saw. Gradually, though, especially as the scenery changed, Elizabeth perked up. When she reached the Alps, she was back to her normal self, admiring the beauty and peace of the scenery as the train sped her towards Paris.

By now the *World* newspaper and *Cosmopolitan* magazine were really drumming up the contest. Numerous headlines of who might be winning; reports on the women's experiences in distant lands; competitions about who might arrive back in New York first; the race really had caught the public's imagination. In an age when very few people travelled far, people were working out best routes, best times, and rooting for one or other of these intrepid women. Even better, the race was becoming very close indeed. Both women had left New York on 14 November 1889. To beat eighty days around the world, they had to arrive back home by 2 February. The *World* newspaper, though, had promised its readers that Nellie could do the trip in seventy-five days, making 27 January her deadline. *Cosmopolitan* had promised that Elizabeth would beat Nellie and do the trip even faster.

Nellie was due into San Francisco on 21 January, giving her just six days to cross the 3,000 miles right across the United States by the erratic railroads to New York. The record crossings of the nation by train at that time were around three and a half to four days. It was doable, but there was no spare time.

After the long train journey up from Brindisi, Elizabeth had arrived in Paris on 18 January, giving her nine days to reach a ship and make the 3,500-mile journey across the Atlantic over to New York. The record for ships crossing the Atlantic that year was around seven days. Timing for Elizabeth was very tight, but again it was just doable.

They should both beat the eighty days in Jules Verne's book, but the timings were extraordinarily close. Who would actually make New York first?

Elizabeth's train into Paris was late, but she hoped there was still time to catch her planned boat from Le Havre. When she arrived, however, she was greeted by confusion and also false information. She was met by a Thomas Cook agent who told her the planned trip on a specially chartered train to Le Havre wouldn't work, as she was too late and her ship wouldn't wait. Instead, she was rushed onto a train to Calais, where she just had time to snatch a quick breakfast before catching the ferry over to Dover and a train to London.

Elizabeth's journey was now becoming confusing and she found herself very much on her own, trying desperately to work out how to get back to New York. She was short of sleep and the panic of finding new ways to travel was exhausting and worrying. Arriving at Charing Cross station in London, Elizabeth immediately went to a telegraph office and sent an urgent cable to *Cosmopolitan*. The magazine quickly came back with new directions: Elizabeth was to catch the *Bothnia*, leaving from Queenstown in southern Ireland.

To reach Cork, Elizabeth had to get a train to Holyhead in north Wales, then it was a scramble with her luggage onto a ferry, and finally a rush onto another train down to Cork. She hadn't washed or changed her clothes for days; what had started as a pleasant cruise was now turning into a nightmare and the chances of winning the race were reducing by the minute.

In Cork, the weather was wild and the little tender taking Elizabeth and other passengers out to the *Bothnia* rose and tumbled in the churning sea. It took two hours of tossing and turning to reach the boat, and when Elizabeth finally managed to get on board, she tripped, bruising herself badly. The weather was appalling and the ship was already rolling around in what turned out to be one of the worst Atlantic storms for years. In her cabin, Elizabeth had totally lost interest in the race. As she collapsed in her bunk, all she wanted to do was get home to her little flat in New York.

Nellie, meanwhile, was having troubles of her own. News had come to the ship that dreadful snowfalls across North America meant there was no hope of her travelling across to New York on the normal railroad. She was told there would be no trains over to the east for at least a week. Nellie almost despaired. After all her travelling and efforts, a sudden snowstorm was going to finally defeat her.

Arriving in San Francisco, she tried to hide her disappointment as she was greeted by the dignitaries of the town and a huge enthusiastic crowd. When she saw the mass of media reports about her arrival, she quickly realised that her trip was indeed now a very big story in the United States.

There was a happy surprise for Nellie. Instead of needing to find a hotel, she was ushered over to the station and escorted onto a private train. The *World* newspaper, once it was alerted to the snow problem, had pulled out all its resources; it knew if it lost this race, the paper's reputation would be severely damaged for a long time. No expense spared, it had chartered a private train and crew to take Nellie south on a network of rail tracks to avoid the snow in the north.

In a surprisingly short time, Nellie was travelling steadily south through California in bouncy but comfortable surroundings. She was joined on the train by her monkey in a cage as well as assistants organised by the *World* newspaper. The driver was aware of the mission, to get Nellie to New York as fast as possible, and the train often reached maximum speed as it headed south via Arizona and New Mexico before turning north to Kansas and up to Chicago. It made brief stops along the way, and at each stop, Nellie was staggered to see huge crowds gathered simply to wave at her. Slowly it dawned on her that she had become rather famous.

The train arrived in Chicago in just under three days, an astonishing time for the distance, and immediately Nellie was escorted off the train as a heroine. She began to enjoy the celebrity status: everything was organised, she didn't have to think; she was escorted first to the Chicago press club and then to a reception at a restaurant. Her short time in Chicago even included a visit to the Chicago Board of Trade, where the traders all stopped work to give Nellie one almighty cheer. Then it was back to the train station to get the final train back to New York. Now, fittingly for her celebrity status, Nellie was given a private carriage.

Nellie arrived in New York at just before 4 p.m. on 25 January; her journey had taken seventy-two days and six hours. She had certainly beaten the eighty days' deadline and, with Elizabeth Bisland still several days out of New York on the Atlantic, she had also, by a good margin, won the race.

It was a glorious time for Nellie and she relished the fame and admiration. Invitations to dinners and events came in fast and Nellie accepted all she could. Throughout February she wrote a series of stories on her trip for the *World* newspaper that were read widely. The newspaper's circulation had risen dramatically during the race and the editors were delighted with the whole event.

The joy wasn't to last. First, Nellie was involved in a major libel case against the *World* newspaper for a story she had written before her trip. The *World* was fined an enormous amount of money, something that annoyed it deeply. Then she signed up for a forty-city lecture tour but had to abandon it quite quickly after finding entertaining an audience was harder than she expected; plus she also fell out with the organiser, who was unhappy with the publicity from the court case. She wrote a book and eventually started writing again for various media, but there were new people coming up and many were better natural writers than Nellie. After the round-the-world trip, she had been hoping for better things. Now, as her story became old news, she found things were moving on and her fame and job opportunities were both fading. Nellie became quite depressed.

The following few years were difficult, but in 1895, when she was 31, Nellie met a 73-year-old millionaire on a train and in a very short time she married him. She enjoyed nine years as a wealthy wife in New York. When her husband died, she tried to take control of his business but found looking after the finances very challenging. It all ended up in acrimonious bankruptcy and this also brought a big split with her mother and sister.

Nellie had to get her life back on track. She took a suite in a central New York hotel and wrote a range of stories and features for various media, often about the plight of women, her main interest all those years ago when she had first arrived in the city. Her life settled down and, with friends in New York, she enjoyed a pleasant social life as well. Maybe it wasn't the life she had dreamed of in the short spell when she was a celebrity, but it was OK. Then, in 1922, Nellie suffered from a bad bout of pneumonia and she never recovered. She died in New York aged 57.

Elizabeth Bisland, feeling dreadfully seasick, had had the most unpleasant voyage across the Atlantic, and when she finally arrived in New York on 30 January, after a trip of seventy-six-and-a-half days, four days behind Nellie, she was just delighted to be back home. She was also very happy not to receive the acclaim for being the first in the race; instead she quietly went back to her sophisticated New York life, concentrating on her interests in fine poetry and literature, and preparing carefully worded articles and essays on serious topics.

In 1891, a year after her trip, Elizabeth married a lawyer and they spent some time travelling, especially in Japan and also in England, where she loved the grandeur and culture. Moving to Washington, Elizabeth became involved in nursing and good works, but in 1930 her husband died. This was a time of deep sorrow for Elizabeth. She again went to visit Japan, a country she had loved from her very first visit all those years before, and then settled down in a charming house near the University of Virginia. There, Elizabeth devoted herself to her first love, writing, and she produced seven books as well as numerous essays. When she was 67, like Nellie she was stricken by pneumonia and died.

Both women had done their very best to succeed in the first ever circumnavigation race, at a time when travel was not easy and communication was slow. Only Nellie Bly, though, is now remembered for her trip around the world. Coming second, Elizabeth Bisland's efforts were quickly forgotten. But in the end, rather than Nellie's fame, it is Elizabeth's beautiful poetry and writing that still stands out, and which may finally prove to be the most enduring.

5

1895 HATTIE McILRATH
THE FIRST WOMAN ROUND THE WORLD BY BICYCLE

In the early days, cycling wasn't easy. Even by 1861, when bikes were developed with a crank and pedals, the lack of brakes could result in a very dangerous headfirst tumble. More than anything, though, they were difficult to mount, with high saddles and also with big wheels that, for women, could easily catch the fashionable long skirts worn at the time. In the 1870s, when the Penny Farthing bicycle was invented, with its enormous front wheel and high saddle, cycling was still a challenge.

Finally, in 1885, a safety bicycle was invented, which was easier to mount and pedal, and with smaller wheels. Now women could really begin to join in this exciting new activity, although there was still considerable opposition, with some arguing that it would be too exhausting for the 'fairer sex' or, even worse, that straddling a bike on a narrow saddle could lead to sexual arousal in a woman. So, just ten years later, for Hattie McIlrath not only to get on a bicycle but then to cycle it right around the world was quite an astonishing achievement, especially when her route took her through isolated and dangerous regions in China and Iran.

Another American girl, Annie Londonderry, also deserves some credit for publicising bike riding for women in the 1890s, but she was more of a publicist and storyteller than a cyclist, and her claimed global trip comprised mainly sailing with her bicycle between exotic ports for photo shoots.

When little Harriet McIlrath was born in rural Ohio in 1873, the United States was still a pioneering country. Many states, such as Oklahoma, Colorado and the Dakotas, had not yet joined the Union; battles were still taking place against indigenous tribes such as the Cheyenne, the Arapaho and the Apache; the great Sioux War was yet to take place. Immigrants were still pouring into New York from across the world, and many were then undertaking rugged journeys to the west to create a new life for themselves.

Harriet's father, though, saw himself as an old timer. His ancestors had headed westwards to the fertile farmland of the Ohio river valley generations before; his grandfather had been a farmer; his father had been a farmer; it was almost inevitable that Harriet's father would follow in their footsteps. But when farm prices fell and life became a struggle, he decided to take on a new role as manager of a local tavern.

It was never going to be a massive success; in the small town of Cecil in north-west Ohio, the population was less than 200. But the railroad passed through, there were local workers, it was a living.

For Harriet, however, in the 1870s and as the seventh in a large family of eleven, it was a great place to be brought up. The wide, open, flat land stretched for miles to a distant horizon in every direction; with her brothers and sisters, she could wander and explore at will. She wasn't a typical American country girl, though. Perhaps it was her mother, who came from an old, established Luxembourg family, who added a level of European sophistication to the upbringing and development of Harriet, or Hattie as she liked to be known.

Growing up petite but attractive and with a light-hearted, adventurous nature, Hattie stood out. There were lots of friends and relations in the area to meet and have fun with, there were also rural activities including shooting competitions. Annie Oakley, the famous sharpshooter in Buffalo Bill's Wild West Show, had been born a few years earlier just a little further south; perhaps her exploits inspired Hattie to take up shooting; certainly by her late teens Hattie was a very good shot. But in such a large family, with her dad busy running the tavern, Hattie and her siblings also had to work hard to help out with chores, with the cooking, sewing and all the work needed to keep the family and household going.

How Hattie met Harold Darwin McIlrath is not known. Darwin, the name he preferred to use, also came from Ohio, part of an extensive Cleveland family that had fanned out into many walks of life, some a lot more successful than others. Darwin was good looking and charismatic, and had a determined zest to emulate the more successful members of the large McIlrath clan.

When Hattie and Darwin married, in November 1892, Chicago became their home as Darwin pursued a career in sales. He was especially interested in products concerned with medicine; he saw good potential in that area. It seems to have been a lively household and just ten months after their wedding a fracas in a private home resulted in Darwin spending a night in hospital after being shot in the arm, and Hattie, along with two others, spending the night in a local police station.

It was a happy marriage, though, and the young couple shared many ideas and became involved in many new interests including wheeling, as cycling was known in those days. In an era still dominated by horse-drawn vehicles, bicycles had become a real craze and fans across the United States were joining new cycling clubs to take part in this healthy, fun and useful activity.

Through contacts with a major local newspaper, the *Chicago Inter Ocean*, one day Darwin heard about the newspaper's interest in this big craze of wheeling. The paper had come up with what it hoped was a dramatic event that would attract new readers: an around-the-world cycling trip. It had been aware of the great circulation boost Nellie Bly's trip around the world had created just a few years earlier, and if the newspaper sponsored a trip around the world, that should boost its circulation, too. It wouldn't be the first cycling circumnavigation. An Englishman, Thomas Stevens, had managed to cycle around the world ten years earlier after numerous setbacks and walking a lot of the route, but he didn't achieve massive fame or even a great deal of interest. By 1895, however, cycling had really taken off and the *Inter Ocean* newspaper believed this time there would be a lot more interest.

Darwin was excited by the newspaper's plan. To cycle around the world, sending back stories from remote and fascinating regions, sounded perfect! With his energy and charm, he managed to become the person selected to make the attempt. There was a great deal of planning to be undertaken: the best routes; how the newspaper could send out money to the cyclist in various countries; how much equipment could be carried. Soon Darwin was totally involved. It would be an amazing journey and he would be paid as well.

While Darwin got on with the managers at the *Inter Ocean* newspaper, home life wasn't going quite so well. Hattie, learning about the trip, realised that he would be away for two or three years or more; what sort of marriage was that? With her determination and energy, she was having none of it. Instead she told Darwin firmly that if he were going, she was going to go with him. She had never travelled long distances; to see the world would be wonderful; she absolutely insisted she should be part of the plan.

Under such pressure, it didn't take long for Darwin to make up his mind. After all, Hattie was young and fit; she was an expert cyclist and, even better, had a strong nerve and was an excellent shot. She hadn't been brought up a traditional gentlewoman in the Victorian style; instead she had seen her father deal with drunk and sometimes violent customers; she knew how to look after herself. The newspaper, too, agreed that Hattie could go on the trip. It could bring in extra interest.

Did Darwin or Hattie really have any idea of what they were letting themselves in for? It seems unlikely. Darwin was a bit of a local chancer: very confident but not particularly well educated. For Hattie, brought up in country Ohio, the move to Chicago had been her only experience of the bigger world. She knew some of the trip would be across remote regions, but she felt confident; after all, in Hattie's mind Cecil, where she had been born, was quite remote.

With a big newspaper behind them to fully fund the trip, arrangements were surprisingly easy. On a big map, they drew a rough route around the world through various towns that looked promising. Two diamond truss-frame Fowler bicycles were obtained, fitted with special anatomical saddles. Luggage would have to be kept to the absolute minimum so that it could be crammed into little leather cases specially designed to fit inside each bicycle frame. Certain repair and medical equipment was vital. When Hattie mentioned security, they both agreed they should carry protection. Hattie knew about guns and the couple purchased and packed two 38-calibre and one 44-calibre revolvers. Neither of them really thought they would need to use them; it was all just part of the procedure and fun. There was virtually no space on the bikes for clothing. A special costume with comfortable bloomers had been designed for Hattie, much better for pedalling than the long skirts of the day, but she could only find room for one change of underwear. She would simply have to buy new items when her clothes wore out.

The date of departure was planned for 10 April 1895, and as the day got nearer, Hattie and Darwin became increasingly excited. They were about to set off to do something magnificent; they had no idea really how long it would take, and most of their thoughts had been taken up by the immediate planning.

The *Inter Ocean* newspaper was already building up the event and special receptions were arranged for Hattie and Darwin. They found being in the public eye a little bewildering but struggled through the interviews arranged for them. There was little packing up to do, as the couple had been living in a rented home. They had no important possessions and were quickly ready for their big trip.

It dawned on them just how big the trip was going to be just a few hours after leaving Chicago. There had been a good crowd to see them off and the local cycle club had accompanied them for a little way out of town. Then they were on their own, pedalling steadily westwards. By the early evening, they had both had more than enough. Finding a hotel in the town of Geneva, after some fast and energetic cycling, they realised that they had covered just 44 miles of their 20,000-mile journey.

For the first time, Darwin began to have doubts, not about himself, but about Hattie. Would she be able to stand up to months of cycling? Hattie, though, thought it all good fun. She was young, fit and feisty; what was the problem?

At various towns along the route to the west coast, they were greeted by cheering crowds and often evening receptions held in their honour. The *Inter Ocean* newspaper had done a great job in generating knowledge and excitement about the event.

As they continued to head west, they began to experience poor roads that occasionally diminished into just stony tracks. At one point, when the roadways were really rough, the best solution was to ride along the railroad beds, on the flat, very narrow border just outside the rail track.

Reaching Grand Island in Nebraska, they stayed the night in a hotel and then, the following day, just 10 miles west of the small town and again riding over the railroad tracks, they pedalled into a hailstorm. Hattie had her head down as she pedalled furiously through the icy bullets and she didn't spot a cattle grid. As she hit it, she was jerked up and the heavy bike toppled over. She fell 20ft down the embankment at the side of the railway. Darwin rushed down to help her. Luckily, apart from a few bruises Hattie was uninjured. The bike was damaged, though. As they struggled back to the nearest town to get the bike repaired, again Darwin started to wonder if he should be making this trip on his own. Hattie still had no hesitation; if he was going to do it, so was she.

Soon they got into a routine, getting up early and covering the greatest distance they could before stopping for a meal. With their muscles tuning up to the constant exertions, cycling became easier, but the weather didn't improve; it just went from one extreme to another. Out of the storms of the Midwest, they now rode into blazing sun. After three weeks of continuous cycling, on 3 May, they reached Colorado and stopped to celebrate. They had covered their first 1,000 miles.

Confidently, they set off again west. The little towns and settlements were becoming much more spaced out. Heading to Stoneham in Colorado, the couple were cycling over flat tracks for mile after mile without seeing any settlement or signs of human habitation. In glaring heat, they ran out of water and after hours of cycling there was no sign of life. Suddenly, unusually, Hattie's resilience left her. She got off her bike, sat on the ground and burst into tears. It was a rare show of vulnerability for Hattie. Darwin soon got her going again and finally they found water at a deserted property, caught a roaming chicken to cook over a makeshift fire, and managed to eat and drink before collapsing on the ground for some sleep. They had no bedding with them.

Getting stuck in the deep snow on the Rocky Mountains; carrying bikes through deep streams; shooting dead a snake that threatened Hattie's bike – the adventures continued as the couple headed steadily west. Darwin by now was a little shocked to realise just how challenging this trip was becoming – and they were still in the United States. Hattie, though, was beginning to enjoy herself. Making it through to the next town, overcoming obstacles, sometimes seeing beautiful scenery; the cycling was now easier and Hattie was totally relaxed. They had nothing to go back to Chicago for; but if they continued, they could save Darwin's salary. It was all looking great.

On 29 July 1895, Hattie and Darwin cycled into San Francisco. Crossing the United States by bike had been an enormous achievement. In the 110 days since leaving Chicago, they had covered over 3,000 miles.

For Hattie, San Francisco was a fascinating town. It was thirty-eight years before the Golden Gate Bridge would be built, but cable cars had already been introduced and there were a lot of attractions and people of interest.

With accommodation paid for by the *Inter Ocean* newspaper, Darwin sent back long written reports to Chicago while the bikes were overhauled and put back into tip-top condition. Then it was time to head off again. The newspaper had booked them accommodation on the *City of Pekin*, bound for Yokohama in Japan, and they set sail for Asia on 12 October 1895.

Japan was a total shock. The language, the people, the food … it was all so different from anything they had ever imagined. It all seemed organised, though. The roads were good and so they set off to see a little of the country; this would help Darwin write some interesting stories to send back to the newspaper.

Inland they found the roads could be rough and the accommodation was so unusual, with mats on the floor, that they didn't quite know what to think of it. They were also worried about drinking the water, so they simply drank the local beer instead. None of it was a real problem, though, and Hattie was very happy. She was with the man she loved and having such fun. If she had known what lay ahead in Asia, she might well have caught the next boat back to San Francisco. But so far, all was well: they had crossed the United States; they had cycled around Japan. Now for China.

The McIlraths arrived in Shanghai, China, in January 1896 and immediately booked into a hotel. After their experience in Japan, they were feeling confident they could cope with China. The town itself was interesting, with its abundance of rickshaws, but it was also very westernised. After China had been defeated in the Opium Wars in 1842, Shanghai, along with four other cities, had been declared a treaty port and opened to trade. Since then increasing numbers of foreigners had based themselves in the town and it was now a thriving international port.

The McIlraths wanted to see what life was like outside the centre of town and planned to cycle a little way out. Local people warned them that this could be dangerous, but they rather disregarded this.

The McIlraths had had no experience of hostility and they tended to think people were being overcautious.

As they cycled away from the main area, they quickly realised that the warnings had, indeed, been sound. Both Darwin and Harriet were shocked when a massive crowd formed around them, pointing and jeering. They quickly cycled on. Then another crowd pelted them with stones and fruit skins. They also had to fight off some dogs, while their Chinese owners simply looked on, grinning as their huge animals went for the cyclists.

Shaken, they returned to central Shanghai quickly. They had a think; there was no talk of turning back, Darwin and Hattie were now determined to keep going, but they both agreed they needed maximum protection. Along with the guns they had already brought, they now purchased a double-barrelled hammerless shotgun and a short, heavy machete. Hattie was not intimidated at all by the thought of having to defend herself; she had seen violent men in her parents' pub and felt she knew how to deal with them. Darwin also bought a stout cane and organised a home-made ammonia gun – squirting that into their faces would sort any dogs out.

Talking to foreign businessmen in the town, they learned a little more about the route they had planned, following the mighty Yangtze river to its source in the far west of the country. Few were encouraging, but they were given letters of introduction to various colleagues and officials in key towns along the way. It was reassuring that there were other foreign businessmen and missionaries at various centres inland along their route. They also purchased some bedding, some basic cooking utensils and some tins of malted milk. If they were stuck in the middle of nowhere for a while, they could survive.

On 3 March 1896, on their heavily laden bikes, the couple headed out of Shanghai, aiming for the town of Wuhan, 500 miles west. The first main stop en route was to be Suzhou, where they had an introduction to the town's administrator.

As they left the populated area, along the road they were greeted by staring locals, who first showed astonishment and then anger. They received many threatening gestures, but no one actually interfered and they simply pedalled on until, suddenly, the flat gravelled road ended abruptly at a deep, wide river with no bridge or ferry. Darwin and Hattie were just wondering what to do next when they spotted a houseboat moored to the bank upstream. It was an incredibly lucky find. On board were a French couple travelling back upriver to Suzhou and they invited the McIlraths aboard. They learned a lot from their hosts as the boat was pulled steadily along by Chinese coolies, or workers, on the tow path, but it was a strange start to their trip across China.

Arriving in Suzhou, they were introduced to an American trader and were taken to meet the local Chinese administrator who, dressed in fine state robes and with a large umbrella held over his head, slowly and carefully read the paper of introduction they had been given and then greeted them. He was very insistent they stay at his palace and for a couple of days they were given great hospitality. They were served with lavish food, and a Chinese boy, who spoke good English, was delegated to help show them the town.

Then they were invited to see the execution of a woman prisoner by the local method of *seng chee*, or thirty-six cuts. To view this was possibly considered an honour, or perhaps a test. Either way, after such good hospitality, Darwin realised immediately it could be offensive to refuse the offer. Hattie, despite being determined to make a success of the trip, realised that for her this was simply a step too far; she really couldn't face it. When Darwin returned, she knew she had made the right decision; the whole thing had been appalling. The poor woman had been marched into a square and tied standing upright to a post. Her forehead was then bound into an immovable position. Then one of the executioners took a sharp, gleaming knife and sliced off her ear, throwing it to the ground. As the woman shrieked and glanced wildly from side to side, her other ear and then her tongue were removed; then slice by slice the woman was cut up. As Darwin explained the gruesome scene to Hattie, he reassured her that the woman had died fairly early on in the proceedings. It was shocking and another cause of concern; what else would they experience as they travelled west?

After thanking the administrator for his hospitality, Darwin and Hattie once more balanced on their heavily laden bikes and, happy to be leaving the town, pedalled off. Following the course of the river and with Darwin's compass helping to ensure the winding tracks steadily headed west, they pedalled on and on. Some of the roads were simply footpaths leading from village to village, and they became used to having to speed through rural settlements surrounded by hooting and jeering mobs. The only wheels most of the people had ever seen had been on little carts; the sight of two Americans pedalling along at speed created fear and distrust. There was also growing general, and sometimes violent hatred against invading foreigners who were spreading out across their land; a hatred that would culminate just a few years later in the Boxer Uprising.

Following the route of the Yangtze river as much as they could, when the track led along the edge of a waterway, they sometimes came across local houseboats that offered accommodation. The McIlraths used these when possible.

In larger towns, Darwin and Hattie often found foreign businessmen or missionaries who offered a warm welcome, happy to help with accommodation and news of the onward route. Steadily travelling west, day after day, sometimes they had easy, flat, gravelly routes along the water's edge, making an easy 30 or 40 miles or more before stopping for lunch. On other days, rain made the paths almost impassable and it was a question of pushing the bikes and stopping constantly to clear the clay that collected in the forks and frames. One evening, after a particularly tiresome and wet ride, they were exhausted, but although they had blankets with them, there was nowhere suitable or dry to lie down for some sleep. There was nothing for it but to keep going, pushing on under the feeble light from their bicycle lamps.

With Darwin feeling frustrated, Hattie was the one to keep their spirits up; her resilience was astounding. She had long realised how bored she had been with her life in Chicago; this was the real world. It might not all be good, but it was new and it was amazing.

The couple went on hour after hour in the dark, sometimes plunging into water as the path led along the edge of rice fields, until finally they came across a mud hut. Shouting loudly, they managed to raise the occupants who, after being shown a generous display of silver pieces, stoked the fire and let them roll out their blankets on the dry floor.

It was an uncomfortable time, but they steadily pedalled on and early in April, five weeks after leaving Shanghai, they reached Wuhu, an established trading town on the Yangtze. Here, there were many western people happy to welcome Hattie and Darwin. They washed and cleaned up; they dined on board HMS *Daphne* and USS *Detroit*, moored up on the river; they were entertained by the British consul and other missions in the town; and they remained in Wuhu so that they could celebrate on 10 April, exactly a year since they had pedalled out of Chicago. A whole year. Looking back, they felt the time had flown. The long days and months of cycling had blurred into a mix of vague memories. Darwin arranged the despatch of several long reports for the newspaper and they collected some money to hide away carefully around their bikes.

On 11 April 1896, with some reluctance, they bid their farewells and started off again on their westward trip. They realised that the most dangerous part of their journey was ahead of them, but there was no thought of giving up. In tricky moments, there was the underlying reassurance that Darwin was being paid for this; this was work, just a slightly unusual job. Their everyday life now was day-to-day pedalling; being continually on one's guard against bad paths and obstacles that could cause an accident or injury; ensuring they had enough food and water to get to the next village; and ensuring their weapons were to hand to quickly deter any hopeful thieves. Hattie kept her revolver tucked right at the top of her carry case, reassured in the knowledge that it was superior to any weapon available to the rural Chinese.

As they sped along, they saw many Chinese men and women and also young children doing backbreaking work in the fields, but these people were never friendly. Instead they were usually greeted by a sullen silence as groups watched them pedal past. Occasionally, the couple fled through villages and even small towns, pedalling like fury as they were pursued by threatening mobs, jeering and howling. Occasionally, clods of earth and stones were thrown at them. Once they were threatened with knives.

Both Hattie and Darwin showed firm authority when approached by local Chinese and that often helped to prevent attack. They didn't look wealthy either; their money was well hidden. Their guns were the final resort. Simply firing into the air caused hostile crowds to stop long enough to give time for Darwin and Hattie to cycle out of any danger.

They were now lucky with the weather and had a week of hard riding in warm, dry conditions. If no houseboats or local accommodation was available, it was easy to build a little fire and sleep overnight beside the track. Reaching the town of Yichang, again there were fellow westerners to welcome them. A boat trip up to see the spectacular gorges on the Yangtse river was arranged for them, although the wonderful sights were mitigated by the terrifying conditions. The river was in full churning flow after a lot of rain, and it was a real struggle to keep the boat safe.

Then there were the goodbyes to be said before Hattie and Darwin once more got onto their bikes and headed out of town. They now had 500 miles of rugged remote riding ahead to reach the western town of Chongqing. The days faded into a big blur as they struggled on, sometimes in pouring rain, sometimes in sun, sometimes on flat, gravelly footpaths, other times on winding, hilly, rocky tracks. On they went. Hattie observed the changing landscapes, the different plants and the different trees, but mainly her focus was on the path ahead. Every mile covered was a mile closer to their goal of cycling around the world. As the weather deteriorated and the higher mountains began, things became really challenging. In pouring rain, they headed up on the hilly footpaths, often having to push their heavy bikes over soft, slushy ground.

At last, the reality of what they were doing hit them both; even worse, Hattie became ill. Feeling terrible, all she wanted to do was to lie down, but with enormous bravery and strong encouragement from Darwin, she kept going. At a village 30 miles up in the mountains, in torrential rain, Hattie could finally go no further. After a night in a dark, damp hut, with centipedes crawling along the walls, rain dropping from the roof and terrible smells from the pigs in the next room, they simply had to move on. This time, though, Darwin had persuaded, threatened and finally bribed some local men to carry Hattie in a special mountain chair. Hattie could hardly stand, but she struggled into the chair and, still in pouring rain, on the party went.

At the next village, the local men rebelled. They wanted more money; then, when they had the money, they refused to go on anyway. It was touch and go, but finally the little procession headed off again. From the end of August until 7 September, it rained heavily all day, every day. The journey was turning into a terrifying nightmare, but now there was no way out. The small group plodded on, stopping in villages overnight to make use of whatever shelter was available, but then on they went again. Hattie slowly recovered and could start walking again, but the journey itself hardly improved; still it rained.

Sometimes they passed groups of sullen locals, standing and staring at them with blank, empty faces. Maybe for the first time Hattie began to wonder if they really would make it out alive. Later, they realised some of the problems they were encountering were caused by opium, the drug that had been the cause of war and anguish in the country for so long. The realisation didn't help the situation at the time; on they pushed. Eventually, they had a small, happy moment when they learned that the town of Chongqing was only 100 miles away, within reach on a bike if roads had been available. Instead the next days were spent climbing hills and wading through ankle-deep mud.

As they slowly pushed their way up a gravelly path to a small village, suddenly and unexpectedly they met a detachment of soldiers. Notification had got through to the officials of Chongqing, the main settlement in western China, that the McIlraths were on their way. The authorities had begun to grow anxious about the couple and had sent out a group of soldiers to meet them and escort them back into the town. It must have been an unbelievable relief for Hattie and Darwin. The deep, dark worry of being totally on their own in appalling conditions in unfamiliar surroundings was suddenly lifted. On 7 September, they reached the town.

They had an introduction to Doctor McCartney, in charge of the Methodist hospital there, and finally, filthy and mud-stained, they arrived on the veranda of his comfortable home. How wonderful it was to step out of the rain and into a warm, civilised, welcoming house! Hattie now recovered quickly. They also learned over excellent meals that they had been very lucky; many foreigners and local mail carriers in the area had been assassinated in recent months, some along the very route they had taken.

The McIlraths had cycled 1,400 miles across China; it was time for some rest and planning for the next part of the journey. If Hattie now thought enough was enough, there were boats she could have taken for a long river trip back to Shanghai. This was the obvious thing to do. The next step, across the remote Yunnan province in far western China, would be more remote, possibly even more dangerous. Dominance in their partnership was swinging: while Hattie had been buoyant and more resolute during their first months in China, now Darwin was showing enormous strength. They had both been refreshed by their nine days of relaxing in Doctor McCartney's care. Darwin felt the final push across the far west of China was doable. Hattie was quieter and less enthusiastic, but nevertheless she decided to carry on. She certainly felt she couldn't leave Darwin to continue on his own.

They left Chongqing in mid-September and for the next three months they continued across the far west of China. It was a real mix of highs and lows: at some points, cycling on flat paths surrounded by beautiful mountain scenery, it was delightful; at other times, struggling up rocky paths carrying their bikes on two poles, it was a nightmare. When the tracks became too challenging, they managed to employ two Chinese people to carry the poles with the bikes, and then they could continue to cover a good distance. Sometimes they had days of intense heat; then, as they climbed higher, they met ferocious snowstorms. Far up in the mountains of western China, they came across a hermit widow; these were widows who, after the death of their husband, gave up all earthly pleasures and, building a pallet of straw high in the mountains, spent the rest of their life in total isolation, sitting on the straw by day and sleeping on the straw by night.

After days on small mountain tracks, the McIlraths finally reached a recognised route of the area, the Great Stone Road. At last, they could pedal properly again. One day they passed eleven small cages hung on eleven trees; in each cage was the head of an executed Chinese person. Hattie had stopped being shocked; she simply lowered her head and quickly cycled past.

By now, the McIlraths were experienced travellers in China; they had learned a lot about the Chinese character and how to deal with threats from local people. Things were becoming a little less impossible.

On Wednesday, 23 December, after almost a year in China, suddenly they could see the hills of Burma (now Myanmar) in the distance. It was a memorable moment. Scurrying down the track, passing numerous Chinese forts and then crossing a swaying suspension bridge, they finally landed on Burmese soil.

They had done it: they had made it right across China. Hattie couldn't contain her happiness. It had been a bleak, challenging time. Burma was British at that time; they felt safe. It was a wonderful feeling. Hattie suddenly flopped down on the sandy track and burst into tears. Darwin yelled like a cowboy. It was as if their journey had ended. On a peaceful track, in improving weather, they could relax mentally as well as physically.

As they cycled down to the town of Bahmo, on the Irrawaddy river, Hattie couldn't help but voice her happiness: the trees looked wonderful, the people looked wonderful, everything looked wonderful. In the town, they were given a good welcome by the authorities, who provided them with a comfortable bungalow and membership of a local club. For a couple of weeks it was perfect; then Darwin especially started thinking about moving on. They had socialised, relaxed, seen the local coffee plantations. After a month of rest and recuperation, it really was time to get going again. They booked onto a boat to head downriver to Mandalay.

The McIlraths spent nearly three months cycling through Burma and found it interesting but a tad monotonous. They found the people happy and friendly, and visited many local sites including watching elephants at work in huge teak timber yards. The roads were filled with carts of all sizes crammed with local produce, which could make cycling tricky, but that was hardly a problem and gave Darwin more copy for him to send back to the newspaper. Exactly two years after Hattie and Darwin had waved their farewells in Chicago, the couple waved goodbye to Myanmar and caught a steamship for India.

Burma had been a happy interlude before the challenges of cycling around the world started all over again. In Calcutta (now Kolkata), Hattie and Darwin were knocked back by the heat and the crowds, by the sheer intensity of life. They made contact with the *Inter Ocean* newspaper and Darwin sent back more stories. They picked up some more money; they reorganised their luggage and they bought maps. Maps! After so long struggling across China, clear maps to help plan their route were a real luxury.

On 4 May 1897, they headed out of Calcutta, west along the Great Trunk Road, a route that would take them right across the subcontinent. There was unbelievable heat, bullocks in the road, crowds to weave through, but there were good hotels and English-speaking people everywhere. The journey had become less of a grinding challenge. At one point, near Benares (now Varanasi), they encountered numerous leopards; sometimes they were entertained by local maharajas. There were few problems as they pedalled along, until as they neared Delhi, Hattie suffered from a bad attack of prickly heat and they had to stay a few days in a hotel, while she recovered. Hattie also adopted a little monkey; it had a sweet face and a gentle disposition. Hattie picked it up, cuddled it and then, to Darwin's patient amusement, tucked it into her pannier. She called it Rodney and it stayed with them as they cycled down through Pakistan to Karachi.

The trip again became more adventurous once the couple took a steamer from Karachi across to Bushehr, halfway up the Persian Gulf in Iran. Initially, there were no hotels, but they found empty rooms where they were allowed to unroll their blankets. Heading north-west for Shiraz, they found the sandy soil impassable on bikes and had to resort to putting their machines onto hired donkeys. Once, three men sprung on them from behind some rocks, but finding that they were foreigners, and meeting with a determined resistance that included Darwin and Hattie both brandishing their guns, they simply left. Just a few days later, another thief attacked and seized the bridle of Hattie's mule. She quickly grabbed her revolver and, yelling at him, literally pressed the muzzle into the thief's face. He retreated.

They reached Shiraz after twelve hours of rough travel with no food, but again there were local foreigners who were willing to help the couple, including English superintendents of the local telegraph system and American missionaries. Their stay in Shiraz was fascinating and visiting Persepolis was a highlight. The ruins of this ancient capital fascinated the McIlraths. At one point they saw an inscription carved into a rockface there, bearing the name of a journalist from the *New York Herald*; it had been made twenty-five years earlier. Hattie and Darwin couldn't let that remain without adding their names and the rival name of the *Chicago Inter Ocean* newspaper, too. They carefully chipped the names into the rockface.

For the next stage of their journey north to Tehran, they employed an interpreter, a trusted man recommended by people they had met in Shiraz, who would also help carry items when necessary. They knew there were no clear roads ahead, so there was going to be a lot of walking and pushing of bikes. All went well until they tried to climb a pass to reach the town of Kashan and hit snow. Their interpreter had gone ahead, but for Hattie and Darwin, well behind and struggling with their heavy bikes, things became difficult. In severe snowstorms they pushed on, often having to carry their bikes across the snow. It was freezing. Below the snow were icy pools of water and they were both soaked through. Hattie tried, but suddenly she could go on no further. Her feet were totally numb and she had absolutely no energy left. Darwin knew that if they stopped that would be the end of it; they would freeze to death on an empty Iranian path. Hattie struggled to move on, but in the dreadful conditions she had nothing left in her. Sinking down on the snow, she couldn't go any further. Darwin, ever resourceful, was about to cut some nearby telegraph lines and try to signal for help when their interpreter, worried about the couple, arrived with horses and a rescue party. For the third time on the trip, Hattie started to cry. Their arrival was an event Hattie would never forget.

With her legs completely numb, she was hoisted onto the back of a horse and slowly the party made their way onwards to the town of Kashan. Hattie had frostbite, but with enormous care and constant massaging for hour after hour, Hattie's white, frozen lumps of feet gradually and painfully thawed.

Hattie remained positive and, despite her condition, still wanted to travel on. She couldn't really walk, so for an exorbitant price the couple hired a diligence – a bouncy vehicle drawn by four horses abreast. With the bikes on board, they headed off for Tehran. With help from a doctor at the American Presbyterian mission in Tehran, Hattie's feet were coaxed back and she luckily made a full recovery.

The real drama of the trip was now over and civilisation as they knew it was returning. From Tehran they took a boat up the Caspian Sea to Baku, where they made new friends and even went to the opera. Then they had a fascinating time pedalling west to Tbilisi in Georgia and finally a boat trip across the Black Sea to see Istanbul before another boat up to Constanta in Rumania. Now Hattie and Darwin were having the time of their lives. They booked into good hotels, were greeted by cycling enthusiasts in every town they reached and were seeing many new sights.

The roads were good, it was late spring and the countryside looked glorious. On they went, pedalling happily westward. After an enjoyable stay in Hungary, they left Budapest on 17 July 1898 and, with smooth clear roads, they easily made Vienna by the next day. Again they booked into a hotel and, with local cycling clubs and contacts, quickly made some friends to help entertain them and show them the highlights of the elegant city.

It was too good to last. As they continued to cycle across Germany, suddenly, out of the blue, Darwin received notification from the *Inter Ocean* newspaper that the trip was to be ended and they were to make their way back to the United States immediately. It was an immense shock. Travelling had become their lives. They had firm plans in place that would have taken them to some of the best places in Europe.

While Hattie and Darwin talked and talked about the sudden change of plan, in Chicago the decision had become obvious. When the couple started out in spring 1895, interest in cycling was immense. But now, three years later, the interest had switched to the new dramatic development of cars. While Darwin's reports from China and Asia had been interesting for readers, details about towns and life in Europe were already well known. Supporting Hattie and Darwin was now costing a lot of money for little return. The newspaper decided it had gained all it could from the trip; it was time to bring the McIlraths home.

Trips around southern Europe, trips up to Scandinavia, all their plans were now thrown out. Instead Hattie and Darwin headed by the most direct route to Paris, across to London and down to Southampton to catch a ship back to New York. It was a strange time for them both. Three years on the road had changed them. Hattie had become a little quieter, a little less spirited. Now 25, she was no longer that happy-go-lucky country girl from Cecil; after so many extraordinary experiences and seeing so much, Hattie had matured into a very confident, very knowledgeable woman of the world.

The couple enjoyed their voyage back on the SS *Pennland*, arriving back in New York on 27 October 1898. The *Inter Ocean* newspaper still intended to get all they could out of the trip, and a big publicity campaign resulted in the McIlraths being met by huge crowds and a mass of local reporters wanting to talk to them about their experiences.

Put up in a top hotel, both Hattie and Darwin were happy to recount their experiences and the life-threatening problems they had encountered as they had pedalled around the world. Then they set off for the final 1,000 miles of their journey across to Chicago. It was almost déjà vu from three years before. At each town they went through, they were greeted by crowds and given a grand welcome. Albany, Rochester, Buffalo, on good roads the towns sped past as they headed west at a steady pace.

When they finally reached Chicago in November 1898, three and a half years after they had left, the welcome was muted. The local cycling clubs turned out to welcome them, of course; friends and relations were there and the managers at the *Inter Ocean* newspaper put on a good reception. But then that was it. Darwin was paid to write a three-quarter-page summary of the trip, but it didn't attract massive readership. There was no real excitement, no offer of a permanent job on the newspaper; in fact there were no offers of anything. The executives at the *Inter Ocean* newspaper had been correct; general interest in cycling had waned. A new era of motorcars and even aeroplanes was coming in. In the three years they had been away, the world had moved on.

Hattie, while in many ways delighted to be back home, nevertheless now had worries that hadn't concerned them for three years. Money, for a start. Hattie's father had by now died; her mother had moved to a rented house in another small Ohio country town and was working as a dressmaker. On Darwin's side, while some of his relations were doing well, there was no opportunity for financial assistance or work from any of them. The McIlraths were back at the beginning, having to find accommodation and earn a living.

For a while, money saved from Darwin's pay from the newspaper covered their expenses, but it soon dwindled. Then Darwin started to earn some money giving talks about the trip, with Hattie assisting, although she didn't want to speak officially at events. She also helped Darwin write a book on the trip. In the end, though, Darwin resumed his first career as a salesman. He specialised in medical remedies and sometimes even advertised himself as a doctor. It was a living.

Soon life settled down and, although no children came along, the couple were happy and they still had fascinating stories that attracted a wealth of interest and new friends. McIlrath's newly concocted cure for blood poisoning and other remedies were making money and the couple moved to Detroit where, they thought, there might be better opportunities. Then, in 1912, Darwin caught pneumonia and died. Hattie was nearly 40.

Since their return, Hattie had developed a good social life and, after her trip around the world, she was never short of admirers. In 1915, just three years after Darwin's death, she married again, this time to a proper journalist, Edwin Pratt. Edwin was 48, eight years older than Hattie; there were no late children, but in lively Detroit there was a great deal of entertainment.

It was a happy time for Harriet, but after many good years of marriage, Edwin died, leaving Hattie, now in her late sixties and a widow for the second time, alone in a rented house in Detroit. Still attractive, still with a zest for life, she once again wasn't going to remain the lonely widow for long. On a trip down to Florida, possibly to see her brother Earl who had moved down there, Hattie met husband number three. She married William Reilly in January 1943 when she was 69 and the couple settled in St Petersburg, Florida. During the next twenty years, before Hattie died in 1963 aged 89, it seems likely she had a lot of fun with new friends in the sun, perhaps sometimes chatting about her previous life and how she had once achieved an impossible journey by cycling right around the world.

Left: Early illustration of Jeanne Baret dressed as a man.
(Pictorial Press/Alamy Stock Photo)

Below: Jeanne Baret, high in the hills above Rio de Janeiro, came across this brilliant red plant and knew it was worth taking back for further examination. It was named after the captain of the ship, Louis de Bougainville.
(Javier Martin, via Wikimedia Commons)

Below: When the *Boudeuse* and *Etoile* reached Tahiti harbour, they were greeted by a crowd of Polynesian men who quickly identified Jeanne Baret as a woman.
(Bougainville at Tahiti by Gustave Alaux/ ANMM Collection)

To begin with, Mary Ann Parker gave little consideration to the convicts held in the hold below for their transportation to Australia. *(Selfwood/Alamy Stock Photo)*

Mary Ann Parker arrived in the very early days of Port Jackson, now called Sydney. *(Chronicle/Alamy Stock Photo)*

To the astonishment of her friends, Mary Ann Parker welcomed Woollarawarre Bennelong into her London home.
(Natural History Museum, London/Alamy Stock Photo)

Ida Pfeiffer was horrified at the widespread Chinese practice of binding children's feet so that, when adult, they would fit into tiny shoes.
(Annie Owen / Alamy Stock Photo)

Ida Pfeiffer travelled alone to the remotest Sarawak native villages, where there was no hope of medical help or any assistance.
(North Wind Picture Archives/Alamy Stock Photo)

Ida Pfeiffer spent the night in a longhouse, sleeping next to trophy skulls from local headhunters.
(Luca Tettoni/Alamy Stock Photo)

After deterring an attacker by pressing her gun into his face, Hattie McIlrath finally reached Persepolis. In those days, no one had considered that scratching one's name into ancient ruins could cause irreparable damage.
(Hansueli Krapt, CCA-SA 3.0 via Wikimedia Commons; John Weiss)

When the Boxer Uprising started across the border from Russia in China, news of the murderous attacks on Westerners were slow to reach Annette Meakin.
(Ann Ronan Picture Library/ Alamy Stock Photo)

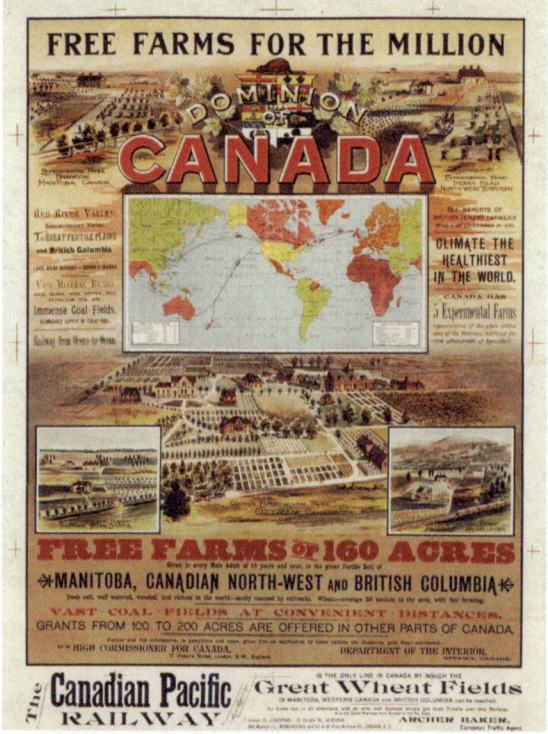

When Annette Meakin and her mother finally reached Canada, they knew their transport problems were over. The government policy of offering free land to settlers had helped to accelerate the development of the early Canadian railways.
(Library and Archives Canada, Acc. No. 1996-63)

There were terrifying moments and also times of serene beauty when Lady Grace Drummond-Hay went around the world in the *Graf Zeppelin*.
(Wernher Krutein/Photovault.com)

After so much training, Valentina Tereshkova was finally ready to go up into space.
(Pictorial Press/Alamy Stock Photo; Rocket picture Dizainera/Istock)

Jeana Yeager and Dick Rutan by their experimental aircraft Voyager.
(Doug Pizac/Alamy Stock Photo)

Very occasionally, after huge seas and knockdowns, Kay Cottee had moments of calm weather when sailing became a real pleasure.
(ANMM Collection, reproduced courtesy Kay Cottee)

6

1900 ANNETTE MEAKIN
THE FIRST WOMAN ROUND THE WORLD BY TRAIN

At the turn of the century, in 1900, eastern Asia was not the world's most peaceful region. In China, there had been a steady rise against foreign intervention, with many of its people protesting against the influence and change to their country being brought about by European and other major nations, and also by the number of Christian missionaries working across the country. Finally, Chinese anger came to a head in what is now known as the Boxer Uprising. The Boxers were a group of Chinese who practised various calisthenic rituals that they believed made them invulnerable but also gave them their name. The Boxers initiated a major violent campaign to drive all foreigners out of China and this was then supported by the empress dowager, who gave an order that all foreigners should be killed.

When Annette Meakin decided to take a train on the new rail track across Siberia, she knew there would be major challenges ahead, but she had no idea she would be travelling into a battle area that would prevent her return.

In late Victorian society, accompanied by her equally charming mother, Annette Meakin could hold her own at any social gathering. When the talk was about music, Annette could join in with confidence; after all, she had studied at London's Royal College of Music. When the conversation turned to literature, Annette again could join in with knowledge, for she was working on her poetry under the world-renowned classicist A.E. Housman at the University of London. With her delightful manners and elegant clothing, Annette really was the perfect guest for a social occasion.

Few would have believed that this well-educated and refined young Victorian woman would soon be leading her mother out of Blagoveshchensk in eastern Siberia, just days before a horrific massacre that left thousands dead. Even more extraordinary, Annette hadn't gone to this remote region as a missionary or for other worthwhile undertakings; instead, after persuading her mother to accompany her because she needed a chaperone, she was travelling simply out of a thirst for knowledge and an extraordinary wish to become the very first Englishwoman to cross Siberia on the region's new train track.

Perhaps it surprised Annette as much as others, this desire to undertake challenging, adventurous trips, alongside her love of formal music and classical literature; but then the Meakin family itself was full of contrast, with a varied history that must have helped Annette develop into this rather unusual young woman.

Annette's grandfather, Samuel Budgett, became famous after an event in 1804 when, in rural Somerset, he found a horseshoe in the road on his way to school. He sold it to a local blacksmith for a penny and that was the start of a buying and selling career that ended up with the creation of a major grocery chain that made a small fortune. His daughter, Annette's mother, had a very comfortable childhood.

Annette's father's side was more mundane, although her father had shown independence when he left his Leicester-based family first for London and then for India, where he managed a tea plantation for a spell before getting married and settling back into English life.

To begin with, Annette's parents' married life was conventional. They established a happy family home in Reigate, Surrey. Annette was their second child, born in 1867, and other siblings followed. All the children were given a fairly standard Victorian childhood with a firm emphasis on education and self-improvement, values enhanced by the family's strong Methodist beliefs.

Things started to change when Annette was 11. Her father had a tendency to give a lot of their money away to good causes and finally his generosity landed him in the bankruptcy court. Her father's health later started to fail and it was decided a major change was needed. When Annette was 14, the family packed up and moved to a warmer climate in Morocco. Her father started an English newspaper out there and the family settled in well. This was the start of Annette's lifelong love of travel. Seeing the colourful, lively people going about their very different lives in an exotic location must have been fascinating for an observant young girl.

It was different enough to cure her quickly of any fear of unfamiliar places and people. When it was decided that Annette needed to return to Europe to continue her education, it may have been her suggestion that she join a school in Germany so that she could learn the language as well as pursue her normal studies. Along with her love of literature, her interest in the wider world and its peoples had now begun.

With her schooling in Germany over, and her parents having returned to England, Annette then settled back at the family's London home. As she grew through her twenties, Annette enjoyed a quiet social life and met a few eligible men. However, she found no permanent partner and she had no career direction either, although she did sometimes dream of becoming a famous writer. To help with family finances, she gave a few desultory piano lessons, a fitting occupation for a well brought up single young woman at that time. When she heard that her older brother James was going to travel to Turkestan and Kurdistan to do some research for his hoped-for career in journalism, Annette had an idea. Why didn't she go with him and also write a report, but from a woman's angle?

Her brother thought it could work, so without any qualms Annette packed her bag and joined him on the long and arduous train and carriage trip across to central Asia. Visiting Bukhara and Samarkand, she made an effort to meet local women and find out about their lives. Her final story was a learned piece of work, and while it didn't attract a great deal of attention, it confirmed Annette's interest in the wider world.

When she was turning 30, suddenly her father died. He was just 59 and, with his quiet religious zeal, good heart and loving nature, it was a big loss for the whole family. While he didn't leave a great deal of money, Annette's mother was receiving a small income from the legacy of her successful father, so while there was no luxury the family could make ends meet.

Her father's death made Annette think. She needed to do something with her life. First, she decided to enrol at London's University College to study classics; then, when she had settled into her Latin and Greek studies, she heard that a new train, the Siberian Express, had started operations.

She was again seized by an idea: she wanted to travel on the train. Her adventurous spirit now replaced her desire for high classics; an excited desperation to be on that Russian train overtook all other interests. The train track had opened from Moscow right across the vast Asian section of eastern Russia nearly all the way to Vladivostok, 5,700 miles to the east. There was a small section still to be completed, but this was covered by a river steamer. The whole journey seemed quite possible and Annette had a gripping desire to be the first Englishwoman to undertake it.

Perhaps Annette also realised she would be able to write a good story from a journey like this. Underneath her quiet exterior, her idea of becoming a recognised writer was growing. Perhaps this trip could be the start she needed.

The huge land of Siberia was certainly an area of interest. Russia's conquest of the region had begun in 1580 when the Cossacks invaded the territory of the Voguls. Since then, with numerous independent tribes living across the region, there had been constant skirmishes and wars as Russia continued to spread its influence eastwards. Progress, however, had been slow. In 1891 the Emperor of Russia, Alexander III, had been persuaded that a rail route right across Siberia would make a huge difference, especially in helping trade between the regions. It would also provide a good link for transporting soldiers to the area. So the railway had been commissioned.

In those days a Victorian woman would never consider travelling on her own; well-brought-up young women were accompanied to almost every event. Annette got on well with her widowed mother, and thought perhaps she might agree to accompany her. Sarah Meakin was by now 67 years old. Quietly religious, but with a strong acceptance of duty, she had already been happy to uproot her family when her husband went to Morocco. Now, with the same stoic family loyalty, she agreed to travel with her daughter into the unknown. Her decision might have been assisted by the hope that dramatic change would help her get over the loss of her husband. Either way, Annette's mother agreed to go with her on the trip.

Annette spent the first few months of 1900 researching her plan carefully. She worked out that they could travel to Moscow, pick up the new Siberian Express to Irkutsk by Lake Baikal and finally take the more basic train to the end of the line at Sretensk. After that, travel looked more challenging, but even getting as far as Sretensk would be wonderful. Annette intended to get off the train every so often to fulfil her wish to visit people living in these remote regions. Finally, the plan was to return the same way, by train, all the way back to St Petersburg and then Paris and London.

Saying goodbye to her books and studies, Annette and her mother packed carefully; luggage on the train would be limited. They also kept their plans secret, as both women realised that their friends would consider it foolhardy in the extreme to travel across Russia on their own. However, they felt happy about the journey; Russia was a reasonably organised society and they were confident they would be safe. Really it was just a straightforward train journey now that the rail tracks were fully open.

Shutting up the house on 18 March 1900, Annette and her mother boarded a steam train for the Channel, then took a ferry and another train to Paris. Here they stayed with friends and socialised happily while Annette made final plans. The weather was unusually hot, so they shed some of the heavier garments they had brought with them, something they would regret once they reached Russia. At least, though, their luggage was lighter and now they could travel with just three pieces of luggage: a valise, a holdall and a tea basket. Their change of clothing was minimal.

At they boarded the Nord Express train in Paris, Annette must have been excited. She had done a great deal of research; now at last the journey was starting. The train itself was extremely comfortable; this route had been organised by the Compagnie Internationale des Wagon-Lits just four years earlier with luxury in mind. On 2 May, they had to change trains on the Russian border because the rail tracks were built with a wider gauge, but apart from that the journey was fast and easy.

Reaching St Petersburg, then the capital of Russia, they had a bit of a shock. While inside the train carriage it was hot and steamy, outside the scenery had changed to a dreary white. As the couple descended from the train, they were met by bitter winds and icy snow. Inadequately dressed, Annette immediately caught flu and spent four days in bed. This didn't daunt her, though; as far as she was concerned, there was nothing too demanding ahead. She was just going on a long train trip across Russia; she would find various hotels, talk to local people and then come back. The big challenge would be to survive so many days and nights in a rattling train carriage. At this stage, going right around the world had not occurred to Annette; it was not in the plans at all.

The night express from St Petersburg to Moscow was a regular route and was first class only, but arriving at the station, Annette encountered a problem of the type she would meet all the way across Russia. Someone had bribed the conductor and taken their berth. They finally appealed to an officer on the train who spoke French, and after an hour and a half of strong haggling, Annette and her mother finally took possession of their sleeping booth. As they sped their way down to Moscow, the snow outside disappeared. The weather was warming up, making everything a lot more comfortable.

Booking into a local Moscow hotel, Annette explored the town. She found it full of coloured roofs and glistening golden cupolas, which she loved; but she didn't want to linger. Annette was now quietly excited by the idea of making a name for herself in literary circles by writing about unusual people and different lifestyles in Siberia; European Russia was already well known and talking to people in Moscow wasn't of particular interest. They arranged to move on quickly to the exciting Siberian Express.

To begin with, everything was quite straightforward. Their sleeping carriage was comfortable enough, although they were sharing it with two other women. The beds were soft and there was a bell to summon a serving man to clean the cabin or to call for a waiter from the buffet. There was also a reading lamp. It all looked very promising and they happily passed the time chatting to other passengers who could understand some English, French or German. The scenery was interesting too, ever changing as the train, with its heavy front engine belching dark smoke, steamed steadily east. It was not a fast journey, the train was slow and made many stops, but there was plenty to entertain the passengers. In the dining car there was a stocked bookcase, albeit mainly of Russian books, and a Bechstein piano; one night a gentleman with a good tenor voice gave a concert. Annette noted that many of the Russian men played cards for the entire journey, hardly looking up. It took five days and four nights to cover the 1,300 miles or so to Omsk.

Leaving the station in a little droshky, a small, horse-drawn open carriage, they found a hotel and quickly laid their own sheets and rugs onto the bare mattresses for a good night's sleep. Their trip in Siberia had begun.

Annette's mother had accepted that this was very much her daughter's trip, but she was equally fascinated by the new people and new ways. Two Englishwomen in town was news, and soon they had made friends and received invitations to dinner, sometimes from the wealthiest in town. Using their German and French as well as English, they found that generally they could understand well enough, and they learned interesting snippets of information, including the fact that Jews were not admitted into society in Omsk.

Near their hotel was a mosque, visited by the local Kyrgyz people, who spoke a Turkish dialect that interested Annette. She decided she would like to visit a Kyrgyz village and managed to persuade one of their new friends to take them in his horse-drawn carriage far out into the open regions away from the town. After several miles of rough tracks, they came across herds of cattle grazing on wide, open land, being looked after by small Kyrgyz boys riding hardy, fierce-looking horses. Cattle played a key part in these nomadic people's lives, with cattle-breeding their main occupation. Horses were also important: horse-meat sausages and *beshbarmak*, a specially flavoured horse-meat stew, were traditional meals, and mare's milk added key nutrition to their diets.

Annette made careful notes as she visited the Kyrgyz yurts, made of wood, covered with hides and felt, and secured with rope that the women had made from plaiting horsehair. By smiling and showing friendship, Annette was allowed inside several yurts and found them all very much alike, containing an iron-bound box that held all the family treasures, and usually an older woman sitting or squatting in the gloomy light, mending clothes or cleaning dishes. There was also often a child or two, not always wearing clothes, and nearly always a young calf tethered by a rope. Annette was fascinated to see that each basic yurt also contained its own musical instrument; all the young people were taught to sing.

With copious notes, Annette was happy to move on again. They hadn't the money to spend too long on this trip; Annette wanted to keep moving to ensure she got as far as possible into Siberia. Reaching the station, they learned the train was at least four hours late, but no one appeared concerned. Timekeeping became very flexible as they travelled further east.

Back on a new train, they found the carriage was comfortable but this time there was no dining car. When the engine broke down and they had to wait hours for a replacement, Annette realised how unwise it was to travel without at least some water and a loaf of bread. Generally, though, station stops were fairly frequent, when all the passengers would pile out to buy food and especially tea.

At some of the more major stops along the route, they got off to look around, staying in a hotel and then catching the next onwards train. They visited universities and museums and found out what they could about life in the regions. Annette was happy to approach anyone to ask for advice or information; a gentle Englishwoman, with an older mother in tow, was very unusual and she nearly always received a courteous, if sometimes incomprehensible, response.

As they slowly made their way further east, they began hearing stories of the vicious winter weather. When they heard that milk was sold in frozen blocks rather than as a liquid, it gave them a good idea of life in the colder months. In some towns, Annette found extraordinary contrast, such as at Tomsk, with its well-built facilities including music and girls' schools, but women still doing their household washing in the river; and at Minusinsk, where they met very poor people occupying dilapidated semi-roofless houses with almost no facilities, and miserable inns that resembled farmyards, but where they also visited a splendid museum. The new train line was already bringing change. Annette saw a lot of emigrants who had volunteered to head east to take advantage of the government's land offer – a small block of land where an emigrant could grow crops for ten years without paying taxes, part of the government's plan to populate and modernise Siberia.

Back on the train, on they went, still chatting when possible to any new passengers and also sitting in silence for hour after hour as they watched the landscape travelling steadily past. Passing through a thickly forested area, they finally arrived at Krasnoyarsk, a town that caused Annette and her mother some surprise. Here, 2,000 miles east of Moscow, there was a thriving modern community and a really comfortable hotel, the best since they had left Europe. The town had developed from 1429, when it became a centre to protect the Russians from the neighbouring Tatar tribes. Now there were good streets, well-dressed people and a variety of facilities, including a fascinating museum and beautiful public gardens; Annette commented to her mother that they could have been in a German town on the Rhine, it was all so lovely.

So far, everything was going well. All the train travel had been tiring, but acceptable. The breaks in the hotels were usually comfortable, the food tolerable. Now, heading further east towards Lake Baikal, things would start to change. First, the weather was becoming hotter. They had left St Petersburg on 12 May; it had taken them three weeks to get this far east. With midsummer approaching, summer weather now arrived. Heading on ever eastwards, Annette and her mother lay on their bunks with closed eyes for hour after hour, simply too exhausted in the heat to stir. They adapted to making use of the rather primitive toilet facilities on the train, but water was usually available, so they could wash their faces and rinse essentials. It wasn't boring – there was always something to look at through the dusty windows. The landscape was changing steadily. Now there was a sense of desolation, made worse by the sight of burned trees and undergrowth; a fierce fire must have swept across the region not that long before.

After travelling east from Moscow for 3,000 miles, Annette and her mother finally arrived at the town of Irkutsk. The railway had only recently reached the town, and after a history of isolation, the local people were slowly becoming used to increased contact with the west. However, the arrival of two Englishwomen still caused much comment. Annette by now had given up her white, long-sleeved, feminine blouse and was wearing a khaki shirt that had a military style; it was more appropriate for the region and also offered good protection against the sun and insects.

There were some surprises. Having paid for a room in the hotel, Annette then found they needed to pay extra for beds. This far east, language was becoming a problem; when Annette tried to obtain a spoon, she was presented with a glass of vodka. But generally the two women were treated well and with respect; there were very few unpleasant moments when they had to walk away fast from objectionable men or possible thieves.

While the food was different and in some cases the lives were very hard, Annette hadn't found anything dramatic to write about. It was all interesting, though, and in Irkutsk once again she found a big contrast: there were good-looking stone churches, public buildings and schools, but there were no paved streets, no waterworks or electricity. She made a note that many Siberians brought their children to school in the town during the winter months, but disappeared back to their countryside homes when summer arrived.

She did hear, however, that there was a labour prison near Irkutsk and she thought that could be of interest. Asking around, she obtained a letter to the director of the prison and then, with her mother, set off on a Russian tarantass – a basic horse-drawn carriage – for the 50-mile drive out to the facility. It was a most uncomfortable ride. They had been advised to travel by sitting with their heels drawn up underneath them and their chins resting on their knees. Evidently this position would help protect the spine from the constant banging, but nevertheless the journey was a painful challenge.

At the prison a German-speaking officer was able to act as an interpreter, and Annette was welcomed into the complex to have a look around. In this remote spot, there were 650 people in the prison and an additional 400 prisoners who lived just outside in a village where they could follow their own handicrafts and trade. Astonishingly, they learned there was a Scotsman in the prison and the governor sent for him. The convict told Annette he was from Glasgow and had also lived in London, but had been working as a soldier in Riga when he was imprisoned. Annette was the first Englishwoman he had seen for ten years. He had no messages he wanted to send anyone. It was a strange encounter. The director of the institution ran a benign organisation, and the prisoners were treated without harshness; they were given two baths a week and adequate food, and there were lessons and even concerts.

There were no women with dramatic stories, though, and Annette was still keen to move on. Back on the train, they reached the edge of Lake Baikal, where they learned that the section of rail tracks around the southern end of the lake hadn't been completed. Instead, a steamboat was waiting to take the passengers across the lake and pick up the train on the other side; it was a large ice breaker with three huge funnels puffing black smoke. Now Annette and her mother were really thankful they had shed so much of their unnecessary luggage in Paris; while their clothing was now becoming quite worn, at least they could easily carry their rugs and all their personal belongings up onto the boat. It took just over four hours to cross the calm lake before they disembarked on the opposite shore.

Once they landed and were waiting for a train, they heard the great clanking of chains. Turning their heads, they saw a group of weary, chained-up prisoners being marched along the dusty road; perhaps not all prisons were as happy as the one they had visited.

The trains on the east side of Lake Baikal were older and shabby; they only offered basic carriages. But Annette didn't think about giving up on the trip. She hadn't found all the stories she wanted to write about yet, and the scenery and people were now changing more dramatically. She really wanted to go as far east as possible on the train track; it would be a journey definitely worth writing about. They could return to Moscow much more quickly by the same route, as they wouldn't need to break the journey with so many stops. Her mother agreed; she was happy accompanying her energetic and independent daughter.

Getting onto the new train, Annette and her mother were in for a shock. After they settled into a compartment, with two-tier shelves on each side to be used as seats or beds, more and more people kept piling in, and there was no sign of the train starting. Suddenly, two rough men pushed their way in, keen to visit two women sitting on the upper shelf above Annette and her mother. With so many people, and now with men's dirty feet hanging just inches from her head, Annette had had enough. Perhaps she now also began to have some anxiety about having brought her mother on such a trip. Annette pushed her way vigorously out of the carriage and charged down onto the platform. Finding a man in uniform who could speak French, she explained the situation. Annette's new friend acted immediately and said he would order an extra private carriage to be put on the train that had sleeping berths and room for a samovar.

Annette and her mother, with their little valise and holdall, were told to wait on a seat. On a remote platform in the middle of Siberia, two Englishwomen in long skirts, sitting quietly on a wooden seat, must have presented an extraordinary sight. While they were wondering quite what to do next, the sky darkened and it started to rain. The train was still sitting there with its carriages packed full of noisy crowds, and at this point perhaps, Annette's mother may have wondered why on earth she had agreed to come on the trip. Eventually, though, the man came back and, while the promised extra carriage was evidently not possible, he had curtained off a section of the luggage van. Escorting Annette's mother with his arm, he helped them clamber up to the empty, curtained-off compartment. It was certainly small, about 10ft by 8ft across; and while there was a small wooden seat, there was no other furniture. However, it was a lot better than being crushed by the locals in the other hot and noisy carriages in the train. Folding their rugs as thickly as possible, they settled down for the next part of their trip.

Annette and her mother spent three days and four nights in the luggage van. It couldn't have been an easy time, yet not once did Annette seem to consider giving up. Something was now driving her to go on as far as she could. The two sides of her character could not have been illustrated more starkly; sitting in a luggage van rattling across the vast empty landscapes of Siberia was a long way indeed from that elegant Victorian woman who loved to immerse herself in music, poetry and fine writing.

The two Englishwomen were now attracting a great deal of comment, especially as they were often dressed in long, flowing skirts and sometimes even hats; day-to-day outfits that were fashionable back home. There was little alternative, though; they only had a few spare items with them. The soldiers who were in the carriage beyond their curtained-off section were fascinated by the two women and took them under their wing, fetching hot water and milk at stations and sharing their bread. Annette and her mother washed their faces every morning with some of the water brought for tea; they struggled through the train or clambered down the steep step onto the ground at every stop to find some sort of toilet, and on they went. At one point, it started to rain heavily and then, for thirty-six hours, Annette and her mother heard heavy rain pelting down on the roof.

The only view out was through a tiny window, high up in the corner of the van, and Annette had to stand on the seat to look out. It was clear they were now passing over low-lying ground that was turning rapidly into a marsh. They were travelling across a region known as Transbaikalia, bordered in the north by frozen marshes and wild reindeer, and in the south by China. A lot of the area is only frost-free in July, and in many places the earth is frozen to a depth of several feet all year round. Before 1664, when the Russians first reached the region, the land was inhabited by several tribes including the Tungus, the Buddhist Buryats, the Daurians and the Mongols – the Mongols' warrior leader Genghis Khan was born there. By 1900 Cossacks and also people who had been exiled from Russia in the east because of their religion had come to live in the area. Annette, though, couldn't see much at all, stuck in the primitive wooden carriage as they rattled on.

Despite their basic train, the track they were travelling on was the newest. It had only just been completed with thirty-four stations between Lake Baikal and Stretinsk, although many of the stations comprised just a tiny log cottage and a water tower.

Pulling into Stretinsk at daybreak, they gladly disembarked and then stood there. There was no real town in sight and they weren't quite sure what to do. The passengers were all dispersing; a group of chained convicts disembarked not far from them and clanked away from the little station. It was all confusion. Finally, they were lucky to find a local soldier to help them. It seemed they had to cross the river by ferry to reach the town of Stretinsk, although Annette could see no sign of it. It was clearly the way to go, though, and they gathered up their belongings and boarded the ferry boat. On the opposite bank they tried to find a droshky, but the first refused to take their luggage. Struggling to make themselves understood, they finally reached a hotel. It was a bleak result when they understood from the manager that there was no room for them; every bed had been taken.

With persistence, finally they found accommodation. Paying off their droshky driver, who Annette thought had insisted on a ridiculous amount of money for the short trip, Annette and her mother made their way into a basic room with a very worn, lumpy bed and a shabby, dirty sofa. They could hear a man in the next room snoring loudly, for the wall between them comprised only a few planks with large gaps between. Privacy was provided by a big sheet hanging over the planks. Annette made her way into the kitchen in the hope of getting some water for a wash, but everything was very challenging. Leaving her mother in the room, she went out to see if she could find something better.

As Annette stepped out of the door, she met a woman who spoke French. It was the luckiest meeting, for Annette was told the woman was travelling on a boat going down the river to the town of Blagoveshchensk and it had comfortable accommodation. Anything was better than the rough room they had been shown and Annette immediately went down to the wharf. She was greeted by a very friendly agent who confirmed that there was indeed good accommodation on the boat, and Annette and her mother could go aboard immediately. Even better, she also learned that, by changing boats down the river, there was a comfortable steamer to take them to Khabarovsk, where they could pick up a train down to Vladivostok, the very end of the line. This was further than Annette had intended to travel; she didn't know that the final section down to Vladivostok had already been completed. The idea of reaching the Pacific appealed to Annette; it would be a fitting finale to the journey before they headed back.

With huge relief, Annette went back to collect her mother and their luggage, and had to argue with the manager before finally paying another very large charge for the short use of the miserable room. Once on board the boat, with a clean, comfortable bed and facilities, Annette could once again relax. The town of Stretinsk didn't look so bad then. It was a Cossack town, populated by the families of those fierce horsemen who had spread from their original base in the east; but Annette also saw a lot of Manchus from north-eastern China, with their hair in long pigtails and wearing wide-brimmed hats and loose, blue cotton trousers. Suddenly, it really brought home to her that they had made it across the whole continent; they were now in a very different land and very near the Chinese border.

Once they set off down the river, apart from the intense heat and biting flies, the journey on the boat was almost pleasant. The scenery on the river Shilka was beautiful, with high granite rocks rising on both sides. It took three days to reach the town of Pokrovskaya, where the little river Shilka joined the Amur, and here Annette and her mother transferred onto the larger boat with even better facilities. The river flowed along the boundary between Russia and China, and they found chairs facing south so that they could look across to China as they chugged down the river. There were few interesting features, though, and few signs of life, and they finally reached Blagoveshchensk, 3,500 miles east of Moscow. The town, once Chinese, was now firmly under Russia control. It was busy and lively, and they had great hopes as they found a comfortable room at the Grand Hotel, where the coffee was good but the eggs were inedible. Suddenly they felt they were back in the real world, and having been away for so long, they asked the manager for news of South Africa and the Boer War.

His answer staggered them: South Africa was a minor problem; it was the war between Russia and China that was the problem now, and here on the Chinese border the conflict was of major concern. Going out into the street, they realised there were many Chinese in the town, from just across the border in Manchuria. They were working in many different areas, often carrying poles balanced across their shoulders, swinging baskets of vegetables and fruits in traditional Chinese fashion.

With the heat and the food, Annette wasn't feeling particularly well, and the situation wasn't helped when the manager burst into their room. His news was bad: he told them they would have to stay in Blagoveshchensk; war had already broken out and all transport was being chartered for soldiers. He told them a Chinese army of 30,000 men was gathered just south of the river, and even if they did decide to travel on, they might well be shot at. They also heard that all the horses were being taken to help the fight as well. Russian troops were being mobilised.

It was now raining heavily, but Annette knew she needed to sort this situation out for them both. It was all very frightening and confusing. She had heard little about the Boxers; when she was planning the trip at the beginning of the year, the group from coastal China had only just started its violent campaign against foreigners. The Boxers originated from a Chinese secret society called Yihetuan, or the Righteous and Harmonious Fists, because of their dedication to a form of martial arts that resembled boxing, hence their name. Their hatred of foreigners was by now spreading quickly across China, and as Annette and her mother were happily travelling east through Russia, the Boxers were storming across the Chinese countryside in a vicious and terrifying campaign against foreigners. Their violent activities included burning churches and brutally killing all the missionaries and Christian converts they could find.

From the end of June 1900 onwards, the Chinese Imperial Army had joined with the Boxers to attack foreign legations in the capital, Beijing. Annette had no idea that, as she talked to her mother in their hotel room in Blagoveshchensk, just a few hundred miles south, hundreds of British and other nationalities, men, women and children, were fighting desperately for their lives, isolated and besieged in their small legation as they fought off vicious attacks from the Qing army and the Boxers.

Annette could sense there were serious problems, though. Finding at last a little droshky, she and her mother drove through dangerous floodwater to reach the offices of the Amur shipping company. Asking around for interpreters, they made good contacts and to their surprise learned there was actually a boat moored on the river that was about to head downriver for Khabarovsk. Taking it could be very dangerous; there was talk that the Chinese fighters were about to cross the border and the boat would be an early casualty. Annette didn't know what to believe, or really what to do, but she concluded that they should get out while they could; it might be the last transport leaving Blagoveshchensk.

Reaching the boat, they found that not only was there space for them, but it was actually quite comfortable. They travelled for three worrying days down the river, right along the border with China, but encountered no problems. Arriving at Khabarovsk, they transferred straight onto the crowded platform and then boarded the train to Vladivostok. The train appeared to be managed by soldiers and there was a strong military presence everywhere, but Annette stopped thinking of war and enjoyed being back travelling. It was a huge relief to be away from the drama, heading south through beautiful hills with valleys and meadows filled with lovely flowers.

Arriving at Vladivostok, Annette and her mother found the town itself full of soldiers and in a state of excitement, but still the news was confusing. They managed to book into a nice hotel overlooking the beautiful bay, and installing her mother safely in their room, Annette went out to find out a little more about what was going on. Everywhere was crowded with people milling around. There were rumours that war between the Russians and Chinese had already started. Everyone not in the military was desperate to leave the area. However, Annette was also told there was no boat out for at least a week, perhaps a lot longer, and there was no telling what might happen in that time.

Annette became seriously concerned, especially for her mother. With persistence, Annette discovered there was a cargo boat at the nearby docks leaving shortly for Japan. Annette leapt at this; Japan would offer a temporary refuge while the situation in Russia settled down, before they could return to Europe. In the meantime, it would be interesting to see the country. Evidently the cargo boat could accommodate a handful of passengers. Somehow, Annette and her mother talked their way on board and they left Vladivostok and the chaos of eastern Russia on Friday, 6 July 1900. It seemed an incredibly long four months since they had left London.

Arriving in Japan, Annette's spirits lifted. It was a fascinating country and, with her usual plan of seeking out people with local knowledge and connections, she met an American woman who took her to see some Ainu families, who were descendants of the original inhabitants of Japan. Annette was fascinated by the women, who had been tattooed above their lips with lead when babies, giving the appearance of a moustache that lasted a lifetime. This was definitely a story she could write about when back in England.

Then, one evening, at dinner, they heard some terrible news. Just four days after they had left Blagoveshchensk, shots had been fired from across the Chinese border at a Russian boat on the very same route they had sailed down. The alarm had been given and a Russian battalion had marched down to the northern bank of the river and opened fire. It turned into a ferocious fight and then a massacre. It was estimated that around 7,000 Chinese civilians had been killed in Blagoveshchensk. When the Russians finally got across the river, they decimated the Chinese towns and drove any remaining rebels into the interior. Evidently the river Annette and her mother had travelled peacefully down was now full of bodies. The situation was incredibly unstable. There was no way they could travel back across Russia.

Travel onwards from Japan to the United States was, however, easy. This was clearly the only route out. On 27 July, Annette and her mother boarded the *Empress of Japan*, which was sailing from Yokohama. The ship was crowded with missionaries escaping from China, many with appalling stories of how they had managed to survive terrifying Boxer attacks.

For Annette, once the ship was under way, the worry and concern about the situation between Russia and China was over. Safely on the comfortable vessel, she had time to go through her notes and was pleased; she thought she had enough to make a book of the journey. Her ambition to become a writer hadn't diminished. It's interesting that Annette didn't talk more to the missionaries during the time they had together crossing the Pacific; they would have had some fascinating stories for her. There were also other stories she missed. During her time in Russia, she didn't make note of the growing industrialisation and very poor working conditions across the country, the desperate situation of many of its people that would lead to the first Russian revolution in just a few years; nor, despite her love for and involvement in serious literature, did she visit any of the places associated with the famous Russian writers of the day, names such as Chekhov, Pushkin and Tolstoy. She did, however, make up for this a few years later when she made another trip to Russia and spent a happy few hours with Count Leo Tolstoy, discussing the works of the great literary figures of the day.

Now, however, Annette was content. She had copious notes and she felt the journey across Russia had been a success. When the ship finally arrived in Vancouver, for her mother at least, there must have been a sense of real relief and happiness at being safely back in more familiar surroundings.

Both women were now very keen to return home. The weeks travelling across Russia and the drama of their last few days in the country had taken their toll. Annette booked seats quickly on the Canadian Pacific Railway. This rail track was also fairly new, having been completed just fifteen years earlier, not without problems. One obstacle had been that the route crossed land in Alberta that was controlled by the Blackfoot First Nation people. It took some persuasion, but finally Blackfoot chief Crowfoot agreed to allow the construction of a rail track across their land in return for a lifetime pass on the railway. As in Russia, the railway was opening up areas right across the country.

The train was modern and clean, with two baggage cars, a mail car, first- and second-class coaches linked by corridors, and also comfortable sleeping cars and a dining car. Compared with the last few trains they had taken across Russia, this was luxury, and Annette and her mother settled down happily. There was one aspect Annette didn't approve of though: every morning attendants came early to change the bed into daytime seats. Annette didn't always want to get up early and then be forced to sit upright for the rest of the day.

Initially, there was compensation for the lack of daytime beds from the beautiful scenery; the train was heading eastwards through the glorious landscapes of the Rockies. But then, as they continued east, the views of the central prairies became flat and featureless. Alighting at Toronto, they sought out newspapers to discover what was happening in China, and they visited Niagara to see the spectacular falls. Annette's younger brother, Sidney, was living in Montreal at the time, and they took a train up to visit him. It was a very cheery reunion and Annette and her mother certainly had some entertaining stories to tell.

Then it was another sea passage, leaving New York for Liverpool on 22 August. A final steam train down to London and Annette and her mother were back home on 31 August, just over five months after they had left. They had travelled over 18,000 miles around the world, with 11,000 miles by train at a time when railways were still being established. For two well-brought-up Victorian women, it had been an extraordinary journey.

Back home, Annette soon immersed herself in writing, completing a series of stories on her travels for the *Gentlewoman* magazine and finalising a book on her journey. This attracted reasonable interest.

Now in her mid-thirties, Annette knew she wanted to make writing a career, and she settled down to creating a variety of works, every so often giving piano lessons and lectures to supplement her income. Her love of travel remained, and eventually she was off again on another journey to Russia. In 1906 her book *Russia, Travels and Studies* was published and this included details of her meeting with Leo Tolstoy.

Then, finally, Annette went back to her first area of interest, women in society. Now, with more writing experience behind her, she was indeed becoming the writer of serious merit that had been her dream so many years before. In 1907, her book *Woman in Transition* was published. It drew on her experience of women in different countries and was recognised as an excellent work. The same year, again with her mother, she visited Galicia in northern Spain to research an idea for a new book, but back in England, just a few months later, her mother died at the age of 75. Sarah Meakin had been a strong background support for many of Annette's adventures, and it was a deep loss. She left Annette a small legacy and this, together with the money from piano lessons, lectures and books, enabled Annette to live comfortably, albeit not luxuriously, for the rest of her life.

Just two years later, Annette brought out another excellent work, *Galicia, the Switzerland of Spain*, and then, in 1911, her book on the United States and a biographical study of religious author Hannah More were also published to good reviews.

Annette was now becoming a prolific and well-respected writer. She had kept up correspondence with her old professor and mentor, A.E. Housman, and now she started tackling complex areas including translating Homer's writings into English poetry, a translation of Pierre Corneille's play, *Polyeucte*, and finally, in 1932, her last major book, the three-volume *Goethe and Schiller, 1785–1805: The Story of a Friendship*, was published.

Annette's later years were not settled; she continued to rent accommodation in many different locations from the Kent coast to north Wales, but in 1956, when she was in her late eighties, she went to live with her niece in Essex. She died in August 1959 and was buried at Highgate Cemetery in London; very definitely a woman of literature but also, together with her mother, the very first woman to go around the world by train.

7

1909 HARRIET WHITE FISHER
THE FIRST WOMAN TO DRIVE ROUND THE WORLD

Like many dramatic inventions that change mankind, the development of the motorcar didn't happen overnight. Steam-powered transportation was being looked at as far back as the late 1700s before it took off in the nineteenth century. In the 1800s, things moved on fast, but it was only when German Karl Benz launched his three-wheel petrol engine car in 1885 that the modern era of motoring really began.

The idea of being able to travel around in your own motorised transport was greeted with enormous enthusiasm, but obtaining one of the new wondrous machines was too expensive for most people. Then, there was the problem of where to drive them. There was a movement to improve roads, especially on main routes between cities, but much of the world was still set up for traditional horse-drawn vehicles.

When Harriett White Fisher decided to drive around the world, she really had no idea what she would encounter. Even with the most vivid imagination, she could not have dreamed of the experiences and adventures that lay ahead.

What on earth was she thinking? Harriet White Fisher was 48 years old and she had established herself as a successful businesswoman. She was now very wealthy and not only had a lovely farm near Trenton in New Jersey, USA, but also a beautiful villa on the edge of Lake Como in Italy.

With a good social life, why, in 1909, would this middle-aged woman decide not only to purchase a car, but then drive it around the world — a world where cars were still a novelty; where, in many regions, horse- and cattle-drawn carts were still the main way of transport and where many roads were simply rough, dusty gravel paths?

Harriet White Fisher, however, felt there was a very clear reason. Her days were becoming humdrum, monotonous even. To begin with, her life had been full of fun and excitement. She had been born in 1861 in Pennline, north-west Pennsylvania, just as the drama and horrors of the American Civil War were starting. Seeking a new peaceful life, her parents moved to a more remote farm property, but right from the start, little Harriet wasn't looking for tranquillity. Toddling and then running around the property, she joined with the boys in climbing trees, milking cows and catching worms to fix on fishing hooks. Daddy felt she needed to become more ladylike, and when she was old enough, he shipped her off to the Ladies Classical Seminary across the border in Cleveland.

It wasn't a natural fit for lively Harriet and, with her independent lust for life, when her parents then suggested she might like to finish her studies at a school in Germany, a popular move for well-brought-up American girls at the time, Harriet leapt at the idea. This was a success and Harriet loved Europe, learning to speak German and visiting as many places as possible. Back in the United States, she tried to go down the traditional homemaking path with a short marriage to Gustav Lindenthal, originally from Brno, then in the Austrian empire. He was a fluent German speaker and that may have been all they had in common. He was also fifteen years older and very involved in his career as a bridge engineer; the marriage quickly failed. His knowledge of engineering, though, interested Harriet and she learned to drive, gaining her licence in New Jersey and also in other states. She rather liked the attention she attracted as a woman driver, which was still unusual in those days in the United States, and being a capable driver also helped her enjoy a good social life.

Finally, though, her parents' hope that their rebellious and independent daughter would settle down properly was fulfilled. Harriet met Clark Fisher, who was running a large and successful anvil foundry in Trenton, New Jersey, and they were married in July 1898. Harriet was 33 and now became the wife of a successful businessman. She tried to assume the role of a dutiful housewife, proud of her hardworking, knowledgeable husband and, in this case, it wasn't her fault when circumstances changed.

First, Clark became seriously ill, too sick even to go down to the factory. Concerned about finances and the future of the workers, Harriet went to the factory initially to sort out the paperwork. Here, she was given a cold welcome by the foreman and shipping clerk; a dirty factory was no place for the wife of the boss. With Clark away sick, some of the workers hadn't even bothered to come in. Now Harriet showed her strengths. She walked over to a small rolling truck and pushed it across to a heavy anvil, lifted the anvil onto the truck and wheeled it off to the despatch area. She then warned the workers that if the factory didn't return to full production instantly, the workers would all be dismissed.

It didn't take long; realising the factory was to continue as before, soon all the workers were back at their posts. Harriet rather liked being involved in the noisy, heavy industry and when her husband eventually recovered, Harriet continued to spend time at the factory, learning all the different processes, from smelting pig iron and tempering steel to bidding for contracts. The company was at the forefront of anvil manufacturing, using top-grade American iron and cast steel, and Harriet found it all quite exciting.

Then, just over a year later, in October 1902, there was a real disaster. Catching the Pennsylvania Railroad for a trip to New York, the train Harriet and Clark were on was hit by another. It was an awful crash with one death and many injuries. Harriet and Clark were both injured, but while Harriet steadily recovered, Clark's injuries were more serious. He gradually deteriorated and two months later died. In his will, he left his property and the factory to Harriet.

Suddenly, amid her grief and trying to come to terms with a new life on her own, she had a real challenge. The factory had been her husband's real love in life; he had been left it by his father and had been determined to build it and make it successful. Now Harriet was the new owner and she made a big decision: she decided there was no reason why she couldn't run the factory herself. She wanted to keep it going, partly in memory of her husband, the only man she had ever really loved, and partly because she felt she had a responsibility to his workers. There was also the challenge itself: no woman had ever owned and run a factory of this size in the United States before; it would be exciting to try and make it work.

Even if she owned it, the workers at least expected a new male supervisor and manager to be appointed, and when they heard Harriet was taking over, they were rebellious. They didn't want to be managed by what they called 'a petticoat government'; for many of them, this woman dressed in a carefully ironed, pretty shirt and long flowing skirt was a ludicrous sight in a dirty, noisy factory. Harriet was having none of it, though, and had no hesitation in telling the workers exactly where they stood. Leave their posts and they would be dismissed instantly. Soon the factory was back once again in full production.

Harriet continued to learn about the business as the months and years went by; checking orders, confirming maintenance and quality, she was hands on in every aspect. Soon she was being called Lady Anvil and the Iron Lady, but the names came with some respect, for the works were not only just continuing, they were flourishing. After a few years, output had doubled and then tripled.

Harriet had two particular strengths. She was very good at getting new orders – once she under-bid rivals to gain a massive contract to supply equipment to the Panama Canal project – and she also kept the workers happy. She got to know them, moving them around to different posts when they got fed up, and asking about their wives and children. The staff at the factory gradually became very loyal to their strong new boss, who supervised by example; although she lived on a farm 4 miles away, she was always at the factory at 7 a.m. to greet the workers. There was never any real discontent or a strike while Harriet was in charge.

It was, however, endless hard work and, by 1908, Harriet was starting to get restless with constant involvement in such heavy industry. She had taken a few trips to her villa in Italy, but somehow that wasn't enough. The idea came to her in a flash: why not go around the world and see new countries, new developments, new people?

The more she thought about it, the more she realised she simply had to do it. It was time to move on. She got out an atlas and started planning; it offered such an exciting diversion from the endless hard work at the factory. The first task was to choose the best form of transport. On board ship, things could become a little boring; after the crash that killed her husband, Harriet would never go on a train again. In 1908, as the idea of a world trip took hold, the first American-made car won the big Vanderbilt Cup race on Long Island, New York. This car race was one of the greatest sporting events of the era, and Harriet's dilemma was solved. The winning car had been a Type 1 Locomobile; Harriet decided she would go around the world in one of those. Resources were not going to be a problem – with money from family, her husband and now the anvil business, Harriet was reasonably wealthy.

Decision made, she purchased a Locomobile Type 1 Model 40 and it turned out to be a beauty. It was the company's top-of-the-line model, powered by a four-cylinder engine with 40hp. The car had sliding-gear, three-speed transmission with a cross-shaft for the double chain drive to the rear axle. For Harriet, it also had larger than normal petrol and oil tanks and excellent suspension, something she knew would be really important if she really was going to take it right around the world.

In the United States and Europe, women were beginning to drive, but it was still a hobby of the wealthy; no woman had driven right across the USA. Harriet's plan to go right around the world was greeted with some scepticism. Now in her early forties, she enjoyed driving, but she quickly realised that she would need some help to drive through the various countries on a world tour. An employee of Harriet's offered the perfect solution. Harold Brooks had a strong background as a motor specialist; he had been working for the Standard Motor Construction Company when Harriet lured him away to help check the engines of a boat she had bought for her villa in Italy. Back in the United States, he had also acted as her personal chauffeur and she knew he was a good and enthusiastic driver. He was much younger than Harriet and strong; he was also friendly and well presented – he would fit in well on a global trip.

Harriet decided they needed to do a test run before committing themselves. With Mr Brooks, as she always called him, sitting firmly in front of the large steering wheel on the right-hand side of the car and Harriet sitting high up beside him on his left, they set off for a trip to Pittsburgh and Cleveland. The car ran beautifully, purring along on the open roadways, and Harriet enjoyed herself, looking down on the world as they sped along at a steady 45mph.

Now Harriet started proper planning. She wanted to call in at her villa in Italy, she wanted to see the Pyramids, she definitely wanted to see the Taj Mahal in India and the elegant Japanese geisha girls she had heard about; it was going to be an ambitious journey. Considering the distance involved, Harriet decided she might need some additional help along with Harold Brooks. Also, travelling with just a younger man might seem inappropriate. In her Italian villa, a tall local girl had worked for Harriet. Her name was Maria and she was so good that Harriet had brought her over to assist in her American home. With her happy, sunny nature, she was an obvious choice and was very willing to join the trip.

Once that was agreed, it occurred to Harriet that as she was taking Maria, why not also take Albert? He also worked in Harriet's home and could turn his hand to anything, from cooking to carpentry to sorting out arrangements. His skills on the trip might come in useful and there was more than enough room in the large car. Harriet asked Albert to join them, too.

By spring 1909, everything was ready. Harriet's house was locked up, a supervisor was installed at the factory, and Harriet had arranged for the car to be boxed up and transported to Paris. Why Paris? She knew that there would be some last-minute provisions to buy once the car was across the Atlantic, and Paris, with its abundance of shops, could provide all the items she needed for the extraordinary trip she was planning.

News had got around of Harriet's planned trip and, just before she left, there was a small send-off party for her that included the presentation of a Boston bull terrier. It was a sweet little dog and Harriet decided to take him with her; she thought a little furry friend would make a good companion during the journey. She named him Honk Honk.

It was quite a group that, on 17 July 1909, all went up the gangplank onto the SS *New York* to set sail for France. The adventure Harriet so wanted was about to begin.

Problems came thick and fast. Reaching Paris, they had to undergo an inspection from the Engineer of Mines and obtain an official permit to drive in France. This they sorted, but then, driving around Paris to see the sights, they decided to visit the pretty park area of the Bois de Boulogne. Hilda had no idea that, outside the city's official borders, petrol could be obtained at a cheaper price, and so there was a rule that any car leaving the capital had to have its petrol officially measured. If the car returned with more petrol than it left with, there was tax and a fine to pay.

But Harriet took all this in her stride. It was part of the adventure she was expecting. In Paris, Harriet soon realised that there might not always be good hotels en route to offer accommodation, so she decided to stock up. The little group visited an army supply house where they bought sleeping bags, blankets, water canteens and a thermos bottle, which Harold packed carefully into the back of the big car.

They also purchased a tent and Harriet wanted to test it before they finally left. She put the tent up in the corner of the Place Vendôme, one of the most beautiful squares in Paris. First, here was an extraordinary American woman in a huge car driving around Paris. Now she was putting up a tent right in the middle of the town. No wonder it attracted a large crowd.

Adding some more equipment, including waterproof bags for sheets and pillowcases, small pillows, rope, rugs and a toolbox, finally Harriet felt they had all the equipment they needed. Harold ensured the weight was evenly distributed as Harriet arrived with more bits and pieces to add to the car. When she finally arrived with a hatbox, he might have wondered what he had let himself in for as he found a place for it on top of the extra tyre.

Nevertheless, with the little dog Honk Honk nestling down on the back seat, it was a happy party that finally left Paris for the proper start of their great adventure.

To begin with, it was a real pleasure for all of them to roll along the roads, stopping at villages and towns for meals and a hotel for the night. There were many sights to see in rural France in 1909, including villages where sheep or cattle shared the same quarters as their owners. Harriet found this made sense; having the animals close stopped them from being stolen and gave warmth to the families at night.

Everywhere they went, they attracted attention; once they were asked to take part in a local fête, and at another town they were herded to a special table where everyone brought them lovely local food.

The first real problem occurred at Lucerne, where they were planning on driving south round the lake before climbing up to cross the St Gotthard pass towards Italy and Harriet's villa in Como. It seemed that motorists were only allowed to go through the pass between the hours of five and seven in the afternoon, and even then, only one car would be allowed at a time with horse-drawn vehicles having right of way. It was suggested they attach horses to their car to pull the vehicle up and that way they could go anytime.

Harriet put her knowledge of German to good use here and they were soon over the mountain and staying in a comfortable hotel with magnificent views. Reaching the Italian border, Harriet's maid Maria was useful. As a native Italian, she could help sort out the new paperwork that was needed to bring a car into the country. New roads were under construction, motoring had taken Europe by storm, and in just a few years, roads and indeed cars were appearing everywhere. They soon made it into familiar territory, arriving at Harriet's villa in Como without further problems. Here the dog Honk Honk made himself at home, examining every corner and trotting happily around the extensive gardens.

Harriet was in no rush and soon the party was well established. Harriet could visit old friends, including titled families who lived in beautiful villas and even palaces; Maria could also visit her family. It was a very happy time. At one point they heard there would be an aeroplane display in the nearby countryside, and they joined a throng of local people who were thrilled when Louis Blériot gave two successful flying demonstrations above the fields. He had made the very first aerial crossing of the Channel just a few weeks before, in July 1909, and now the people could see for themselves the astonishing spectacle of man in the air.

Despite such a happy time, Harriet realised that if she were really going to travel around the world, they had better move on. With everything safely installed back in the car and Honk Honk collected from the garden, finally the little party in the well-laden car set off again. Already their route was meandering; instead of heading east, they headed first down to Genoa on the Mediterranean coast and then west across to Marseille. Here there were arguments in store about the best way to transport the car and also Honk Honk. Harriet was given a strong '*non*' when she mentioned that she wanted to travel on a passenger boat with a dog.

After much discussion and negotiation, it was decided to ship both the car and Honk Honk straight across to Bombay (now Mumbai), and Harold spent time at the custom house to check everything was crated properly. Then Harriet, with Harold, Maria and Albert, boarded a ship, the *Mantua*, to sail east. They stopped off at Port Said and visited Cairo. Here Harriet loved the pyramids, but many of the other sights horrified her. She was puzzled by the number of people she met with sore eyes and made enquiries. She found to her horror that many mothers would add a drop of a poisonous herb into the eyes of their young sons, ensuring the damage to their vision would save them from having to be soldiers when they were older.

They then sailed on to arrive in Bombay on 9 January 1910, six months after the trip had started. Harriet was not in a rush.

It was a joyful reunion with Honk Honk, and Harriet as well as Harold was delighted the car had been transported without damage. As they collected the car and tried to find Bombay's luxurious Taj Mahal hotel, it was clear that India would be a challenge. Harriet's first impressions of the country stayed with her for ever: the hectic, crowded streets, the noise and movement, the sheer intensity of human life. How on earth would they manage to drive through such thronging streets? Harriet remained optimistic, though; outside the towns, hopefully the country roads and tracks would be a lot quieter. Stopping and starting as they made their way along the crowded streets, they finally reached the hotel.

Soon Harriet started to sort out plans for the next stage of the trip; she decided they might need a few more items and she sorted out a lantern, a hatchet, two guns and some cooking utensils. There is no record of the reactions of the carefully trained and dressed staff at the hotel when the guns and hatchet were delivered for Harriet, but the little party was beginning to attract attention. Harriet now also started adding food to the car for the voyage ahead, including coffee, sugar, biscuits, jars of potted chicken and condensed cream. Harold patiently accepted the items and somehow managed to find room for them in the already heavily laden car.

Before they left Bombay, Harriet was given many warnings about her plan to drive across India. She was told that, while by now there were some roads in India, in places these deteriorated into very rough tracks that would be impassable for the car. Then, they would be attacked by robbers, they would run out of petrol, they would be crossing areas with no decent hotels. The problems were innumerable. Harriet explained that they could cover nearly 400 miles with the petrol they had on board, and she had made a note of where they should go to find more petrol. She even arranged for some petrol to be sent ahead on locations she had found on a map. Harriet had no worries at all.

As they drove out of Bombay, the roads were dusty but dry and, at the low speed they were going and with its superior springing, the car rode well. It was the bullock carts and indeed the crowds that caused the problems. Often the bullocks would take fright at the large car and make a sudden turn to get away, tipping the two-wheeled carts over and spilling all their goods. It all seemed quite friendly, though, and on the party progressed.

After about 90 miles, they had left the hectic city well behind them. Climbing nearly 2,000ft into the hills, the air was clean and the scenery beautiful. The little party was beginning to enjoy the trip, but it was late afternoon and they were hot and thirsty. There was nowhere to stay, so they decided to make their first camp. Albert set about to boil the water before drinking, a rule Harriet had insisted upon from the beginning. After boiling, the water was put into a large pigskin bottle, which Harriet tied to a tree and swung around until the water cooled. Despite their preparations, however, it wasn't a successful night. The views in every direction were large mountains with some trees, but they could also see groups of huts. Soon local people started gathering just to look at them. Some of the people were appallingly thin and their clothes were threadbare; it was disturbing. Honk Honk, who had been tied to the front of the car, was concerned at the new surroundings and barked on and off throughout the night. They were glad when daylight came, so they could get up and get going again.

Their destination was Delhi, Agra and the Taj Mahal, just under 1,000 miles away and not always straightforward driving. Many of the roads were narrow and rough, and occasionally the graded pebbly surfaces deteriorated into very steep tracks. They also had to cross many rivers, some by precarious bridges and some approached by deep sand. Harriet and Harold soon got out their Manila rope and organised local helpers and bullocks to tow the car through really difficult stretches. Harriet, always in her long skirt and usually a long-sleeved shirt, would when necessary help out with the pushing and pulling. Just as when she became involved in her factory, Harriet was happy to be hands-on.

Harriet was fascinated by everything she saw. She was getting used to the locals, the animals on the roads, the happy smiling chatter of so many little children everywhere. She wasn't really interested in the political situation in the country, but she loved to stop and visit historic caves and monuments, some of the carvings dating back to 200 BCE. Sometimes they found local rest houses for accommodation, although 'crimson ramblers' or bedbugs were a real problem. Harriet felt pleased she had brought all their own bed linen with them.

One night, Honk Honk had been left outside tied to the car when he was attacked by jackals. The whole party leapt up to go to the dog's defence, with Harriet arming herself with an iron bar that she found on the ground, and little Honk Honk was saved.

The next stop, up a reasonable road at Sarangpur, they found a pleasant spot to camp and Honk Honk was allowed to sleep in the tent with them all. Water was available from a pond, although dead animals were lying on the banks, so Albert was kept busy boiling water. They decided to stop an extra day there so that Maria could do all the washing. They were running short of some supplies, so Harold went out with his gun and came back with some fine pigeons, which they cooked. Then he bagged two chickens and Albert made a curried chicken meal with local rice. Disregarding the heat, the insects and the basic comforts of their tent, it turned out to be a pleasant stop.

After 600 miles of driving, the little party finally made Gwalior. The car was going beautifully; it had made well over 100 miles during the last day of driving and now the roads improved dramatically. They were beautifully graded by the local workers, who worked on them all day long to keep them up to scratch. Here, they were in for a surprise. Checking into a local guesthouse, they learned that the local maharaja had an English secretary. On making his acquaintance, they soon learned that His Highness the Maharaja owned an astonishing thirty-two automobiles; he was a great enthusiast of motoring and wanted the whole country opened up to the new mode of transport.

The guesthouse they were staying in was appalling. It was noisy, rough, dirty, hot and uncomfortable, and when the little party was invited to a meal at the palace, they were delighted to see the other side of India. The huge and ornate palace that greeted them was beyond splendour. Deep-red carpets, furniture covered with gold fabric, elaborately decorated ceilings and splendid chandeliers surrounded them, and at a giant, horseshoe-shaped table, the banquet was superb and was accompanied by musicians playing gently in a high balcony above them. It was hard to leave to go back to their shabby, bug-ridden little guesthouse. Harriet didn't really think about how the local people felt, many of whom were living in dreadful poverty while knowing that, just up the road, other people were enjoying total luxury; she was a very practical woman who simply accepted the situation as it was.

The next day, the road up to Agra was only just over 70 miles. There was a good surface, but it included a major river and there was only a pontoon bridge, made of what appeared quite rotten wood. It was also very unstable. Harriet had her heart in her mouth as their precious car swayed up and down and tipped to terrifying angles from side to side. At one point she thought she had lost the car and it would be tipped right over into the water, but it finally made it across the river, where they were relieved to get back on the road again. Not far away, they found an empty government inspection bungalow they could stay in. From the locals here, they managed to buy some carrots and peas and also some local limes. Mixing the limes with sugar and boiled water, they made their own version of lemonade. Harold shot four pigeons and two partridges, so they had an excellent meal, although it was a bit of a comedown after the banquet the night before.

The next day, Harold had to change a tyre in the searing midday sun, but otherwise they had a good run up to Agra and booked into the Great Northern hotel. It had a lovely fountain in the middle of a courtyard but, despite being a central attraction at the hotel, the fountain had no water; Harriet was getting used to surprises.

In this hotel, she found there was no bedding either, although she did manage to find some mosquito nets. They spent their first day exploring the town; Harriet loved the beautifully embroidered shawls, but she didn't buy anything. Then the day had come to visit the Taj Mahal, one of the key sights Harriet had noted on her must-visit list. They packed a tea basket and arrived late afternoon, waiting for the moon to rise. She said watching the moon lift up behind the exquisite white marble mausoleum was an experience she would never forget.

After wandering around the lovely building, the little group arrived back at their car to find it surrounded by a huge crowd. There were only a handful of cars in Agra at the time and their huge American limousine had quickly become the talk of the area. But no one had touched the car and all was safe.

On 4 February 1910, Harriet decided they had seen all they wanted to and it was time to start heading east again. First stop was Cawnpore (now Kanpur), the site of a famous siege in 1857, and Harriet noticed the bad feelings from all the killings that had taken place in the town. Here she also became very aware of the different caste systems in Indian society; overall she didn't like the atmosphere and was happy to move on quickly.

The heat, the insects, the constant enquiries and stares from local people – it was all beginning to wear them down. The crowds that amassed whenever they slowed down made driving difficult. Harold was getting anxious because so much dust on the road sometimes made it impossible to see where he was going, and he was becoming nervous he might drive into someone. All their luggage had become infiltrated with sandy dust. It was tiring and frustrating, but Harriet was still happy. She was seeing sights she had only dreamed of – the colour, the exoticism of the country – India was showing her a side of life she couldn't have imagined. While it wasn't all good, it was all very exciting. Washing when she could, eating when she could, sleeping on the ground on their own little bedding mats when they had to, Harriet was taking it all in her stride.

Her next main stop on her planned world tour was Japan, a country she was really keen to visit, but she had marked on her map several places she would like to see en route as they continued to head east.

On the boat out to Bombay, Harriet had met Judge Motilal Nehru, an important Indian political figure and also the father of Jawarharlal Nehru, the great friend of Lady Mountbatten and future prime minister of India. Judge Nehru lived in Allahabad (now Prayagraj) and had promised Harriet a ride on an elephant if they visited the town. Harriet was very keen to take him up on it.

On making contact, the judge was busy, but they were invited to stay at one of his palaces and soon they were driving into the most magnificent park, lined with miniature lakes on each side and with a winding drive up to a beautiful white marble building surrounded by flowers and tropical plants. As they reached the building, Harriet couldn't believe her eyes. In front of her were not only seventy-five beautifully dressed servants, all lined up to greet them, but also two huge elephants, dressed in wonderful gold and with silver, hand-embroidered howdah seats, who knelt down to welcome the party.

It was the most spectacular welcome Harriet had ever had anywhere, and made a story she would relate for the rest of her life. With so many servants, everything was taken care of and Harriet enjoyed not only the lavish mealtimes but also chatting to the ladies of the house. She was pleased to hear that some of the older customs, such as marrying girls as young as 7 to boys not much older, were dying out. The Indian women said they also agreed with the British government, which was trying to stop the custom of Sati, the automatic killing of a widow after her husband had died. The tradition was that when a man died, all jewellery and possessions were taken from the woman, her hair was cropped and then she was bound and put on the funeral pyre with her husband's body, where they were burned together. Harriet listened carefully to the details and agreed with the Indian women that it wasn't a good thing.

Judge Nehru was as good as his word and an elephant ride was arranged for Harriet. She had now taken to wearing a local sari, or light silk gown, which she found cool and comfortable. Nevertheless, arranging herself and her skirt carefully on the howdah, high up on the back of a huge elephant, was challenging and a little scary. When the elephant rose, she was very high off the ground, plus it took a while to get used to the constant swaying motion. After a short time, though, she was looking around and enjoying the ride as her majestic elephant moved slowly forward, feeling the way with its trunk and lifting its large, flat feet with great care as it plodded gently onwards through great crowds of people towards the river.

Harriet spent several hours on the back of the elephant at the side of the Ganges, watching the local people including sellers of rice and other items; she also stared, fascinated, at the snake charmers, who were doing good business. At one point, she saw a group of naked men sitting on hot ashes. Being suspicious, Harriet insisted on getting down from the elephant, quite a performance in itself, and then popping her finger in the ashes to see how hot they really were. She quickly took her finger away … it was badly blistered by the intense heat. Harriet got back on her elephant in a slightly more thoughtful mood.

It was another vivid and exotic memory that Harriet would take back to the United States. Really, this round-the-world trip was turning into all she had hoped it would be.

Their visit to the next city on the list, Benares (now Varanasi), was equally interesting but not so enjoyable, especially as the little group took a boat trip on the Ganges to see the burning of bodies and then the remains tipped into the river. There was a great deal of poverty.

On the little group went; the car was purring steadily across the reasonably flat terrain as they headed east into more remote areas of north India. Maria was doing what she could to keep everyone's clothes as clean as possible, Albert was on the constant search for fresh food and supplies, and Harold was continually checking the car and its engine; they all had enough to keep them busy on the frequent stops they needed to give them a break from constantly sitting in the crowded, laden car. Harriet continued to take in all the scenery and one thing that upset her was the large-scale cutting down of trees.

Speaking to local people, she learned that India was suffering from a lack of wood, yet while trees were still being cut down in vast quantities, no new trees were being planted. Harriet was concerned about this and commented that soon India would be without fuel.

On the way south-east, heading towards their next key stop, Calcutta (now Kolkata), they began to run short of food. This was no problem for Harriet, who had made bread on a flat pan over an open fire in her childhood on the farm, and she quickly showed the others how to mix the flour they had available with baking powder and make muffins. There was no snobbery in Harriet: she might have been one of the wealthier women in the United States; she might have been the boss of a large, successful manufacturing company, overseeing many employees; but she had no hesitation in crouching down to cook muffins on an open fire.

The idea of class differences did not really occur to Harriet, but she was aware of position. She was careful not to become over-familiar with her little group and, despite their living together so closely, she still called Harold 'Mr Brooks' and she was happy for Maria to do her washing for her. Along with that, though, she treated them all as good friends. It was a strange hierarchy, but as with her workers in the factory, Harriet made sure it worked. She also took care to ensure Honk Honk had fun. He enjoyed their stops and was allowed to rush around madly in the surrounding bushes, but he never strayed too far, and as soon as the engine started up, he tore back and leapt into his usual position on the back seat.

At one point they travelled for some days without speaking to any local people; the little party, with new provisions carefully packed away in the car, was surprisingly self-sufficient. Once a group of local people waved down the car and said the local maharajah would like to meet them. Harriet immediately had visions of a luxurious banquet and even a soft bed, but they were led into an increasingly remote area and suddenly realised it was a trap. Several naked men appeared. Harriet refused to be shocked; instead she remained calm and told the men with authority that they could not stay there as they were expected at a nearby town for a big reception. It was quick thinking on Harriet's part and delayed any action from the brigands, while Harold quickly turned the car and headed fast back onto the main road. Despite her outer calmness, afterwards, looking back at what could have happened, Harriet realised she was quite shaken.

Reaching the town of Gya, they encountered their first rain and were happy to catch some really fresh water, the first they had since they arrived in India; it even reduced the dust on the road.

After a night in a local dak bungalow, where everyone shares rooms with others and in this case a local missionary joined them to sleep on the floor, the party moved on. That afternoon they reached the Grand Trunk Road on the last lap of their journey to Calcutta. It was the route rather than the road surface that was grand; quite often the road narrowed right down with big washouts on either side. This meant passing any cattle- or horse-drawn cart was almost impossible. They had about 300 miles go to and were now driving through miles and miles of poppy fields, grown for opium. For the first time, Harriet saw men staggering under the influence of the drug, and many times they had to make sharp turns and stops to avoid running over a man who had wandered into their path. At various settlements along the way, they managed to obtain supplies, and it was a happy moment when they arrived at some local English barracks and were given some chicken and eggs.

It was a cheerful, albeit tired and dusty, little group that finally drove into the busy roads of Calcutta, in those days the capital of India. They had travelled 2,300 miles across the country. As they booked into the Grand Hotel, the manager couldn't believe they had driven so far. The car had been magnificent, but nevertheless it had been a long, bouncy trip in endless days of hot sun and dust. All four of them, as well as their luggage, were covered in fine dust and everyone delighted in the opportunity to relax in comfortable surroundings and clean up properly.

After driving a little around Calcutta and meeting some interesting people, Harriet's urge for new experiences returned and she decided they should make a trip to the hill station of Darjeeling. The town, high in the eastern Himalayas, was often visited by resident English and other nationalities as a respite against the Calcutta heat of the summer months; but even now, in early spring 1910, Harriet thought some clean, cooler mountain air would be refreshing for her party.

Harold checked the engine and car carefully, and once again loaded up, they set off. Harriet, sitting erect in the left-hand front seat, helped Harold find the right road by asking local people for directions. After three hours of driving, they at last reached the foot of the mountains. No car had ever gone up this route to Darjeeling before. People travelled up either by a little train or by cart, pulled up the uneven track that wound around the train rails up the mountain. Being the first didn't bother Harriet, who felt sure the car would make it, but first she had to get official permission. That sorted, off they went. What Harold thought of it, twisting the wheel back and forth as the sturdy car bumped its way up the mountain, is not recorded, but he persevered. Like Harriet, perhaps he too had total faith in their big, heavy car.

As they climbed higher, Harriet was thrilled. They were in the Himalayan mountains and the panorama that was opening up was superb, more than she had dreamed of. Local people came out as they passed, some clearly terrified at the purring monster climbing their hills. At one point, a crowd rushed up, stopping the car. It could have been a frightening situation. After all, they had never seen a motor vehicle before; the sight of this enormous, noisy machine must have been extraordinary. Harriet, though, calm and smiling, looked down from her lofty seat and beckoned the locals to touch the car. Soon it was smiles all round and the little party headed on. When they finally reached the Darjeeling hotel, they were over 6,000ft above sea level.

Here they were welcomed by a hot, crackling fire, but while the hotel was hospitable, Harriet wasn't feeling well and it wasn't the refreshing break she had been hoping for. It was probably the altitude, but she was finding it difficult to breathe and had no energy. However, there was some exciting news that got Harriet out of her bed and dressed. The great Dalai Lama, the revered spiritual leader of Tibet, was due to arrive in Darjeeling. There was a fear his life was in danger, so he was escaping across the high mountains into India. When he finally arrived, he was being carried on the shoulders of four faithful followers and was dressed in a red robe with jewelled chains around his neck. The Dalai Lama's party, however, was tired and covered in dust and Harriet thought it a pitiful sight.

Harriet was more interested in the local Darjeeling Indians, who reminded her of the Native Americans back home in the United States, with familiar broad faces and high cheekbones. Another similarity was how the mothers carried their babies strapped in hand-woven silk cloth tied on their backs. She was also fascinated by the rings the local women wore in their ears and noses; some were so big that when they wanted to eat, the rings had to be pulled to one side and tied up with their hair so they could reach their mouths. The women also happily practised polyandry and could take as many husbands as they desired. This made Harriet smile; she thought one husband was more than enough.

With all this going on, there was a lot to interest Harriet in these high hills, but the height did not agree with her and soon they were on the bumpy journey back downwards to Calcutta.

After more socialising in the town, it was time to move on, this time by boat to Ceylon (now Sri Lanka). With the car safely loaded on board, they finally left on 10 March. Arriving in Colombo, the car was quickly unloaded and they spent two weeks touring the island, again fascinated by the sights and people. After a long break, Harriet put on her business hat again and made enquiries about the successful exports of cardamom, cinnamon, coconut oil and especially rubber. Was there a business opportunity there? On good roads and with clean rest houses, travelling was easier than in India. Harriet occasionally took the wheel of the car to give Harold a break, but it was unfortunate she had done so in this country; she was arrested for driving without a proper licence for the car. After some initial disquiet, the situation was sorted out.

One day they were visiting a tea plantation when a baby monkey darted out of the bushes by the car. Harriet climbed out and followed the monkey. After much coaxing, the furry little baby leapt into Harriet's hand. That was it. After getting permission from the owner of the plantation, and to the quiet disgust of the rest of her party, Harriet insisted on adopting the baby monkey as a new pet. From then on, they were rarely parted, with the growing little monkey happily curling up on Harriet's lap and adapting well to the idea of spending its days in a motorcar.

The party, still with Honk Honk the little dog and now including a monkey, boarded another boat to Singapore and then, after a brief stop, sailed on up to Shanghai. Leaving the car, Honk Honk and the little monkey on the boat to be delivered to Japan, they stayed a few days in the busy Chinese town and Harriet didn't particularly like it, finding it dirty and with some abhorrent practices. She especially disliked the way the Chinese women would sell their young daughters, perhaps only 9 or 10 years old, for money. She loved the silks being traded, but was surprised when her attempt to bargain the price down simply resulted in the Chinese seller turning his back on her.

Back on board a ship, finally, on the morning of 26 April 1910, Harriet and her team arrived in Nagasaki. She had reached Japan, near the top of her list of must-see places in her planned trip around the world. Getting the train up to Tokyo, they collected a very excited Honk Honk, the sweet little monkey and also the car, which Harold checked carefully for damage. All was well. He had been ready to undertake various repairs on the trip, but so far the sturdy, reliable car had simply trundled on without problems. Soon everything was ready for a tour of Japan and Harriet was quite excited at the prospect of more new experiences. The country was fascinating and, as they travelled around, Harriet loved it, although she was not so happy about the roads. They had to cross many narrow, slippery bridges and the curiosity of the people was startling; sometimes they were met with such crowds that they had to stop and clear the way. Occasionally, they got lost and Harriet took the lead in talking to local people and sorting things out. She even tried to learn some of the language.

By mid-May they had seen many of the most famous sights in Japan, but one thing Harriet really wanted to do was to see Mount Fuji close up. After many months of challenging travelling, they now nearly met their end. Following directions, as they had understood them, they drove steadily up and up, planning to go through the Hakone Range Pass, where there should be beautiful views, before, as they believed, they would arrive at a hotel. Driving on and up, the road started to narrow and then suddenly they found themselves on a 90-degree turn on the side of the mountain. There was no room to turn around; there were high rocks on one side and a plunging precipice on the other. The road was deteriorating fast into a rough, narrow pathway, but they now had no option but to continue and eventually managed to manoeuvre the big car round the corner and on up the track. Finally, as night approached, they were driving slowly on when, quite suddenly, the track ended. Ahead was a narrow footbridge over a valley perhaps 300ft deep. There was no indication the road would stop and it was only at the last moment that they saw the sudden drop ahead.

There was nothing they could do. In the very restricted space, they unpacked and erected their tent. The only flat piece of road had a small stream of water running across it, which then flowed through part of the tent, but there was no alternative. They had been led to believe they would reach a settlement with a hotel along this road, but they hadn't reached it and now they were isolated for the night. Harriet again showed her leadership. While Albert lit a fire, Harriet took some flour, condensed cream and two teaspoonfuls of medicinal fruit salts they had with them. Mixing it up and cooking it, to their delight it rose like a muffin and Harriet declared it was the best biscuit she had ever tasted. Harriet insisted that after such a perilous drive Harold should take the driest, most comfortable bed in the tent, and Harriet spent the night in the car, with her little monkey to give her warmth.

Sunrise in the morning was magnificent, but even better was the sight of some local Japanese coming up the path. It took quite a while to organise proper help, but with ropes and planks and a lot of assistance from more Japanese who came up the hill to help them, a wider temporary bridge was built. While the others walked across carefully, Harold drove the car over with just 3in of space on each side of the tyres. Finally, after a tense few minutes, the car was across the ravine and the party could again travel on.

After many new sights and new experiences, finally the group made Yokohama, where they crated up the car and then, on 1 June, they boarded the Siberia steamship to continue their journey east. As local journalists crowded round to take pictures of the unusual group, one of them presented Harriet with a little Japanese Chin dog. He was a pretty little thing with big eyes and a silky black and white coat and Harriet felt she couldn't refuse; she named him Jappy. Now there was Honk Honk the dog, Billikins, as she had called her little monkey, and Jappy in the party. The others, especially Maria, didn't really approve of all this – it was all turning into a bit of a zoo – but they accepted it and there was no real dissension. Harriet was, after all, the boss.

They sailed via Hawaii to arrive back in San Francisco on 17 June and were met by a big celebration. Interest in Harriet's trip around the world had been growing steadily, but they were also met with a problem. At the end of the gangplank was a stern official who stopped Harriet and reported that she had no permission to land her animals. It took a lot of negotiation on Harriet's part, but finally the animals were safely brought ashore and installed in Harriet's bathroom at the Palace Hotel.

For a week, the group enjoyed the comforts of the town, meeting many officials and sorting themselves out. Harold stripped down the car and found that, despite all the rough roads and handling, despite the miles, the only problem was that some of the main bearings had become loose.

Back on American soil, Harriet was now eager to get home with her new pets, but there was still a very long trip ahead, nearly 3,000 miles right across the United States at a time well before the main connecting highways had been completed.

Packing up the car, and with both dogs as well as the monkey on board, the party set off on 26 June. It was just under a year since they had sailed from New York. As they reached Lake Tahoe, not only did the car's engine start boiling but Harriet, for the first time in the trip, became very ill. It was probably some sort of food poisoning and Harriet took a little while to recover. Then on they travelled.

Around 150 miles east of Lake Tahoe, the country became desolate and barren, the earth parched and brown. The road was rough and, as they gently bounced along, it made Harriet think of the careful grading done on many of the roads in India. They passed a stagecoach drawn by four miserable-looking horses and also drove past the carcasses of many horses, cows and sheep that had been overcome by thirst in this dry region. At one point, leaving Terrace in Utah for Ogden, they started on what Harriet thought was the worst drive of their whole trip. The road deteriorated into a series of bumpy, rough tracks; there were no directions except from an old guidebook that said to follow the Union Pacific railroad, but even this seemed impossible.

The next couple of weeks were a continuous struggle as they drove across challenging roads; even finding comfortable accommodation was near impossible. They made a detour onto the better roads in Salt Lake City, as Harriet wanted to see some Mormons, but here she was disappointed; to her surprise they were just like other people. The rumours she had heard were clearly unfounded.

On they went, leaving the town and once again travelling along soft dirt tracks. They passed four cars standing not far out of town, waiting for teams to come and haul them out of the dirt. The fun had gone from the trip; now all Harriet wanted was to get home. Heading into Nebraska, things improved a little, certainly for the little monkey who leapt off into the crops beside the road to eat all the grasshoppers he could find. Once he escaped up into an apple tree and had a few happy moments picking the fruit and dropping it down onto the ground below.

In Omaha they stopped at the Henshaw Hotel, where Harriet learned that early aviator Glenn Curtiss had been giving a flying exhibition the day before and was staying at the hotel. They met and had a good chat, including about the flying display Harriet had seen in Italy. What a lifetime ago that seemed!

On 16 August 1910, thirteen months after she had set off, Harriet and her team arrived back in New York City, where they were met by a cavalcade of cars to escort them into town. A big reception had been organised for Harriet, who was now realising that she had become a bit of a celebrity. Finally, she escaped and the group had a merry run back to their homes in Trenton. Harriet's house had been closed for the time she had been away, but soon things were organised: Albert and Maria were back in their rooms and doing their familiar work; Harold went back to his family and Harriet went down to the factory, meeting the manager she had installed there and finding out what had been going on.

Honk Honk was delighted with the home, rushing around the grounds, and Billikins the monkey and Jappy the Japanese dog also settled in happily.

Harriet was soon immersed back at the factory. Just two years after her trip around the world, at the age of 47, she married 29-year-old Silvano Andrew. He had been in the Argentine navy, but Harriet employed him as her new manager at the anvil company. Nevertheless, Harriet continued to be heavily involved in all the business dealings, while Maria and Albert continued to help her in the house, now as a contented married couple. With a husband and also animals in her family at home, Harriet lived happily and without many more dramatic adventures until in 1939, at the age of 78, she died. Over the years, they all must have laughed and reminisced about the times they had had during their extraordinary journey by car around the world.

8

1929 LADY GRACE DRUMMOND-HAY
THE FIRST WOMAN ROUND THE WORLD BY AIR

After early balloons, the idea of powered flight became the next big dream. When, in 1852, Frenchman Henri Giffard built an airship with a steam-powered engine, it was rather an optimistic concept, but nevertheless this heralded the start of a new era in aviation.

German aeronautical inventor Count Ferdinand von Zeppelin became the recognised leader in airships after he launched the first rigid-body airship in 1900. After that, development continued apace with many other countries also becoming involved in developing airships for both passenger-carrying and military uses. There were, of course, numerous setbacks and accidents, some quite dramatic – in 1921, in front of a shocked audience, the British R38 suffered sudden structural failure and caught fire, crashing into the Humber estuary and killing forty-four people, while in 1923 the French navy's *Dixmude* exploded in mid-air near Sicily, killing all fifty people on board.

There were, however, also big successes, and at the time when Lady Grace Drummond-Hay flew around the world, in 1929, there was still hope that the airship would be the future of aviation. When, despite problems, Lady Drummond-Hay completed a circumnavigation in an airship, it heralded a successful era for them, with the German Zeppelins proving their worth by flying regular passenger routes as far as Brazil. Generally, though, flying under a huge envelope of gas was a precarious method of flight, and when the German *Hindenburg* caught fire when landing in New Jersey, in the United States, in 1937, killing thirty-five people, the drama was caught on film to be shown around the world. This marked the end of this stage of airship development.

Grace Drummond-Hay doubted she had ever really, properly, been in love; somehow her life had been too busy for real romance, or perhaps she simply hadn't met the right man. But standing there next to Karl, in the small, intimate control car of the airship as they were being tossed about high over the raging Pacific, she wondered if the deep fondness and comfort she felt when she was with Karl was really what love was all about. Knowing he was there right beside her as they were struggling to keep aloft in one of the most violent storms of the year – not knowing if the howling winds would grab their unwieldy vehicle and throw it carelessly down into the heaving sea below, or simply tear apart the flimsy fabric that was creasing and straining just above them, the very threads of their survival – made a real difference. Staring through the rain-swept angled window into the wild, ever-moving nothingness, their fingers touched. Ahead, if they made it, was the United States. Karl's wife was waiting for him; but now, right now, they were together.

As she stared out of the rain-battered window, Grace made an effort and regained her composure; after all, she was noted for her calm appraisals, her coolness. Her only real passion in life was to be a success, at the peak of her field. This she had probably inherited from her parents; her father especially had dedicated much of his life to improving the prospects of his family, the Lethbridges. When little Grace was born, in London in September 1895, her father was already beginning to fulfil his ambitions to be a gentleman; he was doing very well working as a commercial traveller and was making enough money to live in a nice, solid family home in a good area. They could even afford to employ a servant. This was a definite sign of reaching the middle classes in the well-defined strata of Britain's Victorian society.

When little Grace turned 5 years old, there was some excitement in her life. Her little sister Mamie came along, plus her father had now taken a job with Spratt's, a dog-biscuit company, and things were going well; pet food was a brand-new industry and the prospects looked very good indeed. Even better, aunt Alice came to stay with them.

In late Victorian times, Alice Lethbridge had become very famous as a dancer with twinkling feet, and she was also recognised for her performance of what was called a skirt dance, swirling her skirt to reveal tantalising glimpses of her knees and, occasionally, in really risqué moments, her thighs. It was dramatic and fun, and not so revealing as to raise serious objections. Alice had even toured Australia and the United States; so when, between marriages, she arrived at her brother's house for a short stay, she was full of stories and glamour that must have fired little's Grace's imagination.

As Grace began to grow up, her father's job was indeed turning into a successful career. Providing food for pet dogs was a novel and brilliant concept, and Spratt's had quickly grown into the world's first large-scale manufacturer of dog biscuits. Sales were taking off, he was earning a lot more money and now the family could move to a much more substantial house in a better area, and could afford a few luxuries and even holidays.

At school, Grace learned all the basics easily and then, when she was 10, further excitement came along. With more money available, her parents were becoming keen on travel, and together with their two daughters, they took off to spend some time in South Africa. The region was still settling down after the Boer, or South African, War and the four separate regions – the Cape of Good Hope, the Orange Free State, Natal and Transvaal – had yet to merge to form the Union of South Africa. There was a lot to see and learn, and the trip had a profound influence on young Grace; from then on, she wanted to travel everywhere.

Back at school in London, Grace became a voracious reader, loving exciting adventure books as well as English and ancient classics. Her desire to travel remained and she also started working hard on her French language lessons.

Living in a leafy suburb, with a happy family and lots of activities and social opportunities, life was fun. In her mid-teens, when she left school, Grace wasn't looking for an early marriage to settle down; she still wanted to travel and be part of the wider world. Even at a young age, she knew she could write quite well and began to wonder if a career in journalism could work for her. A few good typewriting and shorthand schools had started up in London and, having left school, Grace signed on; it would be a good next step.

Then, in 1914, when Grace was turning 19, the First World War began. There had been rumours, of course, probably talk over the family dinner table in the evenings, and Grace, with her genuine interest in the world, read the papers avidly. No one, though, was expecting the level of carnage that was about to follow. The war accelerated social change and broke many families. However, the Lethbridges continued to be lucky. While they wanted to do their bit for the war effort, Grace's father was very busy virtually running the Spratt's business now and the company needed him. Grace was keen to take a war job and took a secretarial position.

When the war was finally war over, everyone could breathe again and Grace's childhood desire to travel once more came to the fore. She heard about a job at the Supreme Economic Council in Paris, applied and was successful. In 1919, when she was 23, she moved to the French capital. This was an unusually independent action for a young girl of that era. Although Paris was recovering from the devastation of war, it was still the heart of European culture and fashion. Young Grace, who had grown into a smart, well-dressed woman and was now earning a good salary, could have been set for a wonderful time.

In fact, Grace's life took a very different course. How she first met Sir Robert Drummond-Hay is not clear. Perhaps they met at a theatre or some social event; either way, they met and started chatting. Grace was charmed. There was a huge shortage of eligible young men after the war. To attract the attention of such a distinguished, refined and good-looking man thrilled Grace, and Robert, even if by now he had reached his early seventies, could still be considered a catch. His seniority, his knowledge of the world and his previous work as consul in exciting places such as Stockholm, Tunis and Beirut, his position as a member of the British aristocracy; all these aspects were an attraction to Grace, who had inherited her father's ambition to get on in life.

In return, Robert was flattered to receive such attentive interest from such a young, attractive woman. After a full life and a long marriage, his wife had died in 1918. His four children were all grown up and following their own lives. A new bubbly, young partner would help him live again. He may also have been attracted by Grace's intelligence and her interest in world affairs; here was someone not only who listened to him but with whom he could discuss current events. He proposed and Grace accepted.

They were married in a church in Hampstead, north London, in June 1920. Grace was 25 and Robert was 73.

Grace, now as Lady Drummond-Hay, quickly assumed the customs and styles of her new position in society. Elegant dining, being welcomed at top hotels and being shown the best rooms; it was very easy to get used to this new life and it boosted her confidence enormously. Now travel became not just easy but the norm, and included visiting property Robert owned in Morocco and Egypt, spending time in Nice and Monte Carlo, and wintering in Cairo. Often, on the way back from Egypt in the spring, the couple would stop in Rome or Florence for Easter and then call into Paris so Grace could pick up some new clothes before the couple returned to London for the coming social season. There must have been some moments when Grace just sat back and thought about things. Marrying such an older man could never be perfect. It had, however, brought her a lot of good things. Was that enough?

In Egypt for the winter of 1922–23, on one fateful evening they went to a ball in Cairo. In those days, many wealthy and interesting people spent their winter months in the city and there was a round of social activity. On this eventful day, German American Karl von Wiegand attended the same ball.

Karl had been born in Hesse, Germany, in 1874, but his family had emigrated to the United States four years later. He was celebrating his 21st birthday in California when little Grace was born in London. As the new century arrived, Karl, now with a wife and young daughter, joined the *San Francisco Examiner* and found his niche, soon becoming a well-respected reporter.

In 1917 he became an official foreign correspondent for the successful and still-growing Hearst organisation, about to become the biggest media conglomerate in the world. Karl was soon acknowledged as its leading journalist. In 1922 he interviewed Hitler and was the first to alert the United States that this German activist should be taken seriously.

When Grace met Karl at the party in Cairo, she was immediately impressed and her ideas of writing and journalism came flooding back. Grace was beginning to feel unsettled in her role simply as a society lady. There were no children to give her added fulfilment. Grace came up with a deal: if Karl would teach her journalism, then she would feed him any story ideas she found from the elevated circles she was mixing in.

Under Karl's guidance, in October 1923, Grace completed one of her first attempts at professional writing, a story on the harem women of Egypt. It was a serious, considered piece and attracted attention, especially as it was written by a member of the British aristocracy. She then wrote several more stories and London's *Sphere*, an influential weekly newspaper, was happy to take them.

Thanks to her position in society, Grace had little problem in arranging meetings with top people for new stories. It was rather exhilarating to be ushered into the presence of famous politicians and leaders – generally middle-aged men who were more than happy to chat to this clearly intelligent, but also personable and friendly woman. Getting ideas, sourcing information and writing articles; as the months went by, Grace became very busy indeed. In her London home, she would obtain information and interviews by telephone; overseas telephone calls became normal. Karl was continually offering advice and comments, usually by phone and by letter; Grace commented later that talking to Karl always gave her a fresh outlook on things. Typing away and sending off article after article, Grace was very busy. Her elderly husband was now taking very much second place in her life.

Prolific writing, covering serious situations rather than just fluffy, feminine stories, was steadily making Grace a well-known name: Lady Drummond-Hay, the reporter; Lady Drummond-Hay, the newspaper correspondent. Her title was still very useful, but Grace also loved the fact that she was now being recognised for her work, not just her status. This keenness for success was more than just wanting to boost her ego; she found she seriously enjoyed the cut and thrust of obtaining good stories for the British media. It offered a stark contrast from the quieter, more refined atmosphere of the home and life she shared with Robert. It was another exciting step when she was taken on as a full-time correspondent for the *Daily Express*. Now she would be paid to travel to cover various stories; her childhood dreams were coming true.

It was probably thanks to Karl that, in the summer of 1925, she was in Berlin, interviewing Gustav Ernst Stresemann, the German Minister for Foreign Affairs, and she sent back an in-depth report on Germany's attitudes to the proposed Security Pact and other issues. Then she went on to Vienna, where she covered anti-Jewish riots in the capital, commenting on how these were assuming a new and grave aspect. A few weeks later, Grace was interviewing King Alfonso of Spain and describing the war in Morocco as a new crusade: how it was developing into a great battle between east and west, between Islam and Christianity. In November 1925, Grace was reporting as the *Daily*

Express's special correspondent in Palestine, commenting that Syrian rebels were stirring up trouble.

Grace was joining Karl in the realms of recognised, leading journalists; in fact, being a woman reporting on such serious matters drew her even more attention. On several of her trips, Karl was also there, and at some point their relationship became deeper. Karl was married with grown-up children. He had married young and his wife, from Ohio, had given up a lot to accompany him on his various moves. Dedicated to his work, he really wasn't looking for an affair, but Grace was young, enthusiastic and very pretty. As for Grace, she was fond of her older husband, but she admired Karl and found him attractive. Being thrown together in strange places, they almost inevitably became lovers.

After six years of marriage, on 15 October 1926, Robert died. He had just turned 80. Grace was 31. The last ten years had been a big learning curve for Grace, but now she knew what she wanted; she enjoyed her glamorous lifestyle and she also enjoyed being recognised, even respected, for her work in a job that she loved. Grace was on her way to a new future. She didn't see Karl as much as she would have liked, but her career was totally absorbing and her life was very busy indeed. However, by the late 1920s more women journalists started to come on the scene and ambitious Grace was constantly on the lookout for new ideas to keep her star alive.

It was more than likely that Karl told her about the exciting new Zeppelin airship being built in Germany. As the recognised foreign correspondent for the Hearst Corporation and with his German background, Karl had already signed up to be involved in the airship's early voyages and Grace quickly realised this could have real potential for her as well.

The design for the new LZ127 *Graf Zeppelin* was ambitious. It would be 776ft long, the largest airship ever constructed, and it included some exciting new technical advances. Its girders were made of a special light aluminium alloy called duralumin, reducing the weight of the airship. It was lifted by seventeen giant gas cells filled with a total of over 3.5 million cubic feet of lighter-than-air hydrogen; each cell was lined with material from the intestines of cattle to help prevent leakage. A big advance was its five 2,650hp Maybach propeller engines, which were reversible and could also burn Blau gas. In older airships, when their fuel was burned off, the airship steadily lost weight, creating unwanted ascent. Then the ship would have to vent hydrogen to reduce lift and stop it floating up too high; it was a difficult balancing act. For some of its fuel, the LZ127 *Graf Zeppelin* intended to use the newly invented Blau gas, which weighed around the same as air. This helped a lot in reducing the problems of unwanted changes in height.

The idea was for the new airship to demonstrate that passengers could be carried quickly, safely and in comfort across the Atlantic, offering real competition to the established transatlantic liners of the day. Carrying mail would be another advantage offered by the airship.

As the *Graf Zeppelin* reached completion, in the summer of 1928, plans were made to commence a series of test flights and then to launch its new services with an initial flight over the Atlantic to New York. In Britain, squabbling over the development of airships, which finally settled on the construction of two rival vehicles – the R100 and the R101 – meant that these projects would not get off the ground until the following year, late in 1929.

As Grace discovered more about the German airship project, she found it increasingly appealing. If she flew and reported on the flights, it would be something very different and would lift her above all the other women journalists, and not just literally. She had loved the excitement of travel; how thrilling it would be to experience a ride in this enormous gracious flying vehicle! Women were already flying quite long distances in little open-cockpit biplanes, but there was no competition from women journalists covering airship travel. The whole idea offered Grace enormous scope. Once more, Karl stepped in.

When Karl suggested to his employers that a woman's view of the airship could be very useful to boost female readership, the Hearst

Corporation was willing to sign Grace up as a reporter. For Grace, joining the biggest media group in the world was a triumph, a definite step up in her already successful career. Her happiness was dented, though, when Karl told her their relationship would have to end. It was all very well when their friendship was confined to Europe, but now, working for the same organisation, and no doubt with Grace making visits to the United States, it was all getting a little too close to home.

This was the first real emotional problem Grace had encountered in her life, and her stance was to try to pretend nothing had happened. She threw herself into her work and writing, and in early autumn headed down to Friedrichshafen on Lake Constance in southern Germany to get all the details about the *Graf Zeppelin*. Karl would be there, but while she ensured she looked her best in her smart but feminine style, she was also determined to be cool and professional.

When she first saw the enormous LZ127 silver airship, silently sitting there above her, its fabric shimmering in the quiet air inside the giant hangar, it must have taken her breath away. The sheer size of it was overwhelming. Looking up at its shiny silver surface, glistening so far above her, the thought that this beautiful cigar-shaped bubble could carry the little passenger car high up in the sky caught her imagination. Despite the attention to detail, despite the strength of the construction, the airship looked vulnerable and flimsy, sitting there in the hangar; it also looked very unwieldy. How on earth would it be controlled in the air?

Grace quickly became enthusiastic. Test flights and then a proving flight across the Atlantic in September 1928 were planned, and as reporters for the Hearst Corporation, both Karl and Grace were accepted on the passenger lists for the flights.

As Grace clambered up the steps into the gondola for the first time, she couldn't help but be impressed. It was all so well planned, with so much attention to detail. Certainly, in the front, the control and chart room, the radio room and the small kitchen area were quite compact; but behind this was a luxurious dining car, and it even had embossed wallpaper and comfortable chairs as well as large, sloping viewing windows. The corridor behind ran back to ten sleeping cabins and they too had been designed with comfort in mind, with beds that would convert into daytime silk-covered lounges. There were also two toilet compartments and two small washrooms right at the back of the gondola. There was no bath or shower on board; because of its weight, the amount of water that could be taken on board was limited. Wastewater was carefully stored to be used as ballast when needed.

On the early test flights, Grace found the take-off and indeed flying quiet and undramatic. The big airship was simply towed gently out of the gigantic hangar, its long handling lines were released by the ground crew, and it rose quietly and sedately up into the sky. Looking down on the little houses, the boats on the sparkling water, as they slowly trundled through the air, it seemed a lovely way to travel.

Grace had no qualms when she stepped aboard for the start of the first Atlantic voyage and, as they took off, there was no rush, no drama. Chatting in the dining car by day and relaxing at night in comfortable sleeping quarters, it was all very easy and relaxed, and Grace was really enjoying her involvement with the airship. Karl was there, but Grace retained her composure, and there were other men on board who occasionally paid her attention when she wasn't tapping away at her typewriter, preparing her reports for the Hearst Corporation.

On the third day of the flight, however, there was some drama. A large section of the fabric covering the port tail fin was damaged during a storm, just east of Bermuda. Now the giant airship was beginning to be thrown about violently, and the mood on board changed from laughter to apprehension. What was going on? The commander, Hugo Eckener, throttled back the engines, but in losing control of direction this caused even more problems. He directed the radio operator to make a distress call.

It might well have been this moment when Karl started to reform his views about Grace. Standing near to her as the unstable airship was tossed vigorously around in the sky, he warned her that the end could come at any moment. Grace took the news calmly. At least they had experienced the wonder of flying in an airship; if this was the end, so be it. Karl was enormously impressed at her control and quiet response. At the same time, newspapers in the United States were speculating that the airship was lost and the US Navy was preparing a rescue mission; an American radio station broadcast a prayer followed by a minute's silence.

On board, the crew weren't giving up that easily. Hugo Eckener's son and other riggers, roped on for safety, climbed outside the airship and steadily repaired the torn fabric. Every so often they had to clamber back in while the commander revved up the engines to get more power and regain control of the unwieldy airship, now being moved quite vigorously in the north Atlantic gale. Slowly and steadily, though, the riggers managed to effect a repair. After many worrying hours, at last the work was completed. Hugo regained height and speed, and once again the giant airship set off on its way to the west.

When news reached the United States that the airship was safe, the response was enormous. Hearst couldn't have hoped for a better news story! The airship finally reached the USA at 10 a.m. on 15 October, four days after leaving Germany. Heading up the coast to Lakehurst, south of New York, it descended gently, and, with the facility to adjust its buoyancy by releasing hydrogen or dropping ballast, it finally made a smooth and gentle landing at 5.30 p.m. that day.

Despite the hiccup, the flight was hailed as a huge success; Hugo Eckener and the crew were welcomed with a ticker-tape parade in New York and an invitation to the White House to meet Calvin Coolidge, the US President.

Grace wrote to her mother that she had loved every minute of the trip. She had written copious copy and her descriptions of the flight had been very well received by American audiences. William Randolph Hearst was delighted. In his newspapers, she was now described as a remarkable British noblewoman and famous journalist, world-renowned for her beauty, wit and piquant views. Britain's famous 'Lady reporter' was now making a real name for herself in the United States, too.

While Grace returned to Britain by ship, Hugo Eckener and his crew flew the airship back across the Atlantic. Overall, these flights had gone very well, but when Hugo reached the home base of Friedrichshafen, he had new worries to face. Earlier that summer two new luxury ocean liners, the *Bremen* and the *Europa*, had begun service on the Atlantic route. Both ships were luxurious and fast, offering real competition to the airship. Even worse, aeroplanes were developing at breakneck speed; Britain's Imperial Airways was already organising a regular weekly air service to Karachi.

Hugo realised he really had to move fast to ensure the commercial success of the *Graf Zeppelin*. He organised some flights in the spring of 1929 to attract attention and one included the idea of an Aerial Grand Tour, with a flight down to Greece and Jerusalem. Grace went on this flight and again wrote some enthusiastic copy for the Hearst Corporation's newspapers.

It was really thanks to William Randolph Hearst that Hugo Eckener's next publicity idea took off. Hugo had long thought an aerial trip right around the world would surely establish the airship as the real future of air transport; but money was very tight. William Hearst now came up with an idea: if the airship would take off and return to the United States for a round-the-world trip, and if the Hearst Corporation's newspapers could be given sole media rights to cover the story in the USA and Europe, he would provide nearly half the cost. The deal was done.

When Grace was first told about the planned trip around the world, she was excited but also had reservations. Three weeks or more in the very confined space of an airship would be challenging. Then there had been that problem in mid-Atlantic. There had already been some dramatic airship crashes; Grace was more than aware that a flight like this could really be very dangerous. The airship would be spending long hours high in the sky, flying over vast oceans and some uncharted territories; it was definitely not going to be a flight for the faint-hearted. There was little option really, though, for Grace. She had signed on with the powerful Hearst Corporation and they wanted her on board. She tried to put her fears aside and look at the positive aspects. Perhaps, as the only woman on board the first ever flight around the world, her future as a leading global journalist would be assured.

Planning what to take with her, Grace soon began to look forward to the trip. Karl would also be on the airship for the three-week voyage. Although the relationship was meant to be over, Grace couldn't help being excited by the thought.

By the summer of 1929, Grace was in New York getting herself prepared. The planned route would be over 20,000 miles, flying from Lakehurst in New Jersey right across to Germany, then over the Soviet Union to Japan, then over the vast Pacific Ocean to San Francisco, and finally back to Lakehurst. Flying time, assuming cruising at an average of around 70mph and not taking into account any severe headwinds, should be just under two weeks; but extra time was needed to stop for checks and any repairs, to take on more fuel and supplies, and also, in order to fulfil William Randolph Hearst's expectations, to add news value to the trip.

The idea of a round-the-world voyage by air quickly made international news. The start of the flight was scheduled for 8 August 1929, and by early evening, large crowds were beginning to gather as Grace was driven up to the airship. Once on board, Grace unpacked her clothes carefully in her little cabin and then headed back into the dining car to meet the other twenty passengers. There were some interesting people to be introduced to, including the famous Arctic explorer Sir Hubert Wilkins and, of course, Karl. This wasn't a time for warm greetings, though; he was busy talking to the crew and taking notes, absorbed in the preparations going on for this momentous flight.

Grace knew the facilities on the airship would be good. Despite limited supplies of water for drinking and washing, catering was of a high level, with excellent food, wines and even champagne on board. Air pressure was not a problem for the passengers; the airship generally cruised at around 1,500 or 2,000ft. It could climb higher when necessary, but generally low-level flight at around 70mph would be the norm.

The members of the forty-man crew, under the command of Hugo Eckener, were all impressive; the navigators, helmsmen, engineers, mechanics, radio operators and stewards had all been selected with care for their expert knowledge and expertise; they all looked the part too, in their smart uniforms.

For the whole world, it was very exciting. There had been an aerial circumnavigation before, in 1924 when four aviators belonging to the United States Army Air Service finally managed to complete the trip in a fixed-wing aircraft after 175 days and with numerous stops. Since then, however, despite the steady development in aircraft design, a round-the-world trip had proved problematic. Now, here was a massive new airship about to attempt the flight with very few stops and in a very fast time. It could even carry passengers. No wonder many thought this was the start of a huge new era in science, aviation and travel.

In the late evening, as the time came for departure, an enormous crowd gathered. After final checks and to a resounding cheer from the crowd, the men below released the main tether lines and the giant airship slowly lifted up and away from its mooring mast. In the dark stillness of the night, the giant airship was described as a huge phosphorescent fish, hovering in the moonless darkness, its shimmering lower sides brilliantly lit by searchlights. It was a dramatic spectacle for the crowds on the ground, and also for the passengers on board as they crowded at the open windows, looking down and waving goodbye to the mass of upturned faces. Then, rising steadily into the sky, with its engines turned on and increasing power, the LZ127 *Graf Zeppelin* turned and slowly headed north-east to start its momentous voyage around the world.

Looking out of the windows, Grace was quietly excited. She watched the buildings of New York slowly appear below her as the glistening silver airship cruised smoothly and sedately through the sky, past the Statue of Liberty and then, finally, out over the coast and into the North Atlantic.

Against a backdrop of gentle humming from the engines, the airship now headed steadily east and the passengers began to settle down for the long trip. There was some movement and a few bumps, but nothing that gave the giant airship and its crew any cause for concern. Chatting in the dining car, looking out of the window as the airship headed on above the endless sea, sipping coffee and enjoying good meals, it was all very enjoyable, although perhaps just a tad monotonous. However, using the washroom, arranging her cabin, changing into night clothes and then choosing what to wear in the morning, for Grace the time passed surprisingly quickly.

Grace liked to wander into the control room and watch was going on, and she was also fascinated by the technology in the little radio room. But that was Karl's sphere; she was very aware that her job now was to write for the Hearst Corporation's female readers, and she thought the cooking arrangements might be of interest. The small kitchen was very well equipped, with electric burners and ovens, an electric water heater and even a refrigeration unit, vital to keep food fresh on the voyage. Grace noted that no open flames were allowed; after all, they were in a hydrogen-filled airship. Grace added a description about the elegant white, blue and gold china embellished with the LZ mark of the airship; every detail of the trip had been carefully thought through and organised. She realised it was no wonder Hugo Eckener had jumped at William Randolph Hearst's offer of financial assistance; the whole project must have cost an incredible sum.

Both Karl and Grace spent time typing out reports. Grace took on a more emotional stance than was usual for her, writing sometimes rather gushingly about her sincere love of the airship and how it was carrying her and her companions in safety and comfort through trackless paths high above the sea; how it was all appealingly beautiful. This new style of writing took a little effort, but Grace was prepared to work hard to satisfy her new employers, the Hearst Corporation.

After a steady flight lasting fifty-six hours, the airship was back above familiar territory, crossing Lake Constance to the giant hangar at Friedrichshafen. The trip had been uneventful and had gone totally to plan. Grace spent five days in a hotel in the town as the airship took on fuel and restocked. After some final checks, it was announced the *Graf Zeppelin* was ready to start the next leg of its round-the-world voyage.

This was to be the longest leg of the journey, a 7,500-mile journey from Friedrichshafen all the way across Asia to Tokyo, a journey that included crossing hundreds of miles above the vast emptiness of Siberia.

As the airship headed north, cruising steadily at just a couple of thousand feet, Grace made constant notes about what she saw and about life on board; the airship's radio office was kept busy, dispatching the copy provided by Grace and the other journalists on the trip. As they approached Berlin, they were low enough to see the mass crowds congregating, and Grace quickly tapped out a report. As the airship slowly motored east over Berlin's airport, Grace's story, along with film and copy from the other journalists, was on this occasion dropped down by a little parachute. The following day, in all the Hearst newspapers, Grace's story about cheering multitudes filling Berlin streets made front-page headlines.

Initially it had been planned to fly over Moscow, but this had to be cancelled due to adverse winds, leading to a vigorous complaint from Joseph Stalin's government. Despite the technology on board, despite the modern design and equipment, the airship was still very vulnerable to weather conditions.

As the airship purred on steadily east, the temperatures dropped, especially at night. There was no heating in the cabins and Grace found she had to resort to sleeping in the fur coat she had sensibly brought with her; at last, here was a story for her female readers. She wrote about how she was travelling with 1 million cubic feet of gas but no heat and about how merciless cold was driving through the cotton walls of the flying tent. She said that before they left, the passengers had envisaged charming evenings with men in formal jackets, enjoying elegant dining and fine wines. Instead, Grace wrote, leather coats, woollies and furs were the evening attire, and hot soup and steaming stew were more welcome than cold caviar and chicken salad.

Nevertheless, despite the cold, things were still going reasonably smoothly. Looking out of the windows, Grace saw the land change from densely wooded hills into endless, monotonous marshlands, and it all began looking very remote indeed. Hour after hour, the big silver airship was cruising above forests, small lakes and rivers with no sign of human inhabitation anywhere. For no particular reason, Grace now began to consider what would happen if the airship had an accident. She started to fret that some of the passengers were secretly smoking; under a big store of hydrogen, that was inviting a problem. Before she had taken off, she had of course heard about earlier disasters, especially in 1925 when the United States' *Shenandoah* airship was caught in a storm and broke apart, killing fourteen people and how, just the previous year in May 1928, the Italian airship, the *Italia*, had crashed in remote polar conditions.

Any form of flight was still quite new and airships had massive potential for disaster. Chatting to Karl in the dining car, she found it almost impossible not to touch him, to move close beside him, but she retained her composure and drew comfort from his quiet, matter-of-fact views on everything.

On the great airship trundled, heading steadily eastwards and finally reaching the Soviet Union's Stanovoy mountains, a region that had not been fully charted. Large areas of larch forests gave way to high, bare summits, with the highest peaks reaching nearly 8,000ft, way over the airship's operational height. Winds for the airship were not favourable, swirling around the mountains. For the crew, keeping the giant airship under control and on course became very challenging indeed.

Slowly, steadily, the airship nosed its unstable way upwards, through 4,000ft, to 5,000ft, to 5,500ft, yet still the top of the pass was above them. With higher mountains to the side, it edged its way forward as it fought the buffeting winds. Inside the passenger car, it was cold. Below, if something went wrong, there was no hope of rescue. They were miles and miles from anywhere. Now, through the sloping windows, there were terrifying peaks closing in on both sides as the airship slowly clawed its way forward, rocking slowly in the gusting winds. Grace watched Karl as he sat there, talking quietly to other passengers. How could he be so distantly polite when they had been so close? Karl must certainly have been impressed by this fearless, talented young woman who was showing no outward sign of fear in what was turning out to be a very treacherous situation.

Hour after hour the passengers stared either blankly at each other or at the dramatic views out of the windows as the airship slowly edged its way forward and upwards. Finally, it reached the summit and, at its flying limit and swaying sometimes quite dramatically from side to side, the airship steadily struggled across the top of the pass. There was just 150ft to spare below them and the jagged mountains still rose up on either side. In the passenger car, the tension was tangible. Then, suddenly, they were through. As the height of the mountains reduced, the airship also descended. Soon, once again, they were in quieter, warmer, more stable air. The immediate danger had subsided. Grace wrote later that she loved the giant airship with a deep and poignant emotion; in difficult conditions, it had steadfastly carried them all to safety.

It had been a very frightening time, but the airship and everyone in it had survived. The mood in the dining car quickly changed, and so did the relationship between Grace and Karl. In the wild relief that followed, all restrictions disappeared; once more they became close.

It had been a long flight, but after four days and nights, suddenly the coast of Japan was in sight. Reaching Kasumigaura airfield, northeast of Tokyo, there was a tumultuous welcome waiting for them. A crowd of a quarter of a million had rushed out, wanting to see the quiet approach of the glittering silver *Graf Zeppelin* and then watch it come down from the skies. The news coverage was immense; that was the longest sector of the flight and the *Graf Zeppelin* had completed it successfully. Now the giant airship really was on its way right around the world. Emperor Hirohito entertained Hugo Eckener and some of his team and passengers to tea, and Grace was back on form, vigorously typing out reports not only on the trip but on the welcome they had received, what the Japanese women were wearing, what was going on in the capital. Interest in the voyage was building up everywhere, and Grace was providing her employers at the Hearst Corporation with the sort of stories they had hoped for.

After four days in Tokyo, on 23 August 1929, it was time once more to leave. Next stop was the Pacific. While the passengers were talking confidently about an exciting return to the United States, commander Hugo Eckener was quieter. He knew more than anyone that crossing the Pacific was fraught with danger. Inside the comfortable, isolated passenger car, you could almost pretend you were on a ship or a train, but the Pacific was well known for its turbulent weather and sudden storms. Hugo fully recognised there could be enormous problems and real danger ahead. If they made it, it would be the first ever non-stop flight across the Pacific Ocean.

New passengers had come on board, including Lt Cdr Ryunosuke Kusaka, who was later involved in planning the Japanese attack on Pearl Harbor, and the airship, restocked and ready to go, slowly and gently lifted off on 23 August, two weeks after it had started its voyage from Lakehurst in the United States.

Despite her instructions to write about the trip from a woman's angle, Grace was increasingly interested in the operational side of the airship. The radio room fascinated her. It was fitted with the most modern equipment available, and three officers served there, working on radio navigation and weather reports as well as communicating with ground stations and ships, and sending telegrams and reports out from the passengers. With both Karl and Grace sending regular reports, as well as other journalists on board, the radio team had been kept very busy indeed.

As the airship headed east into the vast airspace above the Pacific, Grace wanted to learn more about the structural side. When, in a leather flying coat, Grace clambered up the ladder and out along the small walkway inside the ship's hull, Karl watched in admiration; later, he even wrote about it. Here was one truly exceptional woman.

With the *Graf Zeppelin* making its way out into the Pacific, after two days Hugo Eckener's fears were justified. A huge storm was reported in the area of the Aleutian Islands. Hugo abandoned his planned Great Circle route, the same route that was followed by the passenger liners of the day. Instead, although it would add time to the journey, he turned the big airship south to avoid the worst of the heavy winds. Nevertheless, the turbulent weather was soon throwing the airship around like a balloon and the helmsmen were hard pressed to keep it on course.

Suddenly, the airship was caught in a rushing air current that lifted it up 300ft in just a few seconds; then, just as quickly, the bow dipped steeply and the airship plunged fast downwards. It was becoming a roller-coaster of a ride, with equipment and personal items being thrown all over the place. Once again the passengers went quiet as they hung on, not knowing if the whole airship would at any moment be torn apart, dropping them all into the churning water below.

Grace quietly took it all in her stride; at one point, she and Karl struggled forward to look out from the large windows in the control room as the giant airship slowly pushed its way forward through the storm. With rain battering down and the view changing constantly as the airship swung and swayed, there wasn't really a lot to see.

It was the most violent storm the airship had encountered, a terrifying time for the passengers and frightening for the crew as well, but within a couple of hours the worst was over. Soon the airship was back on a steady course, heading east. Returning to her typewriter in the dining car, Grace began pounding out stories. She knew the Hearst Corporation was syndicating her stories around the world, so she wrote copy that she hoped would appeal to a wide audience. Survival of a violent storm should surely be of interest to readers everywhere.

Then, finally and amid great excitement on board, the great silver airship reached the American coast.

Their first sight of land was north California, and Hugo Eckener had timed the arrival so they could fly above San Francisco at sunset. With a Stars and Stripes flag flying in one window, he allowed Grace to steer the great airship as it headed in above the narrow bay entrance and over the town. It was a memorable occasion for everyone. Grace found the airship slow to respond and very heavy to manoeuvre; it brought home to her what a wonderful job Hugo had done in taking them all right around the world.

Now the *Graf Zeppelin* headed slowly south, and in the growing early morning daylight of 26 August, after 6,000 miles and seventy-nine hours of flight, it reached Los Angeles. Here there was a problem. A temperature inversion made it difficult to bring the airship down and large quantities of hydrogen had to be released to reduce lift. There were no facilities to replace this amount of hydrogen in Los Angeles, but Eckener had no option. Finally, the 315 men waiting patiently on the ground could reach the ropes and tow the airship to its mooring mast. Another sector of the round-the-world trip was over. Again there was a tumultuous welcome, and as the passengers disembarked, the applause and cheering were deafening. They were all greeted as heroes and whisked off by waiting cars to a big reception.

Grace was happy. Her relationship with Karl, a relationship that she now knew to be so important to her life, was fully restored. The Hearst Corporation was delighted with her continual flow of excellent copy. Life was good. As the only woman on board, she received a great deal of attention in Los Angeles. Now it was time for the final leg back to Lakehurst to complete the round-the-world voyage.

What should have been a simple, enjoyable flight started off badly. The lost hydrogen had reduced lift; the airship was much heavier than usual, and when Hugo tried to lift off, he found he was heading straight towards some power lines at the edge of the field. After some dramatic moments, they managed to just clear the lines, and then there was a very bouncy passage above the deserts of Arizona and Texas – the summer weather was creating strong thermals and unwanted lift.

Finally, on 29 August 1929, the great airship reached Lakehurst, New Jersey. Soon after 7.30 a.m., a great cry went up from the excited, waiting crowd as they spotted the giant silver airship slowly approaching through the early morning haze. By just after 8 a.m., it was down.

The welcome was extraordinary; Grace told a reporter she was the happiest girl in the world. The *Graf Zeppelin* had achieved many records in its three-week flight around the world and Grace, after so much excitement and adventure, was thrilled but exhausted. The flight had been a triumph and Grace now had the record of being the first ever woman to travel around the world by air. However, rather than this record, it was the fact that her continuous reports had made her a household name across the United States and, to a certain extent, in Britain that really made Grace happy. Close again to Karl, and with an assured future as a leading journalist ahead of her, it was no wonder Grace felt optimistic about the future.

Grace was now in her mid-thirties and her name was recognised everywhere. She established herself in a comfortable flat in north London, and from here started travelling around the world again, following various stories. She had enjoyed her trip around the world and started to take flying lessons in a little Gipsy Moth at the Airwork School of Flying at Heston Air Park in London. She continued to cover stories about the *Graf Zeppelin*; the airship went on to be very successful, flying and carrying passengers as far as Brazil before, in May 1937, Germany's second great airship, the *Hindenburg*, crashed in New York, ending the entire airship programme.

As a top name, Grace was invited to many social functions, but whenever remarriage was suggested, she would comment strongly that nothing – not money, jewels or position – could compensate her for that glorious feeling of personal freedom. She was, however, also still seeing Karl, who was continuing in his career as a foreign reporter.

Karl was now a professional nomad, rarely spending any time in one place, so it was not a settled relationship. Karl was also always aware of his family situation. He had four children and he cared about them all; he was especially proud of his daughter, Charmion, who was carving out a very successful career for herself as an artist.

As she reached her early forties, Grace undertook a series of lecture tours across the United States, speaking on the international personalities she had met during her career, but the constant travelling was having its toll. Grace began to suffer health problems and started to reduce her trips, concentrating on European stories. In 1940, with Britain now at war and her doctor advising a warmer climate, Grace left England first for America and then for Hawaii. Here she linked up with Karl and from then on travelled with him, helping him with his work rather than following her own career.

Covering a range of stories, they spent time in Shanghai and then left for the Philippines. Their timing couldn't have been worse. They arrived in Manila on 7 December 1941, the very day the Japanese attacked the American naval base of Pearl Harbor in Hawaii. Karl and Grace had made a bad decision, for just ten hours later the Japanese attacked Manila and then occupied the city. Karl and Grace tried to escape without success, and they were put into the Santo Tomas internment camp. They were separated to sleep in men's and women's dormitories, which had virtually no facilities and were a far cry from the luxurious first-class accommodation Grace had been enjoying during the previous few years.

At this time, however, their conditions compared with some Japanese internment camps were fairly reasonable, with just about adequate food, although the situation would deteriorate badly as the war went on. Karl and Grace, though, were lucky. Karl was now approaching 70 and his health, especially his eyesight, was causing problems. Appealing to the authorities, he was able to emphasise his German background. Japan was not at war with Germany, and after just two weeks, Karl was given permission to be transferred up to Shanghai, and Grace was given permission to assist him. They left aboard the SS *Takaoka Maru* and were housed in a Shanghai hotel under Japanese house arrest, where they remained until September 1943. Then, as part of an American–Japanese exchange agreement, they joined other Americans on the SS *Gripsholm* to be taken back to the United States. Although neither of them was in the best of health, it must have been a joyous moment for Grace and Karl when they stepped on board, now free and firmly together.

In the United States, as the war ended, Grace hoped to restart her journalism career but she hadn't had a story published since 1940 and many things had changed. For Karl, too, things were different. Now in his seventies, he was still writing some stories for Hearst Corporation newspapers. Grace needed money and agreed to work as Karl's assistant while she considered what to do next; she had an idea that writing books might be the next step for her.

Grace and Karl were staying at the Lexington Hotel in New York when Grace's health suddenly deteriorated further. Suffering a coronary thrombosis in her hotel room, she died on 12 February 1946; she was 50 years old. As Karl transported her ashes back to Britain, he must have thought about this elegant, bubbly, independent woman, the times they had shared and also that exciting airship trip when they travelled east together – giving Grace the record of being the very first woman to travel around the world by air.

Harriet White Fisher, in her new Locomobile Type 1 Model 40, ready to set off for her drive around the world.

Buying a little tent in Paris, Harriet White Fisher caused quite a stir when she decided to try it out in the Place Vendôme.

On Harriet White Fisher's drive around the world, her car survived many precarious trips, including river crossings in India.
(The Brooks Family Collection)

Driving up the remote Hakone pass in Japan, the road suddenly stopped at a plunging precipice. With no room to turn round, Harriet's party had no alternative but to set up camp and hope for help.
(The Brooks Family Collection)

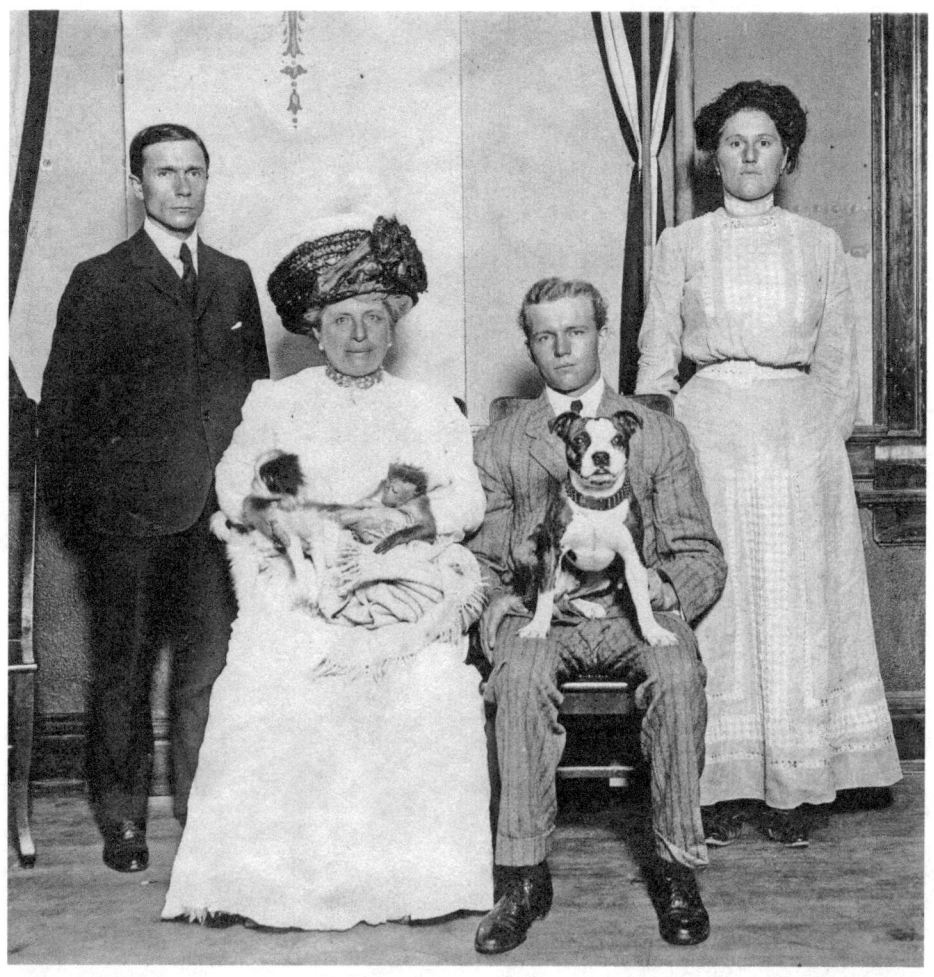

Harriet White Fisher and her team, including her two dogs and the little monkey that she picked up on her trip.

Journalist Lady Grace Drummond-Hay knew it would be a scoop if she could fly on the *Graf Zeppelin*, the largest airship ever constructed.
(Chronicle / Alamy Stock Photo)

The *Graf Zeppelin* had been designed with space and luxury to try to compete with the ocean liners on the transatlantic route.
(Aviation History Collection / Alamy Stock Photo)

In the cockpit of the *Graf Zeppelin*, Lady Grace Drummond-Hay was once again with the married man whom she loved.
(www.airships.net)

Valentina Tereshkova was close to her mother, who had worked so hard to bring her up.
(By kind permission of Lady Cecil Cameron)

When Valentina Tereshkova was working in a factory, a friend suggested she join a local parachute club. From the start, Valentina loved being in the air.
(By kind permission of Lady Cecil Cameron)

Every aspect of the flight had been practiced many times before Valentina Tereshkova finally set off on her historic journey into space.
(Archive Collection / Alamy Stock Photo)

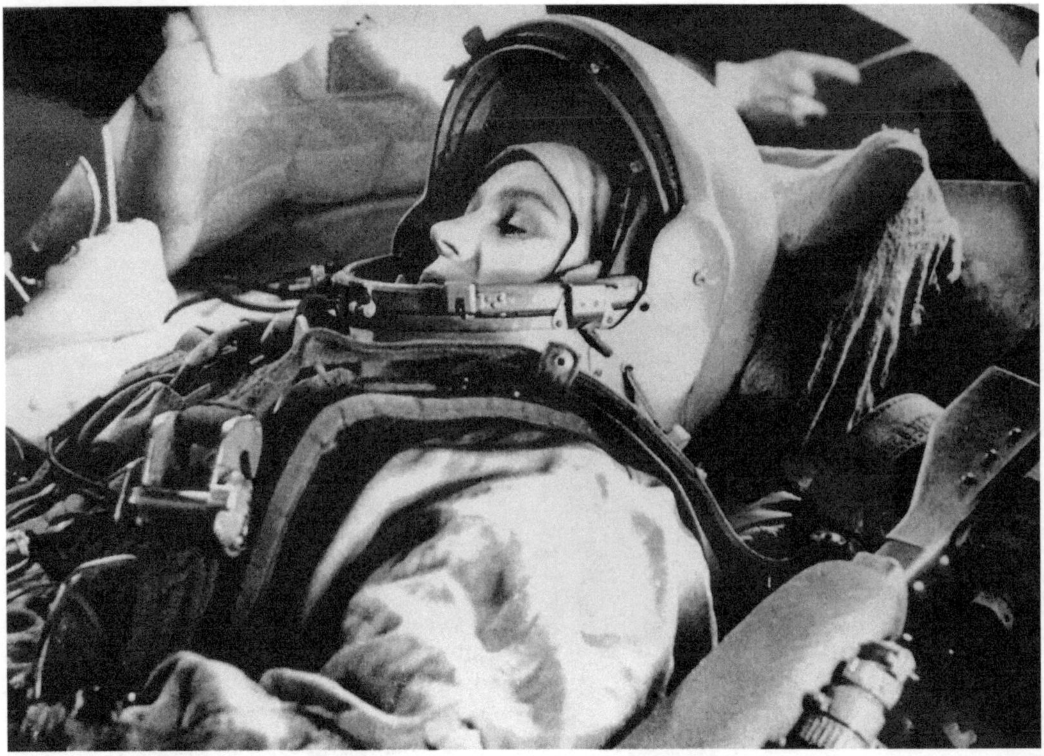

After her flight, Valentina Tereshkova's life had changed forever. Here she is with Communist leader Nikita Khrushchev.

Jeana Yeager with her co-pilot spent nine days squeezed into their experimental Voyager aircraft as they flew 24,000 miles around the world without stopping or refuelling.
(NASA / Contributor)

After her momentous flight and a time of receptions and presentations, Jeana Yeager was happy to go back to a quieter life with her horses. *(Aviation History Collection / Alamy Stock Photo)*

9

1963 VALENTINA TERESHKOVA
THE FIRST WOMAN ROUND THE WORLD IN SPACE

The prestige for the first country that managed to get a human into space was going to be enormous, so it was no wonder that in the 1950s and early 1960s the most advanced nations in the world were working hard on their various space programmes.

It turned out to be an extraordinarily close race between the Soviet Union (which included Russia) and the United States. Finally, in April 1961, Soviet cosmonaut Yuri Gagarin went up in Vostok 1 to become the first human to travel beyond the Earth's atmosphere and reach space. On his descent, he ejected from the spacecraft and landed by parachute.

Just over three weeks later, the astronaut Alan Shepard shot up into space in the Freedom 7 capsule to become the first American in space; instead of ejecting and landing by parachute, he stayed inside the capsule for the entire descent before splashing down in the ocean.

Both flights were a triumph for technological development, but both projects also faced unexpected problems and enormous challenges. The work continued, with improved technology sending more men into space and then, in 1969, to land on the moon.

There was no similar urgency to send the first woman into space. Russian woman Valentina Tereshkova achieved more prestige for her country when she clambered into Vostok 6 and went up into space in 1963, but then it was another nineteen years, when space technology had advanced by leaps and bounds, before the Soviets sent a second woman into space, in 1982, and the Americans finally sent their first woman up in 1983.

Across the Russian region and the rest of the Soviet Union, which covered so much of northern Europe and Asia in the twentieth century, it should have been a time of great fear and misery. Leader Joseph Stalin was at the height of his repression. Nearly one and a half million people had been taken in mass arrests; half of them were then shot. Thousands were dying in Gulag labour camps. For many, the year 1937 was a time of constant fearful expectation, when a terrifying knock on the door could come at any time, when fathers and husbands would suddenly, instantly, disappear. Trust had evaporated; people now became suspicious of others; old neighbours and friends, even relatives, were avoided. Who was reporting on whom to save themselves?

Yet amid this Great Terror, there was a quiet rural area of gentle rolling hills in the central plains of eastern Russia where life was still being ruled by the seasons, by the soft warmth of summer and the frosty fingers of winter, where families and friends still talked and hugged, where age-old traditions kept communities close.

The villagers of Maslennikovo, 180 miles north of Moscow, were aware, of course, of what was going on. Stalin's plan to move the Soviet Union forward at any cost had touched every area of the vast country; but in this tiny Russian hamlet the shield of isolation had helped keep things stable, had helped keep trust and love and laughter alive.

In the midst of this village, on 6 March 1937, at four o'clock in the morning when Elena Tereshkova called out that her baby was coming, there were no thoughts of Stalin and his terrifying purges. Instead, her husband left their small, neat wooden house and rushed across the village to fetch his mother. When they arrived back at the house, little Valentina Tereshkova had already arrived.

Valentina was a much-wanted baby; her mother had lost twins before her and the home in Maslennikovo was now full of joy and happiness. Despite the difficulties in the country surrounding them, for the Tereshkova family life was progressing well. Valentina already had an older sister, Ludmilla, there were relations around the region for support. Valentina's father, Vladimir, was a tractor driver and his earnings, while not bringing in riches, were regular and adequate. Her nearby grandparents had sheep and a cow, so milk and butter were plentiful. Both Valentina's parents loved music and that added to their lives as well. Her mother loved classical composers such as Beethoven as well as Russia's Tchaikovsky and Glinka, and she also loved Italian composers and singers; she was a good singer herself. Valentina's father was also very musical; after his day in the fields, sometimes family and friends would get together to listen to Vladimir play the accordion.

But the tentacles of Stalin's regime were now spreading further. Valentina's uncle, her father's brother, was suddenly arrested and imprisoned. Then, on 29 September 1939, when little Valentina was just 2, her father Vladimir was drafted into the Russian army to fight in the Soviet–Finnish war. In January 1940, he was killed. Valentina, when she grew up, believed the Finnish war was a whim of Stalin; she held her country's leader totally responsible for her father's tragic death.

So now, even in the remote, tiny hamlet of Maslennikovo, things were changing. Five months after her father's death, Valentina's little brother, Voloyda, was born; this brought some joy to relieve her mother's heartbreak, but also added to her difficulties. Voloyda was another mouth to feed in a family where there was now no wage earner.

Little Valentina knew her mother was unhappy, but she couldn't help but enjoy life in the country. There were no toys, but there was lots of fun to be had with other children outside. There were horses and dogs, a pond with ducks, and relations to spend time with. For Valentina, it was a sunny childhood.

The village school was a mile away, with a loved and respected teacher, but for the first seven years of Valentina's life, she had education enough at home. Her grandmother's house, a little farmhouse with few facilities, defied expectations with its beautiful furniture, carpets and a small room filled with fascinating books. For this family, a farming family in a remote country region, education was paramount.

Valentina didn't start school until she was 8 years old, in 1945, when the family moved 20 miles to the nearby town of Yaroslavl. Her mother desperately needed to earn money and she had heard there were job opportunities in the town. For the family, life now became very different. The Soviet Union had been at war with Germany since June 1941 when Adolf Hitler launched his invasion, and in the town the repercussions of this were much more evident. Food was rationed, but even with ration books only very basic items were available. Valentina's mother's job as a loom operator at the huge textile factory in the town paid very low wages; life was quite hard. Valentina remembers her mother, though, as a shining light, protecting and day by day looking after her young family.

Educational standards in the Soviet Union were very high, and one thing Valentina didn't lack was good instruction. While citizens weren't allowed to travel, at school she started learning French and was given access to foreign classics. Valentina's mother, thanks to that little library in her parents' farmhouse, had already read Tolstoy, Pushkin, even Shakespeare, and her influence too must have helped Valentina in her studies.

It wasn't until Valentina was 16, and leaving school, that people were told about Stalin's crimes. Originally hailed as a great leader, the Father Saviour of their country, it was a shock for many when the extent of his cruelty was revealed. The worst aspect for Valentina was his treachery; he had betrayed those who loved him. This all helped Valentina start thinking about politics and her country, a place she loved, her homeland.

When Valentina left school, she had the idea of training to be an engine driver, but money was needed desperately. Instead, she started work at a tyre manufacturing plant and then moved to join her mother in the textile factory; she also joined the Textile Technical Institute, where she studied in the evenings. It was thanks to her job in the factory that Valentina joined the Komsomol, the Communist Youth League. Her family had had no real interest in politics; living a busy farming life, they were a long way removed from the political powerhouses of the giant Soviet Union. For young Valentina, though, the Komsomol was an interesting organisation to join. It provided a number of leisure activities, including volunteer work and sports as well as political clubs. Perhaps from her mother, Valentina had developed a great belief in self-improvement, and the Komsomol group fitted in well with her growing belief in a better future for everyone. Valentina was growing into a serious young woman with definite views.

The Komsomol helped Valentina make new friends; she found a boyfriend and enjoyed going to the theatre, seeing Chekhov and *La Traviata*, which became her favourite opera. For a poor rural family, there was no lacking in classical knowledge. Even her mother occasionally saved a small amount of money to buy records of Verdi or Tchaikovsky to play in their small flat. Valentina learned to play the domra, a Russian stringed instrument, and even joined with friends in a folk-music group for a while.

It was in part thanks to former Russian leader Vladimir Lenin that, for many years in the mid-twentieth century, Russian women had enjoyed better rights than in many other countries. Lenin had believed that petty housework and drudgery crushed women and they should be allowed to enter the workforce and be economically free from men. The idea became ingrained and the 1936 Constitution of the Soviet Union guaranteed equality for women and equal rights in all spheres of life.

Thanks to this early doctrine, by the 1950s women in the Soviet Union were involved in many occupations and Valentina would not have been surprised to hear that some were parachuting. From its earliest days, the Soviet Union had been dominant in the sport as well as in the military uses of parachuting. The country had held the third ever world parachuting championships in Moscow in 1956, and a year later the Soviet Union's Nadejda Priakhina was achieving world records in parachuting accuracy.

One of Valentina's friends at the factory was Galina Shashkova, who had taken up parachuting at the local aero club just out of town. She suggested Valentina might like to give it a go; after all, Valentina already enjoyed physical activities such as swimming and skiing. So one day Valentina went to the airport with her and watched some jumping. Seeing the little black figures falling away from a plane high in the sky and considering the willpower and perhaps even strength required, Valentina decided it was not for her.

However, not long after there was a small Komsomol advert put up in the factory where she worked. Young men and women were invited to join various clubs including shooting, radio, boating and parachuting. Valentina now started to become interested in aviation; she read books about pilots and the idea of flying appealed to her, especially from the engineering side. Then she thought about parachuting again – the opportunity was there, perhaps she should find out more.

She went up to the airfield for a second time and joined a group of newcomers where the instructor, Viktor Havron, was talking about the history of sport parachuting. Now, as part of a group, it all seemed easier. Early in 1959, the year she was turning 22, Valentina decided to learn.

The training took a little while. She had to fit her visits to the airfield around work, but having learned about the round parachute, how to exit from the plane, how to land with feet together and then roll onto her side to mitigate the shock, she was ready for her first jump.

On Wednesday, 21 May 1959, with other club members and struggling under the weight of the heavy parachute, she clambered into a small, green aeroplane and, bumping across the grass airstrip, they took off. She loved it from that very first jump; from the cold air rushing in through the open door, to the view of the Earth far below and the freedom of jumping out into nothingness. Valentina was hooked.

She spent more and more time at the club, clocking up over 100 jumps and mastering the techniques of pulling on the lines to try and steer the round, white canopy floating far above her. She was still working hard and through her evening studies, in 1960, she obtained a diploma as an engineer. By now, she was becoming more involved in the Komsomol's political activities and becoming a strong believer in the idea of communism. She believed everyone should love their motherland and do what they could to help themselves and their country.

In April 1961, fellow countryman Yuri Gagarin became the first human to orbit the earth in space, an event that was followed with excitement and pride by Valentina and her friends at the aero club. They celebrated together, talking about how he had come from a very disrupted childhood in the country and how amazing it was that he had got so far. It may also have been mentioned, as her fellow club members chatted excitedly about the event, how the Soviet Union's chief rocket engineer, Sergei Korolev, was keen on gender equality and was now considering sending a woman into space, something that would be another big political coup for the Soviet Union.

It was only when Valentina got home, however, and told her mother about the amazing news of Gagarin's flight, that an idea started forming in her mind. Her mother listened carefully and then commented that, now a man had flown in space, it should be a woman's turn next.

This made Valentina really think. Could she possibly join the Soviet space programme? Whether she flew or not, being part of such an exciting organisation would be tremendously exciting and give her a new challenge in life. Gripped with enthusiasm, she managed to find out the best contact and then quickly wrote a letter to the Central Committee of the DOSAAF in Moscow, an organisation for co-operation between the army, air force and navy, and asked if she could be considered for a training course in new space technology.

Something – her parachuting, of course, but also perhaps her work in a factory, her interest in engineering, her willingness to study out of hours and perhaps her support for the Komsomol – caught their imagination. She was asked to appear before a committee in Moscow. A visit to the capital was in itself both exciting and a little daunting.

It was an easy train ride down to Moscow, though, and the interview and then the subsequent tests must have gone well, for she was finally informed that she had been chosen to go to the Cosmonaut Training Centre, one of just five women selected. It must have been an extraordinary moment for Valentina; suddenly, from being a fairly ordinary worker in a factory, she was being given the opportunity to do something remarkable. However, there was bad news too. Valentina was of a quiet, thoughtful and serious nature, but nevertheless this could have been a time for some celebration. However, she was strictly told she wasn't to inform anyone of what was happening. The Soviet space programme was cloaked in secrecy.

By this time, the world had entered the Cold War, with a major battle between the United States and the Soviet Union for technological supremacy; space and space travel were critical elements that developed into a space race. The Soviet Union didn't want anyone to hear of its idea of putting a woman into space.

The secrecy was a problem for Valentina as she was very close to her mother, so she made up a story saying she had been selected for a special parachute team and had to go to Moscow for training. Nevertheless, it was an exciting time for Valentina. Now, at 24, Valentina was ready to start a new life. Her friends, though, who saw her off at Yaroslavl station in December 1961, must have wondered what she was up to.

Valentina spent eighteen months at the Cosmonaut Training Centre at Star City, 15 miles north-west of Moscow. As she first stepped through the doorway, Valentina felt really welcomed; it was such a friendly atmosphere. Right from the start, though, there was little time for socialising. Along with the other four women on the programme, Valentina was quickly introduced to a full-on and wide-ranging training regime that covered many areas from geophysics and rocket technology to physical fitness and medical monitoring. Some of the tests were very physically demanding, including thermal chambers and undergoing centrifuge vestibular tests. With a rocket launch and then time in space, every part of the body would be affected.

The training included parachute jumps, but the sport that Valentina used to enjoy now became hard work and challenging. There was a continuous programme of parachuting in spacesuits and landing both on land and in water.

The women, together with the men training with them, developed a close-knit group; they knew they had been selected for something very special and they were all working together, helping and supporting each other. They each had their own accommodation in Star City, basic but very adequate, and Valentina settled in well.

The training went on day after day and month after month: radio communication, space navigation and orientation, how to deal with emergencies, even what to do if they landed back in an area where they could not be found quickly. These were the very early days of space exploration; the landing place of returning cosmonauts was in no way exact.

An especially challenging aspect of the whole programme for Valentina was that the girl who was finally chosen would be going up into space on her own. There wouldn't be a team with her. This was possibly one of the most daunting aspects of the whole programme, but Valentina was willing to do it. Her heart was now set firmly on going up into space. Her training included time in a sound chamber to cope with isolation, although nothing could really emulate the experience of being alone so high up in space, circling the Earth. The thought of being completely on her own didn't terrify her; she was confident in the programme and the extensive support team.

Valentina went home to visit her mother a couple of times, and chatted about certain aspects of her training. But it was very difficult not being able to explain exactly what she was doing, and her mother must have wondered why her daughter was being so reticent. Secrecy was a vital aspect of participating in the programme, however, and Valentina wasn't going to risk jeopardising her chances, even for her family.

In 1962, one of the girls in the group became ill and had to leave the programme. They had all become good friends, so this was sad; but it also brought home the fact that not all of the girls would be going into space. Of the four who were left, only one would be chosen as the pilot of the spacecraft and one more would be selected as a back-up.

There were tough examinations in November 1962, and three of the four girls, including Valentina, were then identified as the candidates suitable to continue on the programme. They were commissioned as junior lieutenants in the Soviet Air Force and a detailed profile was started on each of the three girls to help with the final decision of who would finally go into space.

In early 1963, the training became more intense. The space programme would launch Vostok 5 with a male pilot and Vostok 6 with a female. Vostok 1 had been launched by rockets and had been the first spacecraft to carry a human into space, when Yuri Gagarin went up in April 1961. Vostok 5 and 6 were later models. With their huge bulbous module heads and overall design, at the time they were at the cutting edge of space transport.

By April 1963, the main training was pretty well complete. Valentina was given a few days off and went home to Yaroslavl to see her family. Again this was a wonderful but difficult time for her; when she got back, she would hear if she had been selected as the woman to pilot Vostok 6, so it was hard to relax and almost impossible not to let slip any hint of what she had really been doing. Her mother especially was becoming very concerned about the changes in her daughter, but there was nothing she could do. Back at Star City, she packed up a few things and then, along with the other girls and the men who had also been training with them, flew to the cosmodrome at Baikonur in Kazakhstan. Here they were given the final news: the man from their training group selected to pilot the spacecraft Vostok 5 was Valery Bykovsky; the woman chosen to fly Vostok 6 was Valentina.

It was a memorable moment for Valentina. She was now 26. Coming from a poor, rural background, after so much work, after so much effort, she had been chosen to be the first women ever to fly into space; the very first woman in the world to attempt this. There were no big celebrations, though, for Valentina, or commiserations for the others. Everyone was very friendly and supportive of each other, and they realised they were all a team still working together. One of them might be going up into space, but they all had jobs to do. Valentina's immediate back-up was Irina Solovyova and the two of them got on really well.

The launch days approached fast; Vostok 5 was due to go up on 14 June and Valentina's Vostok 6 on 16 June. As Valentina spent her time working on the final flight preparations, every aspect of her life now began to be watched by scientists and doctors. The time for Valery Bykovsky's launch came and everything went well; Vostok 5 successfully reached its planned height and began circling the Earth.

Now it was Valentina's turn. The night before her flight, her back-up Irina joined her so they could drink tea together. All the training was complete, everything was ready. Tomorrow was the day.

The doctors administered an enema before Valentina went to bed; meals now consisted of carefully planned space food, offering key nutrition rather than flavour or substance.

At seven in the morning, on Sunday, 16 June, Valentina got up and did half an hour of exercise. Then it was time to get ready. In a designated final area, Valentina was kitted out for the flight. She was helped into her special underwear and thermal layers and finally into her spacesuit and boots; various wires were attached to monitor many aspects of Valentina's health. When all was complete and fixed, finally special protective covers were put on over her boots.

Valentina was ready.

She walked carefully out to climb into the special bus that would take her to the spaceship. Her back-up, Irina, accompanied her. It must have been a difficult time for Irina, having to be totally ready and prepared to step into the spaceship at the very last moment if something went wrong to prevent Valentina taking off.

Yuri Gagarin and a few others accompanied Valentina in the bus and it was a happy atmosphere; this was the culmination of so much preparation, so much hard work. She had no time for thoughts of anything other than what lay immediately ahead.

Leaving the bus, after saluting the chairman of the State Commission who was standing close by, Valentina stepped onto the platform lift that would take her to Vostok 6, attached to the top of the rocket launch system. Technicians at the Vostok helped remove the covers from Valentina's boots and then helped her into the specially contoured seat of the capsule. Once she was there, firmly strapped in, they shut the hatch.

After eighteen months of intense training, Valentina was now on her own. The moment had come.

There were still many checks to go through and these occupied Valentina for nearly two hours. Her radio name was Chaika, meaning Seagull, and in these early days of electronic communication, her contact through the radio link and flickering screen had to be checked constantly.

Finally the systems that would lift Vostok 6 into space were ready. Valentina received a final word, wishing her a happy flight, from rocket engineer Sergei Korolev, and then, in a roar of white-hot flames, the rockets ignited and Vostok 6, with Valentina tightly strapped on board, lifted up into the sky.

To begin with, there was no sitting back looking out of the two small porthole windows, as Valentina needed to constantly monitor the equipment and controls. After a few minutes, though, Valentina could look up. The Earth was already disappearing. More checks, more instrument watching, and finally the Vostok had reached its planned height. Over 125 miles up into space, Valentina was able to watch her Vostok capsule separating from the rockets.

There was no spare room in the Vostok capsule, but initially Valentina was comfortable. Her chair had been carefully designed, and while she was surrounded by equipment and technology, she didn't feel claustrophobic.

Now that the Vostok capsule, her little home high above Earth, had been released from the rocket and was on its own, it started a constant, steady orbit around the world. Valentina was pleased the angle of the craft enabled her to see out of the porthole down onto the Earth, and she said afterwards that, right from the start, the view was overwhelming. It was incredibly beautiful. Initially the surface was lit by the sun, but Valentina was circling the Earth in just eighty-nine minutes, so although she had no sensation of speed, there was constant change from light to dark. From that height, the Earth looked astonishingly blue, but the areas of land as well as the sea stood out clearly. Valentina could identify many areas including the icecaps of the two poles and the ice of Greenland. The Suez Canal and Red Sea stood out too, a long dark ribbon of water between the yellow sands of Egypt and Saudi Arabia; and as she circled, she started to identify more areas, picking out major rivers and other features not blanketed in cloud.

Life was busy, though, and Valentina had many jobs to do. She made contact with Valery Bykovsky, orbiting in Vostok 5; at one point, they were within 3 miles of each other before they separated again. Valentina was very aware that she was captain of the vehicle, and while most of the operations were automatic, nothing in this early stage of space exploration could be left without regular supervision just in case something was beginning to go wrong. She had also been given a number of experiments to carry out, including activities with seeds and insects. One of her jobs was to use a special camera to take specific film and photographs of the Earth and its atmosphere from various angles. In her logbook, she noted her physiological reactions to being in space, including her heart rate, pulse and breathing, as well as aspects of her environment, such as cabin temperature. Radio reports had to be sent regularly down to Baikonur, and Valentina even sent a radio report down to the Kremlin on the progress of the flight.

With so many things to do, Valentina had little spare time to gaze out of the window and contemplate what she was doing. Sitting there in her special chair, her thoughts must, however, sometimes have strayed away from her work into the sheer marvel of her surroundings. After all those ideas and dreams of what she could do with her life, here she was high up in space, circling the Earth, the very first woman ever to do this. For an ordinary Russian girl from a poor rural background, it was an extraordinary achievement.

On 17 June, at 3 p.m. Moscow time, she flew over her hometown of Yaroslavl and the Volga. She stared out of her little porthole, desperate to see any sign of her town, but it was too small, too far below, and anyway the area was covered in thick, white clouds. Valentina had to keep an eye on time. At this height and circling the Earth so fast, there was no night and day. Time instead had been set according to Moscow clocks, and Valentina had been given specific times to eat and drink, to relax and to sleep. During her first period of sleep, she was woken by a very strange feeling. It took her a while to realise that her hands were floating up in front of her. She had been fully trained in how to cope with low gravity, but this caught her unawares. She tucked her hands back under the belts of the tethering system and went back to sleep.

The initial plan was for Valentina to return to Earth after twenty-four hours, but there had been an additional plan that if the flight was going well, and Valentina was up for it, the flight could be extended. Valentina felt that the first twenty-four hours had gone well; she was feeling OK and she radioed down to the State Commission that she was willing to extend the flight. This was settled and the plan was that she would now land on 19 June, at around the same time as her colleague Valery Bykovsky in Vostok 5.

So, in her little spaceship, Valentina continued to orbit around the Earth. Initially her sleep patterns, her food and her work and experiments had all gone well. She did some very limited exercise in the enclosed space, and she could wash, albeit only with an impregnated cloth. It wasn't home comforts by any means, but it was survivable.

She was still being overwhelmed by the beauty of the flight, but increasingly, as she looked down, she felt how small and vulnerable that little blue planet was, floating in such alien darkness. It was an awareness that helped to drive her desire for world peace and co-operation for many years after her flight.

As the flight went on, things became more challenging. At one point, she was very sick and, because of the restricted movement in the capsule, she developed agonising cramp in one leg. Then an uncomfortable rash developed under one of her biomedical sensors.

There was mention after the flight that the automatic orientation system for her Vostok capsule had been incorrectly set up and on board she had to make a manual adjustment; but this was never officially confirmed. That, however, was what all the months of training had been for and Valentina would have been quite capable of dealing with it. There were also rumours after the flight that there had been concern about Valentina's performance in some respects; but Valentina was not a robot and to be sitting alone so high up in space in what was still a very experimental system must have been more than challenging, both mentally as well as physically.

It was a relief for Valentina when, after two days and twenty-three hours in space and completing forty-eight orbits, it was time to go back down to Earth. She now had to take some control of the capsule and was in constant communication with her team on the ground as re-entry was commenced. This was not easy; it was possibly the worst, most physically uncomfortable aspect of the entire trip as well as being the most dangerous. As the capsule descended, initially it was fine, but then, as it ploughed into the higher atmosphere, the noise built up and the pressure grew. Bright yellow flames surrounded the shaking capsule – it was clear something momentous was taking place. The physical discomfort was becoming intense; Valentina was having to withstand high G loads and also, for a short time, it felt impossible to breathe. It was a very difficult and frightening time, but Valentina had known what to expect and it only lasted for a short period. The next step was automatic and came suddenly: an electric impulse opened the hatch and triggered Valentina's chair to be ejected. Valentina had gone through this so many times on the ground. She knew what would happen. Very quickly, the chair separated and a big parachute blossomed up above her.

She had been under a parachute many times, but this was different. Landing in her space outfit didn't make it easy, and even worse, she looked down and saw she was approaching a lake. This was not good, but there was little she could do. How ironic it would be if, after becoming the very first woman in space, she ended up dying by drowning.

She had been fully trained for water landings, though, so it might have been OK; but luckily the wind blew her over the edge of the lake and she landed in a nearby field. Suddenly, in an instant, her feet hit the stubble and she bounced over onto her side. Valentina was down; she had returned safely to Earth.

The only injury she had was a big bruise on her face where the metal rim of her helmet had banged into her on landing. She quickly communicated her location to the rescue team and then removed her large helmet and inner fitted cap. It was a scene of peace and tranquillity: it was a soft summer's day; there were men working in a nearby field; she could feel the warmth of the sun and a gentle wind. Valentina must have felt a surge of relief and probably real joy; for all her confidence in the technology and her team, in 1963 space travel was still very new indeed. So much could have gone wrong. Now here she was, her helmet and oxygen system off, breathing sweet air as she stood firmly on the ground of planet Earth. She had done it.

Still, though, Valentina had work to do. First, she got herself out of her spacesuit and then she gathered up her parachute. The farm workers came over; they must have been delighted to be the first to meet this woman cosmonaut and were very happy to help. Searching the land around, the capsule was found; it had fallen to Earth just a quarter of a mile away. Valentina picked up her various items and carried them over to stack them neatly by the capsule ready for the rescue. Her willing helpers found the heavy chair and manhandled that over to the capsule for her. Then she asked for a lift to the nearest village with a telephone. Through a special arrangement, she was able to get through to the Kremlin in Moscow and report briefly to Soviet premier Nikita Khrushchev that she had landed and all was well.

Valentina had come down in the Altai region, around 400 miles north-east of Karaganda in Kazakhstan, and after phoning the Kremlin, she simply went back to the field to wait. It wasn't too long before a rescue plane reached the area. She was taken directly to a centre in Kuybyshev, a space facility in Samara, 600 miles south-east of Moscow, where the first Vostok rockets had been assembled. Here

Valentina had to undergo a series of thorough medical tests and she was also reunited with Sergei Korolev who, after so many years helping to direct the Soviet space programme, must have been delighted with the total success of the mission. Valentina now had the first taste of what her life would become; she was greeted with many flowers, with people wanting to say hello and congratulate her, with kindness, warmth and gratitude for what she had done for space exploration and for the country.

Valery Bykovsky had also landed safely, and on 22 June 1963, the two of them were taken to Moscow to deliver personal reports to the leaders of the Soviet Union.

Landing at Moscow's Vnukovo airport, the group were met by Nikita Khrushchev and many other officials. Her mother had been brought there, too. By now she had, of course, learned what her daughter had been up to; her flight had been big news all across the country, and indeed across the world. It must have been such a shock when she learned the truth; she would have been upset that her daughter had deceived her but would also have taken enormous pride in what she had achieved.

There was a huge reception organised in Red Square and, along with other cosmonauts, Valentina stood beside Khrushchev on a podium. As she looked around, all she could see were applauding crowds and a sea of flowers and banners.

There was no time to rest for this new heroine of the Union of Socialist Soviet Republics. Just two days later she went to the opening event of the 1963 World Congress of Women in the Palace of Congresses in the Kremlin, where she had to give an address to 2,000 women from 119 countries. Valentina's new career as a public speaker and ambassador had begun in dramatic fashion. Her main message came naturally; she had seen planet Earth from so far away, seen how beautiful it was, but also how fragile it was, hanging there in space. Valentina felt strongly that the people of the Earth needed to unite and look after the planet for future generations. The message came from her heart. As a cosmonaut, she had not seen any frontiers, just the planet as a whole.

Ceremonies, presentations, meetings and talks, a full programme was now organised for Valentina. There was no longer any secrecy, Valentina and the Soviet Union had done it; a woman had been up and orbited the Earth in space. She was honoured with the title of Hero of the Soviet Union; Valentina Tereshkova had become a recognised name, a star, right across the world. Her family could not have been prouder.

While she now had a full programme and was given accommodation in Moscow, she kept her flat at Star City and that remained her real home, even though she couldn't spend a great deal of time there. Amid the non-stop activities of her new life, though, Valentina did find time to get closer to fellow astronaut Andriyan Nikolayev. She had met him during training and he was also deemed a hero; he had been the third Soviet cosmonaut to go into space when, in August 1962, he had orbited the Earth sixty-four times in Vostok 3. All the cosmonauts in this early Soviet space programme were close; they were a team of specialists undergoing extraordinary experiences together. Valentina and Andriyan also shared a vaguely similar background: he had been brought up in a farming area on the Volga outside Moscow and his father had died when he was fairly young, in his early teens. In the autumn of 1963, things became more serious between the two of them and, encouraged by the authorities who recognised the potential of a good news story, on 3 November 1963, they were married at the Moscow marriage palace. Her mother wasn't particularly happy about the arrangement; she just hoped her busy daughter was happy.

The wedding, of course, attracted a huge crowd. Nikita Krushchev was just one of many top names who were invited; he had been very supportive of the union from the first and, as predicted, it was a wonderful boost for the Soviet space programme too, this love story between two cosmonauts. Early 1964 was a busy time for Valentina, especially as she found that she was now pregnant, but the talks and visits continued. In February 1964, she was invited to Buckingham Palace in London, where she met Queen Elizabeth II; despite both women being pregnant, the talk remained focused on the space flight.

On 8 June 1964, Valentina gave birth to a baby daughter, Elena. She could have stopped now. She was still only 27 years old; she had achieved the incredible and now she had a family, too. This was not in Valentina's nature, though; her eagerness to keep learning, to keep doing things, hadn't been dimmed. She still wanted to serve her country and continue to progress – perhaps this desire became even stronger after her daughter was born.

Star City remained her base and pre-school help for little Elena was well organised and readily available. Her mother came to live with her as well, although by now she was suffering health problems. Valentina was travelling extensively, meeting top leaders and heading Soviet delegations, as well as attending and being guest speaker at many major events. She also signed on at the Zhukovsky Air Force Academy to study for a doctorate in engineering science, a qualification she finally achieved in 1976 after mixing her studies with many other activities. Valentina was on numerous committees and a member of many major national and international organisations, and she was also in constant demand as a guest of honour at many events. Awards, including the Joliot-Curie Gold Medal of Peace and the United Nation Gold Medal of Peace, were still being showered upon her.

Valentina was one very busy, very active woman. In the early 1980s, her marriage ended, and not long after she married a surgeon, Yuli Shaposhnikov; they remained together until he died in 1999.

By then Valentina's interests were increasing becoming directed towards politics. Her country had given her the most amazing opportunity; a girl from a very modest background had been supported to fulfil her dreams. She wanted to do what she could for her country and for women. She became more involved in political activity through the turmoil of the disintegration of the Soviet Union, and failed twice to get selected for the national State Duma, one of the chambers of the Russian parliament. Finally, in 2011, when she was 74, Valentina, as a member of the United Russia party, managed to join the State Duma. Her politics were by now quite clear-cut. She had been vigorously opposed to the ideas of Mikhail Gorbachev and had now met and supported Vladimir Putin.

Time, however, changes people and the energy that she had enjoyed in her youth couldn't continue at such a high level. As she got older, Valentina increasingly started to spend time at her small brick dacha or country home on the outskirts of Star City, and kept in close contact with her daughter and also with her two grandsons, Andrei and Aleksei. In her later years, she might almost have been seen as an ordinary Russian woman – as ordinary as one could have been after becoming the very first woman to go up and circle the Earth in space.

10

1986–88 JEANA LEE YEAGER AND KAY COTTEE
THE FIRST WOMEN ROUND THE WORLD NON-STOP

After Valentina's trip around the world, all the main circumnavigation records had been broken. Women had travelled around our Earth by sea, air, land – and finally up in space.

In the following years, with infrastructure, technology and communications all advancing steadily, the world seemed to be growing smaller. In many places, women were no longer restrained by social pressures and, with modern materials and equipment, more recent women explorers and adventurers haven't had to face the same obstacles and problems experienced by the early pioneers. By the 1980s, thanks to modern vehicles, boats and aircraft, travelling around the world had become almost commonplace.

There was still one record to be broken, however. While Valentina had travelled around the world in space, she had been a long, long way up. No woman had ever travelled completely non-stop around our world by land, sea or air. It was time for this final record to be broken.

The idea of going right around the world non-stop was hardly considered until the middle of the twentieth century. Before then, a requirement to take on supplies and also repair the damage done by the constant battering by the oceans prohibited any idea of sailing such a long distance without stopping. A plane faced different problems: fuel was needed to keep it aloft, and no plane was available that could fly such distances and also carry enough heavy fuel to cover the entire journey.

In 1949, however, there was a breakthrough when a United States Air Force's B-50 Superfortress was refuelled in the air and made a record non-stop voyage. Then, twenty years later, England's Sir Robin Knox-Johnston sailed into history with a non-stop circumnavigation in his boat *Suhaili*. However, it took another two decades before a woman achieved the record of travelling right around the world non-stop, and then, extraordinarily, it almost became a race between two women from opposite sides of the Earth.

Jeana Lee Yeager from Dallas in the United States and Kay Cottee from Sydney, Australia, had a lot in common. They had both been born in the early 1950s; neither of them was excited by academic learning; both of them married while still in their teens and both marriages failed after just a few years. Jeana and Kay were also both 34 when they finally achieved their dream of going around the world non-stop. There was one big difference, though: Jeana was going to try the non-stop circumnavigation by air; Kay believed that with the right experience, equipment and a little bit of luck, she could sail right around the world non-stop by sea.

Neither woman initially set out to set a record, though. For Jeana, the idea was put to her; for Kay, the idea just evolved.

Jeana's background had nothing to do with aviation; in fact, her real love had been horses. Being brought up in Texas, when her older sister was given a horse, little Jeana was immediately hooked. In 1955, when she was just 3 years old, she found a chair and, after much struggling, clambered onto the back of her sister's patient pony. After that, there was no stopping her.

As Jeana grew into a bright and bubbly girl, she did well at school, but her lessons didn't interest her; all she wanted to do was to get back home and ride horses. In many ways it was an idyllic childhood and at their home property, in sunny Texan weather and with 23 acres of pasture, life was good.

At 19, Jeana then found another love in her life. Jon Farrar was good looking and kind and also a man with excellent prospects; he was already a deputy lieutenant in the local sheriff's department. They were married just before Jeana's 20th birthday and for a year or two it was a very happy time. Slowly though, Jeana began to realise that she was getting frustrated. She knew Jon was a wonderful, devoted husband, but somehow it wasn't enough. As the years flowed steadily past and she reached her mid-twenties, Jeana was becoming almost desperate to do something, anything, away from the static atmosphere of her traditional home and familiar surroundings. There was a whole world out there to be discovered and Jeana felt she simply had to move on. How was she to tell her lovely husband, though, and what should she tell her family? It wasn't easy; Jeana had grown into a caring, sensitive woman and hated the thought of causing so much upset. However, she felt she had no option and the decision was made. Jeana's older sister had already left to move up to Santa Rosa in California and Jeana decided to join her for a fresh start.

Now Jeana could experience the new, independent life she had dreamed of. She had taken drawing and drafting lessons at school and managed to get a job as a technical illustrator for a local energy company; then she looked around for a way to make new friends and maybe add some real excitement into her life. There was a small but active airfield operating in the town, and Jeana's thoughts turned to flight. It looked fun and perhaps would offer some new opportunities. Saving her money, she went to the airfield and booked some flying lessons. It was very different from horse riding and Jeana really had to work hard; for the first time in her life, though, she was happy to study. It took a while, but as she progressed, she started to really enjoy herself. She was making new friends and she also loved being up in the air. Looking down on Santa Rosa and the countryside below, the little houses, the wooded hills and the far horizons, Jeana at last felt she had found the sense of freedom she had been looking for. She gained her pilot's licence in 1978 as she turned 26.

Soon aviation was dominating her life; Jeana had found her future and was interested in learning as much as she could. In summer 1980, when she attended an air show, she had lots to talk about to the pilots there, but one, former United States Air Force fighter pilot Dick Rutan, made a big impression. Dick was now working for his brother, aircraft designer Burt Rutan, as a test pilot for his Rutan Aircraft Factory. This all sounded very exciting and Dick was also very attractive. It wasn't long before Jeana agreed to move up to be with Dick at the aircraft factory in Mojave, 80 miles north of Los Angeles.

Jeana's happy personality and willingness to try new things helped her quickly fit in. She got on well with Dick's brother Burt and, with a pilot's licence, she was soon allowed to fly the company's aircraft. Relaxing with Dick in the hot air of the Californian summer, she realised she had come a long way from her steady times in Texas. Horses had become a memory and Jeana was very happy in her new life. The trauma of leaving her kind husband and moving away had been worth it.

One day, over lunch, the Rutan brothers and Jeana were discussing the new developments in plastic fibre composites. The conversation turned towards how the lighter weight of the new material could help planes fly even further. Working out weight and flight with the amount of fuel that needed to be carried, could a new plane be designed in these new, incredibly light materials that could travel really long distances – what about even right around the world? As they finished their lunch, they made sketches on paper napkins and their excitement grew. Talking about the idea, the final decision was made surprisingly quickly. Yes, with a special plane in the new lightweight materials, a non-stop round-the-world flight should be possible, and they would try to do it.

Jeana, along with the two brothers, thought the idea was terrific; a real challenge that they could all work on together. However, to achieve such a long flight, they realised they would need to come up with a radical new aircraft. Brother Burt was the key here; he already had enormous experience in designing aircraft. Jeana's experience in technical drawing also helped, and she drew up the formal plans and also prepared a perspective view of the airplane. It was an extraordinary design.

The body of the aircraft was to be made in a honeycomb design from a mix of the latest lightweight materials, including fibreglass, carbon fibre and Kevlar. While the length of the fuselage would be just over 25ft, its wingspan would be an astonishing 110ft. The radical design included propellers and engines at both the front and the back of the plane. Overall, unladen, the plane should weigh just over 1 ton. Weight was imperative, for Burt had calculated that for every extra pound of weight added to the fuselage, an extra 6lb of fuel would be needed.

After months of hard work, the little team felt they had a plane that could work. Jeana came up with the name Voyager.

Now it was time to actually build this extraordinary-looking aircraft, but that needed money. Jeana and Dick were by now very close, living together in an old military house lent to them by Dick's parents. Their office was the kitchen table and they decided that, with such a groundbreaking project, it should be fairly easy to find backers. They carefully put together proposals, researched the best names and companies, and then sent out details to literally hundreds of possible sponsors.

Things turned out to be far harder than they had anticipated, and Jeana and Dick spent a dispiriting and frustrating eighteen months looking for sponsors. Every so often, with excited anticipation, they spent hours preparing extra details for people who showed an interest, only to be let down. They travelled vast distances to meetings and spoke enthusiastically about the project to people who showed initial enthusiasm, but disappointment followed disappointment and no one would take that final step and come up with any money to help build the new plane.

While Jeana didn't have a serious technical background, sharing Dick and Burt's enthusiasm, she felt the plane could achieve fantastic distances. Yet no one was willing to help them. It was a hugely frustrating time, but none of them wanted to give up on their dream. While they undertook various flying jobs to help cover their living expenses, they came up with a brand-new idea. Along with doing as much of the work as possible themselves, they would also launch a VIP club, the Voyager Impressive People club, with members each contributing $100. In those days this was an innovation, a very early form of crowd funding. They weren't offering a lot in return but, amazingly, it worked. Money started coming in, including smaller donations from businesses that were impressed both by the idea and also by Jeana and Dick's determination to literally get it off the ground. In 1983, they had enough money to begin construction. Fund raising was continuous; sometimes they were down to their last few dollars, but the dream persisted and on they went.

It took a long year and a half to create the aircraft, but finally, by 1984 and under Burt's careful supervision, the basic plane had been built. Now it had become a reality, it was easier to attract interest.

Jeana had by now become totally absorbed by the project; after they had devoted so much time and energy to the plane, she felt it simply had to work. Weighing a lot less than either Dick or Burt, she agreed that she would be the best choice to do the first flight in this incredibly light, innovative flying machine. It was a brave decision, but she had confidence.

On 22 June 1984, just six years after she had first gained her pilot's licence, Jeana squeezed herself into the tiny cockpit and started up the engines. To begin with, she simply taxied up and down the runway to get a feel of the plane. It was unlike anything she had flown before: it was very light and she found that the exceptionally long and narrow wings offered a strange sense of balance; the plane wasn't particularly responsive either.

Finally, it was time to test it properly. She taxied out to the end of the runway and took a deep breath. The designs had been good, the engines were good, but she couldn't help but be nervous. Could they have they missed something vital?

Taking off, the plane lifted up into the air very fast and also very easily. It was a natural glider. Looking out of the window, Jeana saw a crazy long network of shadowy shapes flowing across the runway. It really was an extraordinary design – but it flew. It didn't take long, though, for the first problem to appear: oil was bubbling out of the front engine.

Calm and controlled, Jeana simply switched off the problem engine and, flying on just the other one, continued with her early checks. Everything else worked well and after forty minutes she slowly turned and then, softly and gently, glided the plane down onto the long runway. Along with the oil leak, Jeana explained to Dick and Burt that there had been other problems too and she had found handling the plane really hard; the rudder could barely do the job. However, Voyager had flown! It was time to celebrate. Relations and well-wishers joined Burt, Dick and Jeana for a big party that night. Stage one of the project had been accomplished.

Stage two was testing and the team continued to test and make modifications. It took long months of adjustments before the team felt they had achieved a viable aircraft that could actually achieve the distance they were hoping for.

On top of building the aircraft, there were numerous other areas to be covered, including communication, navigation and human factors. To go all the way around the world, the flight would probably take around nine or ten days to complete. To reduce weight and drag, the cockpit area for the pilots was minimal, just over 3ft wide and just over 7ft in length; the person flying the plane would sit in the seat and the co-pilot would squeeze into the little space behind to try and get some rest. Could two people really manage over a week in such cramped conditions?

Jeana and Dick also had to be realistic about structural and engine problems, and they talked long and hard about what would happen if they came down in the sea or in an inhospitable region of the world. There was no room for survival equipment on board, though. Because of weight, everything had to be cut back to the very minimum.

Finally, all the modifications, all the checks, all the preparations had been made. By now the voyage was beginning to attract serious attention; news that two young Americans really were going to attempt to fly around the world non-stop in a crazy-looking aircraft was creating a lot of interest.

After four long years of planning and building, everything was finally ready. Jeana had even cut her hair short just to eliminate any chance of it catching in one of the plane's open control cable tracks; they really had tried to be as prepared as they possibly could.

On 14 December 1986, the day dawned clear but chilly. Jeana got up, very aware that she was about to start on another major adventure in her life. This time, though, things were a lot easier. Leaving her kind husband and upsetting her family and friends had been very hard emotionally; now, although she was slightly nervous, there was optimism and cheerful support all around her. Jeana had a quick shower, put on her carefully chosen cotton underwear and tracksuit, and went out to the airfield. As the flimsy-looking white aircraft was gently taken out of its hangar, only family and members of their special VIP club, who had done so much to help fund the flight, were allowed on the airfield.

What would the next few days bring? Would that weird-looking aircraft fly them right around the world? Jeana didn't like to think about it anymore; she simply concentrated on saying a few goodbyes and then clambered into the 3ft-wide cockpit. Struggling around the pilot's seat, she reached the tiny space behind and sat down as comfortably as she could. Then Dick got in; initially he was going to fly the plane and was responsible for taking off. All was finally ready and Dick started up the engines. The flight of the Voyager had begun.

Jeana's eyes were glued on the instruments as the glittering white aircraft with its long, drooping wings very slowly began to move forward. They had never flown with so much fuel on board before and the plane seemed incredibly heavy. Finally, they began to pick up speed, and on and on they went, with the runway flashing past faster and faster below them. Still they were on the ground, though, and the people watching started to get nervous. A lot of the fuel had been stored in special tanks in the wings, and now they were completely full, the weight was dragging the wings down. As they accelerated up the runway, the tips of the wings started to flex up and down, and as they sank, they began to scrape along the ground. Then small sections of the end of each wingtip started to chip off as the plane gathered speed. The long runway was also beginning to run out too. Dick and Jeana became very aware that it could all end in a sudden disaster before they even took off.

Finally, though, as the speed steadily increased, the long wings started to flatten out and lift as they grabbed into the air, and then, as the small crowd of onlookers held its breath, the big white Voyager finally rose, quietly and majestically, into the sky.

Checking the broken ends of their wingtips, and reading all the instruments, Dick and Jeana hesitated. This was the time to go back if they weren't happy about anything. It was tempting; did they really want to go through with this long, very risky voyage? Everything looked OK, though; the plane was flying well. The decision was made. They would go. They slowly turned the Voyager and started to head west, soon reaching the coast. Now, levelling out at around 7,000ft and flying out over the Pacific, the couple felt they really were on their way. The journey had begun.

They picked up some good tail winds and started to settle into a routine. Changing pilots was a real struggle in such a cramped space, but they each needed to take turns at the controls so that the other could try and rest. On the control panel, they taped a strip of paper marked with the days so they could tick them off; flying night and day across the world meant time would soon cease to have any real meaning.

The little lightweight aircraft was unlike modern aeroplanes and could not climb high enough to avoid the worst weather. Soon they were flying into problems. Seeing big cumulus clouds ahead, they gently turned to go around them. As they bounced through the edges of a storm, the Voyager handled well. Speed was good; engine temperature, fuel, it was all looking as it should.

On and on the Voyager went. Generally flying at between 5,000 and 10,000ft, they were averaging around 115mph. They had around 26,000 miles to cover; it was going to be one very long flight. Inside the tiny cockpit, the conditions were hot and extremely cramped; in the small 3ft-wide space behind the pilot's seat, trying to stretch out for some intermittent sleep was almost impossible. The physical problems of spending time in such a tiny cockpit were huge. An aluminium pee tube had been organised to be lowered from the bottom of the aircraft, connected to a funnel behind the pilot's seat. An antiseptic liquid had been brought on board to try to keep things clean. Rations had been limited to what was necessary to keep them healthy. Even water was in pre-measured packets. Jeana planned to live mainly on crackers and peanut butter, with fruit juices, shakes and other meal plans to keep them going.

And on they flew. The autopilot gave them both time off, but constant monitoring was still necessary in this experimental aircraft.

After nearly twenty-four hours' flying, they reached Hawaii, where some friends took off to meet them and fly alongside for a little while; Jeana felt good to have human contact so near. Then off they went again, all alone as they headed into the dark western sky. That night they flew through turbulence that was enough to ruin any chance of sleep, not just from the shaking but also from a nagging fear that the lightweight aircraft might not be able to withstand such a constant battering. Looking out at the long, narrow wings and watching how they flexed up and down in the gusty air was very frightening. Just one crack, just one small fracture in the wrong place, and that would be the end of the plane and their lives.

The new materials were, however, turning out to be as good as they promised, and on and on they went. While Dick was flying, Jeana was not only monitoring the systems, but recording speeds, positions, engine performance and a fuel log. Checking the oil system was also crucial and sometimes it had to be replenished, which took twenty minutes of hard hand pumping from an awkward position.

As they crossed the dateline, right in the middle of the Pacific Ocean, a pointer handle fell off one of their instruments and just sat there at the bottom of the casing. This dial had given back-up information to help calculate how much fuel they had left, a critical aspect of the trip. After some minutes of anxiety, though, both of them decided there was nothing to be done, so they taped over the gauge and just got on with the job of flying to the constant horizon far out in the west.

After forty-eight hours of non-stop flying, they hit bad weather and learned that Typhoon Marge was just ahead of them. They tried to avoid the worst of the conditions, but at one point the little aircraft was being bounced around and the tips of its long, flimsy wings were rising and sinking dramatically. Jeana started to seriously worry. Could the aircraft's innovative, lightweight materials withstand this new, really violent battering? Whatever her fears, stuck in their tiny, enclosed cabin, there was no option but to carry on. Controlling the aircraft became a struggle in such turbulent conditions. The constant movement made it even harder for Jeana and Dick to change positions, and even when they made it into the little space behind the pilot's seat, there was no real rest for either of them. In such a cramped position and against the constant throbbing of the engines, a period of good sleep was almost impossible. Tiredness, worry and physical discomfort started to take their toll.

As they headed into their fourth day in the air, they crossed the north of Malaysia and motored on through another band of rough weather to Sri Lanka and the Arabian Sea.

Now they were beginning to worry about the performance of the plane and especially about their fuel consumption. Both Dick and Jeana had noticed what looked like fuel streaming from the cap of the left-tip tank; what other problems were there? If only they knew exactly how much fuel they had left on board.

After more hours of steady flying, both Jeana and Dick felt the plane was flying at a different weight than the numbers showed. Certainly the rate of climb they could achieve didn't fit in with their weight calculations. They were both getting tired; had they made a mistake with their numbers? How much fuel did they really have left? Communication wasn't always easy and, apart from giving weather forecasts, there was little anyone on the ground could have done anyway, except check the figures Jeana and Dick sent back.

At the little control office at Mojave's airfield in California, tensions were rising. The big support team were trying to help all they could, preparing graphs and tables and various what-if scenarios. They concluded that the Voyager did not have enough fuel left to fly across Africa and potential landing sites were talked about. But Dick's brother Burt wasn't happy with the number crunching they were doing and felt they had been sent the wrong numbers.

No definite plan of action resulted from the information Dick and Jeana were managing to send back, so the Voyager simply went on.

There were many challenging moments as Jeana and Dick continued to head steadily west. There were hiccups in the equipment, panics over fuel consumption and bad thunderstorms. To clear mountain ranges in Uganda and other areas of Africa meant the aircraft had to climb to 15,000ft, and it was a struggle to coax the plane up to reach that height; flying now with oxygen masks added another layer of difficulty. Still they headed on, the sturdy engines continuing to hum, driving the little white aircraft steadily through the air. Hypoxia and fatigue were beginning to hit both Jeana and Dick; at one time, with a pounding head and watering eyes, Jeana was sick into a little bag, but still she kept flying. Dick, suffering from lack of sleep, was struggling to concentrate on anything.

Things were now becoming very hard, far more challenging than either of them had imagined, but there was no let-up. They crossed the west African coast and then levelled out at around 7,000ft over the stormy Atlantic Ocean. Looking down, they could see the grey, turbulent water just below them. Nothing else was in sight. They simply had to keep going. On the eighth day of the journey, after 184 hours of constant flying, with the engines still purring their familiar sound and with the Voyager's elongated, thin wings stretching far out each side of their little home, Dick and Jean finally spotted a coastline in the distance. Costa Rica. They had at last made it back at least to the American continent.

Hope and optimism rallied them. They didn't dare even think about home; they just kept flying, swapping positions, making themselves eat some food and drink some water, both of them fixed on the one idea of simply getting back and completing the trip. The constant worry was their fuel supply; in their over-tired state, they really were losing track of what was left. Radioing back all the information they had from their instruments, they received encouraging messages from the team waiting for them at Mojave. It was clear that both Jeana and Dick, in their state of exhaustion, were on the verge of not being able to go on. As their concerns grew, they even shut one engine down; the little plane could still fly, and with luck they might conserve enough fuel to get back.

Luck, though, was running out. Heading up the California coast, with only about five hours to go, new information from their instruments confirmed the increasingly lightweight feel of the engine; the fuel supply was now at a critical level. There was one final step they could take, and this was to use up the small amounts left in the very bottom of the fuel tanks. They decided to try and draw this through. They weren't certain it would work and it was a difficult job. Switching the final valve, there was a panicky moment when nothing happened. Then trickles of fuel started to flow.

Now optimism returned. All they needed was 125 litres to get back; there might be enough. The Voyager and its two exhausted pilots continued to head north through the night until dawn began to lighten the eastern sky.

At 7.30 a.m. on 23 December 1986, the Voyager appeared above Edwards Air Force Base in California. Jeana and Dick hadn't thought about their return or any sort of welcome; in their worn-out state, all they could think about was getting home and trying to put the plane down safely. But as they approached the airfield, the sun was shining down on a massive crowd and a collection of cars, motorhomes and other vehicles, all congregating in the area. Traffic was still backing up, trying to approach the airfield as Dick and Jeana got ready to land. The crowds meant nothing to them; it took all their effort and concentration to continue to fly the aircraft. They hadn't landed it before with so little fuel; the plane was now so light it almost floated. They were worried that, in their exhausted state, their height perception might be faulty. It would be dreadful if, after virtually completing the flight, they made a hash of the landing. Steadily they lowered their landing gear and locked it; they were ready.

Keeping the plane as steady as possible, slowly, slowly, they turned the Voyager towards the airfield and started to descend. 1,000ft, 500ft, 300ft, 200ft – the crowd went silent as the elegant white aircraft steadily approached the runway. 100ft, 50ft, 15ft; suddenly the wheels were down and the flimsy aircraft rolled gently to a halt. After a flight of 24,987 miles, taking nine days, three minutes and forty-four seconds, Jeana and Dick had achieved the first ever non-stop, non-refuelled flight around the world.

As Jeana tried to get out of the aircraft, she found her legs were rubbery and shaky. She also felt woozy. She sat down for a while on the fuselage, trying to pretend everything was normal. What was wrong? With so many people looking on and cheering, this was really embarrassing. She managed to wave to the crowd, and then slowly stood up. Both Dick and Jeana were having problems, but helpers and medical staff rushed up and they were quickly taken to waiting ambulances. At the nearby hospital, they underwent some immediate checks; Jeana had lost 9lb, about 10 per cent of her bodyweight, in the nine-day flight.

After two hours of medical help and tests and then a shower, Jeana and Dick both felt much better. They were cleared by the doctors and felt well enough to face the media and attend the big reception put on by family and friends. Dick's brother was included, of course; it really was a team of three that had got this idea off the ground. Jeana and Dick were astonished to learn that millions had watched their landing on television and that interest in their flight was international. It took a while for them to realise what they had achieved; the world record they had dreamed of, had worked so hard for, had been accomplished. They had done it! Within Earth's atmosphere, Jeana had become the first woman ever to travel around the world non-stop.

In the meantime, over in Sydney, Australia, Kay Cottee was still in the final stages of pursuing her dream of sailing around the world. For Kay, it hardly resonated that an American had just beaten her to achieve the first non-stop circumnavigation by a woman. Kay wasn't looking for fame and glory; her motivation was the challenge of doing something on her own, of using her skills for a real achievement.

Kay's introduction to sailing had started almost immediately after she was born, when her parents took her onto their boat to have fun sailing around Sydney harbour. As she grew up, Kay had spent all her free time sailing, first in small dinghies and then on larger boats. School work, friends and family all played a part in her young life, but for Kay there was nothing quite as good as being out on the water. After she was married, together with her husband she built a boat. After they separated, Kay joined her sister who ran a yacht charter company. By the time Kay reached her thirties, she still loved the freedom of being on the water, but she was, by now, also a hugely knowledgeable yachtswoman.

The idea of long-distance sailing first gripped her when she took part in a Solo Trans-Tasman Race from New Zealand to Sydney. It was then that she started thinking seriously about doing a long ocean trip, and this quickly developed into an idea of going round the world; not a normal round-the-world sailing trip either, but a solo non-stop trip. The challenge of doing something no other woman had done before appealed to her. She had spent so much time on the water, she had already sailed through storms and knockdowns, she had been involved in repairs and refitting on all sorts of yachts; her knowledge and experience were extensive. Kay had a close friend who encouraged her and soon her mind was made up.

Like Jeana, it took Kay a long time and a lot of work to find a sponsor, but eventually her boat, *Blackmore's First Lady*, was ready. Kay also spent a great deal of time on planning; she believed that really detailed preparation would be the key to success on the voyage. One problem, of course, was food; no fresh food would last the six months or more that the non-stop voyage was expected to take. Kay tasted and tested all kinds of dried and tinned foods before she sorted out what to take. Her attention to detail was immense. She even enrolled on an evening self-defence course in case she came into contact with rogue sailors or pirates; out on the ocean there would be no help on hand for a lone woman. Once her friends and family knew Kay was serious, they rallied around to give her as much support as possible. Finally, in the Australian spring of 1987, 33-year-old Kay felt everything had been done. She was ready for the trip.

On Sunday, 29 November 1987, just a year after Jeana had touched down in California, and in a flood of sudden tears as she said a mass of goodbyes, Kay set off across Sydney harbour and out to sea. Turning south-east, she headed off towards the southernmost tip of New Zealand. She was on her way.

Kay's challenges were very different from Jeana's and on a few occasions she was in real fear for her life.

Just four days out to sea, Kay found out that rogue waves really do exist. The weather had deteriorated and suddenly Kay heard a huge roaring noise from behind, so loud it deafened all other noises. Looking back, she saw the largest wave she had ever seen, with a top that was foaming and breaking. Surging towards her, it collapsed onto her little boat with a huge crash, slewing it sideways and then rolling it onto the side, with the mast horizontal to the waves. Down in the cabin, Kay clung on tightly while the water crashed the boat around and everything tumbled about; it seemed forever before her sturdy little boat straightened up.

Luckily there was little damage apart from a lot of cleaning up to do. It shook Kay a little, such a drama so early in the trip, but Kay just put it behind her as one of those things and carried on, continually adjusting the sails in the changing conditions. The rogue wave had caused one key problem, though: the surging water had swept the wind generator away, so from that early stage in the voyage Kay had to be careful to conserve power.

Heading into the southern latitudes, the weather continued to deteriorate. By Christmas Day it was raining and also blowing 60 knots, generating enormous waves. Kay started the day after just two hours' sleep by struggling up on deck to further reduce and adjust the sails; then she spent an hour below, bailing out the bilge. The vessel was continuing to fill with water and she never did find out the cause. With a weather report warning of another violent storm ahead, Kay turned the little boat to the north to try to avoid the worst of the gale.

Approaching Cape Horn in mid-January, bad weather came in with a vengeance. Kay estimated the waves again to be 50 or 60ft high. At one point she was going so fast that she felt she was out of control. Huge waves were approaching her from the stern and she had serious fears about being pitchpoled, with the stern rising up so steeply that it might somersault the boat. The little boat, though, despite its violent motion, managed to keep afloat and ride it out. There was little respite for Kay as she alternated between being soaked and blown about on deck and struggling below for a short spell to try to dry out, complete her log, eat some food or even get some sleep in the violently rocking cabin.

In calmer moments, there were urgent maintenance jobs to do. Kay started a test of the engine to find smoke pouring out. It took Kay two hours to discover that the insulation around the main power cable to the starter motor had chafed through. It was a major job, but Kay repaired it.

It had been a long, hard, physically exhausting three-month sail from Sydney, but at last, as she headed north-east into the southern Atlantic, the weather eased off. By the end of February, Kay was at last enjoying perfect sailing conditions in warm weather. She could sleep on deck as the boat sailed steadily along, ever eastward.

Even good weather, though, was not without problems, and one day, along with several dolphins, she spotted two huge whales heading directly towards her. She quickly turned the boat and the whales dived down and disappeared. Then, just after the scare from the whales, she woke up with a badly swollen knee and couldn't bend her leg. She had no idea what had caused it. Worries and problems were coming non-stop.

Now, as she headed towards the Cape of Good Hope at the southern tip of Africa, she was reaching busier shipping lanes. Collision at sea is a serious hazard and Kay took to scanning the horizon every thirty minutes, which meant constantly interrupted sleep. But sometimes the journey nevertheless became enjoyable. Some nights, with a flat sea and no wind or moon, the sky seemed totally filled with the light from millions of shining stars, light that was reflected in the mirror ocean below. It was the most stunning sight. Kay was also pleased she was coping with the isolation well; spending months alone at sea can play havoc with the mind, but Kay found she was dealing with it fine.

Another good thing was the autohelm, which was working well, especially in reasonable weather. Good conditions, though, never lasted long and soon Kay was back up on deck, battling to change sails and keep direction in increasing winds.

As Kay headed south again, in huge ocean swells, she faced more knockdowns, one tipping the mast well underwater. Each time the little boat righted itself quickly, although the mess in the cabin took a lot of clearing up. One evening, Kay was down in the cabin when she heard a tremendous roar and the bow of the boat started rising – and rising. It rose higher and higher, until the boat was almost vertical before it finally began to level out. Kay, wedging herself and hanging on tightly, realised with horror that she was completely out of the water. She braced herself as the boat came down, and waited. It seemed like forever, but finally the boat landed, hitting the bottom of the trough with an ear-splitting crash. Amazingly, the boat had remained balanced and landed well, causing little serious damage.

Then came a sailor's worst nightmare. In turbulent seas, at the top of a swell, Kay spotted the lights of another boat. As it got nearer, she could see it was a big boat and it was heading straight for her. The boat just kept on coming, and now it was near enough to see the great steel structure of a large ship, lurching closer into view on the top of a wave before it disappeared again into a deep trough. Terrified of a collision, she grabbed a flare and set it off. Finally, the large ship lumbered pass just 300yds away.

The day was not over as, very soon after this scare, Kay suffered another knockdown. As the boat recovered, Kay finally felt she could take no more and, down in the little cabin, she collapsed onto her narrow bunk, thinking about the vulnerability of life. Trying to keep dry, making sure she ate and drank and got some sleep, checking weather and navigation, continually on the go, looking after the boat and the sails, Kay had finally run out of both mental and physical energy.

In the middle of the southern Indian Ocean, miles from land, there was no way out, no easy coast to pull into; Kay knew she simply had to find the strength to keep going. As the little boat sailed sturdily on, Kay regained her drive and was soon back in control. On she went and at last, after many weeks and many dramas, she sailed into Australian waters. Keeping well south of the land, radio communication now became clearer and easier, and Kay could at last chat confidently to her team and to her family. At last, Kay could dream of being home. The final days and hours went agonizingly slowly, though, as she started to reach the familiar waters of south-east Australia.

On 5 June 1988, after 24,000 nautical miles and 189 days and 32 minutes, and amid a welcome from hundreds of little boats with noisy sirens going off, Kay sailed her 37ft yacht back into Sydney's Watson Bay and crossed the finish line.

Now, like Jeana, she was greeted with a huge reception and awards. Being the first woman to sail non-stop around the world was a magnificent achievement. She too had completed her dream.

Both Jeana and Kay spent the months following their trips attending receptions, receiving numerous awards and giving talks right around the world. It was a heady and busy time for both of them as they finally recovered from their amazing and exhausting voyages; it was a shame they didn't meet, as they would have had a lot to talk about.

After that, both women were happy to move on. The non-stop voyages had been successful, but enormously challenging. By the late 1980s, both women were looking for a new life.

For Jeana, having spent so many years with Dick, after the flight around the world they finally decided to go their separate ways. Jeana wanted to pursue her idea of flying helicopters and she still loved her horses and had a plan to start harness racing. A more reserved person than Dick, she had found the media attention and having to speak to large groups difficult, and she wanted a quieter, less public life. In 1994 she married again, to another pilot who also shared Jeana's love of animals, and Jeana was happy to return to her home region in Texas to devote herself to horses.

Kay established her own boat-charter business and also became a motivational speaker. After marrying a television producer, she moved up the east Australian coast, where she continued working with boats but also took time to enjoy her hobbies of painting and sculpting.

Jeana and Kay's non-stop voyages marked the end of an era for women circumnavigators. After over 200 years of trailblazing, women had travelled around the Earth by sea, by land and in the sky. As the 1990s came in, things were changing fast. The world appeared to be getting smaller; new technology was progressing at lightning speed, providing huge advantages from new types of engines and equipment to satellite and computer communications, micro weather forecasting and even electronically warmed clothing.

For travellers today, it is a very different world from the rugged, dramatic and quite often life-threatening journeys of yesteryear. In more recent years, women have walked, driven and flown enormous distances. Women have rowed across oceans and skied across Antarctica. Nothing, however, in the modern era can take away the extraordinary achievements of these early women, who completed real firsts in global circumnavigation in such different times.

BIBLIOGRAPHY

BOOKS

Baker, Aloha Wanderwell, *Call to Adventure!* (West Hartford, CT: Boyd Production Group, 2013)
Begin-Kruysman, Lisa, *Around the World in 1909* (Staunton, VA: American History Press, 2014)
Birkett, Dea, *Spinsters Abroad: Victorian Lady Explorers* (Stroud: Sutton Publishing, 2004)
Bly, Nellie, *Around the World in 72 Days* (New York: Pictorial Weeklies, 1890)
Botting, Douglas, *Dr Eckener's Dream Machine* (London: HarperCollins, 2001)
Brook, Margaret, *My Life in Sarawak* (London: Methuen & Co., 1913)
Bruce, the Hon. Mrs Victor, *Nine Lives Plus* (London: Pelham Books, 1977)
Bullock, John, *Fast Women* (London: Robson Books, 2002)
Clayton, Nick, *The Birth of the Bicycle* (Stroud: Amberley Publishing, 2016)
Clode, Danielle, *The Woman who Sailed the World* (Sydney: Picador, 2020)
Coleman, Deirdre, *Maiden Voyages and Infant Colonies* (London: Leicester University Press, 1999)
Conquest, Robert, *The Great Terror: Stalin's Purge of the Thirties* (London: Bodley Head, 2013)
Dear, Ian, *Great Ocean Liners* (London: Batsford, 1991)
Dick, Harold G. and Robinson, Douglas H., *Golden Age of the Great Passenger Ships: Graf Zeppelin and Hindenburg* (Washington, DC: Smithsonian Books, 1985)
Edington, Sarah, *The Captain's Table* (London: Conway, 2011)
Erickson, Carolly, *The Girl from Botany Bay* (Hoboken, NJ: Wiley, 2004)
Friss, Evan, *The Cycling City: Bicycles and Urban American in the 1890s* (Chicago, IL: University of Chicago Press, 2015)
Garrioch, David, *Neighbourhood and Community in Paris, 1740–1790* (Cambridge: Cambridge University Press, 1986)
Gillen, Mollie, *The Founders of Australia* (Sydney: Library of Australian History, 1989)
Goldman, Wendy Z., *Women at the Gates: Gender and Industry in Stalin's Russia* (Cambridge: Cambridge University Press, 2002)

Goodman, Matthew, *Eighty Days* (New York: Ballantine Books, 2013)
Hanbury-Tenison, Robin, *The Great Explorers* (London: Thames & Hudson, 2010)
Hartley, Janet M., *Siberia: A History of the People* (New Haven, CT: Yale University Press, 2014)
Hill-Murphy, Jacki, *The Life and Travels of Isabella Bird* (Barnsley: Pen & Sword History, 2021)
Hunt, St John, *Dutch South Africa: Early Settlers at the Cape 1652–1708* (Kibworth: Matador, 2005)
Innis, Harold Adams, *History of the Canadian Pacific Railway* (Newton Abbot: David & Charles, 1972)
Kruysman, Lisa Begin, *Around the World in 1909* (Staunton, VA: American History Press, 2014)
Letofsky, Polly, *3 MPH* (Denver, CO: Global Walk Inc., 2010)
Lothian, Antonella, *Valentina* (Edinburgh: Pentland Press, 1993)
Lovell, Julia, *The Opium War: Drugs, Dreams and the Making of China* (London: Picador, 2012)
MacKenzie, Charlotte, *Mary Ann Parker Origins* (Raleigh, NC: Lulu, 2022)
McIlrath, Darwin, *On Wheels Around the World* (Chicago, IL: Inter Ocean, 1898)
Meakin, A., *A Ribbon of Iron* (London: Archibald Constable & Co., 1901; reprinted by Forgotten Books, London, 2018)
Meakin, A., *Hannah More* (London: Smith, Elder & Co., 1911)
Morningstar, James Kelly, *War and Resistance in the Philippines* (Annapolis, MD: Naval Institute Press, 2021)
O'Rourke, Shane, *The Cossacks* (Manchester: Manchester University Press, 2007)
Parker, Mary Ann, *A Voyage Round the World* (London: John Nichol, 1795; accessible version thanks to Cambridge University Press, Cambridge, 2010)
Payne, Michelle, *Marianne North* (London: Kew Publishing, 2011)
Pfeiffer, Ida, *A Woman's Journey Round the World* (London: Petter, Duff & Co., 1852)
Pfeiffer, Ida, *The Last Travels of Ida Pfeiffer* (Salt Lake City, UT: Project Gutenberg Literary Archive Foundation; online retrieval www.gutenberg.org, 2023)
Preston, Diana, *A Brief History of the Boxer Rebellion* (London: Robinson, 2002)
Reis, Professor João José, *Slave Rebellion in Brazil* (Baltimore, MD: John Hopkins University Press, 1993)
Ridley, Glynis, *The Discovery of Jeanne Baret* (New York: Broadway Paperbacks, 2010)
Robinson, Jane, *Wayward Women: A Guide to Women Travellers* (Oxford: Oxford University Press, 1991)
Ross, Michael, *World of Her Own* (Chicago, IL: Chicago Review Press, 2014)
Ross, Robert, *Status and Respectability in the Cape Colony, 1750–1870* (Cambridge: Cambridge University Press, 1999)
Runciman, Steven, *The White Rajah: A History of Sarawak from 1841 to 1946* (Cambridge: Cambridge University Press, 1960)
Salmond, Anne, *Aphrodite's Island: The European Discovery of Tahiti* (Oakland, CA: University of California Press, 2009)
Sheehan, Laurie, *Mary Bryant, the Convict Girl* (Kinloss: Librario, 2006)

Smith, S.A., *Russia in Revolution* (Oxford: Oxford University Press, 2017)
Tench, Watkin, *Sydney's First Four Years* (Canberra: Library of Australian History, 1983)
Tereshkova, Valentina, *The First Lady of Space* (Bethesda, MD: International Space Business Council, 2015)
Van Wyhe, John, *Wanderlust* (Singapore: NUS Press, 2019)
Welsh, Frank, *A History of Hong Kong* (London: HarperCollins, 2010)
White Fisher, Harriet, *A Woman's World Tour in a Motor* (Philadelphia, PA: J.B. Lippincott, 1911; reprinted by Forgotten Books, London, 2018)
Wood, Michael, *The Story of China* (London: Simon & Schuster, 2020)
Yey, Wen-Hsin, *Shanghai Splendour: The Making of Modern China* (Berkeley, CA: University of California Press, 2007)
Zheutlin, Peter, *Around the World on Two Wheels: Annie Londonderry* (New York: Citadel Press, 2007)

ARCHIVES, OFFICIAL BODIES AND COLLECTIONS

Airship Heritage Trust
Ancestry UK
Australian Association of Maritime History
Austrian National Library, Vienna (Austria)
Bodleian Library, Oxford
Bridgeport History Center, Connecticut (USA)
British Library
British Museum
British Newspaper Archive
British Pathé
California Historical Society, San Francisco (USA)
Chicago Cycling Club (USA)
Chicago History Museum (USA)
Cuyahoga County Archives, Ohio (USA)
Defiance Development and Visitors Bureau, Ohio (USA)
De Montfort University Archives, Leicester
English Heritage
First Fleet Heritage, Ocean Grove, Victoria (Australia)
Golden Eagle Luxury Trains
Hoover Institution Library, Stanford University, California (USA)
Housman Society, Bewdley
Institute for English and American Studies, University of Rostock (Germany)
Institute of Historical Research, University of London
Justus Liebig University Giessen (Germany)
Library of Congress, Washington (USA)
Library of the University of French Polynesia
Lloyd Sealy Library, New York (USA)

MacOdrum Library, Ottawa (Canada)
National Army Museum
National Association of Cape Horners
National Geographical Society, Washington (USA)
National Historical Museum of Brazil
National Library of Australia
National Library of France, Paris (France)
National Library of Mauritius, Port Louis
National Museum of History, Seychelles
National Museum of the American Indian, Washington (USA)
Naval Historical Society of Australia
Naval Museum, Madrid (Spain)
Navy Records Society
P&O Heritage/DP World
Royal Geographical Society
Royal Museums Greenwich
Sarawak Heritage Society, Kuching (Malaysia)
Sea Museum, Sydney (Australia)
Smithsonian National Air and Space Museum, Washington (USA)
Society for Geography in Berlin (Germany)
State Library Victoria, Melbourne (Australia)
The National Archives
The Times Archive
Trenton City Museum, New Jersey (USA)
University of London Institute of Historical Research
University of Melbourne (Australia)
University of Pennsylvania (USA)
University of Pisa (Italy)
University of Rostock (Germany)
Wren Library, Trinity College, Cambridge
Zeppelin Luftschifftechnik GmbH, Friedrichshafen (Germany)

INDEX

Ainu families 147
Alexander III, Emperor of Russia 133
Armenia 56
Australian Aboriginal people 36, 42–4

B50 Superfortress 230
Baret, Jeanne 11–35
Batang Lupar river, Sarawak (Malaysia) 73
Batavia (Jakarta), Indonesia 29, 45, 47, 73
Bennelong, Woollarawarre 43, 50
Benz, Karl 151
Berchtold, Count Leopold 60, 61
Bisland, Elizabeth 89–106
Blackfoot First Nation 148
Blackmore's First Lady 243
Blackwell Island Asylum for the Insane 88
Blagovestchensk 13, 144–5, 147
Blau gas 184
Blériot, Louis 159
Bly, Nellie 87–106
Bombay (Mumbai) 160–1
Boxer Rebellion 117, 130, 145
Bound feet, Chinese children 54, 68
Botany Bay 36
Bougainville, Louis-Antoine de 17, 22, 24, 27, 29–30
Bougainvillea plant 24
Bougainville Reef 28
Brooke, Sir James 72–3
Brooks, Harold 156–73, 175

Bryant, Mary 48, 52
Budgett, Samuel 130

Calcutta (Kolkata) 95, 123, 167–8
Canadian Pacific Railway 148
Canton (Guangzhou) 54, 66, 68, 98
Cape of Good Hope 39, 178, 246
Cape Horn 45–6, 245
Cape Town 39, 41, 47–9, 72
Cawnpore (Kanpur) 164
Ceylon (Sri Lanka) 94, 100, 170
Chicago 104, 109, 127
China Sea 91, 97
Chinese Imperial Army 145
Cockerill, Colonel 87–8
Commerson, Philibert 13–31
Compagnie Internationale des Wagon-Lits 134
Convicts 39–40
Cook, James 36
Coolidge, President Calvin 187
Corcovado mountain 61
Cossacks 134, 144
Cottee, Kay 243–8
Curtiss, Glenn 174

Daily Express 182–3
Danube river 56
Darjeeling 169–70
Darwin, Charles 51
De la Giraudais, François 22
Diego Ramirez Islands 46
Dirnböck, Jakob 57

Dordogne 34–5
Droshky carriage 135
Drummond Hay, Lady Grace 176–200
Drummond Hay, Sir Robert 180, 182–3
Dubernat, Jean 33–4
Dyaks 72–4

Eckener, Hugo 186–97
Eora People 43
Equator, Crossing the Line 23

Fairfax Plantation 89
First Fleet 38, 41–2, 48
First Fleet Marines 44
Fisher, Clark 153
Fisher, Harriet White 151–75
Fleet debtors' prison 51
Fowler bicycles 111
French East India Company 30
Friedrichshafen 185, 188, 191

Gagarin, Yuri 215, 219
Ghengis Khan 142
Graf Zeppelin 183–5, 188–98
Great Barrier Reef 28, 47
Great Exhibition 71
Great Trunk Road 123
Guangzhou (Canton) 54, 66, 68, 98
Gweagal People 36

Hakone, Japan 172
Hearst Corporation 184–8, 191, 195–9
Hearst, William Randolph 187–9, 191
Hindenburg 177
Holy Land 55–7
Hong Kong 66, 96, 98, 100
Hornos Island 46
Housman, A. E. 130

Ile d'Aix 21
Inter Ocean Newspaper 109, 111–14, 123–7

Jakarta (Batavia) 29, 45, 47, 73
Jardin des Plantes, Paris 15

Kanpur (Cawnpore) 164
Khrushchev, Nikita 224–5
King, Captain Gidley 38
Knox-Johnson, Sir Robin 230
Kolkata (Calcutta) 95, 123, 167–8
Komsomol 213, 215
Korolev, Sergei 215, 220, 225
Kusaka, Lt. Cdr. Ryunosuke 125
Kyrkyz people 136

La Commelle 12
Lakehurst 189
Lethbridge, Alice 178
Livingstone, David 70
Locomobile Type 1 155
Londonderry, Annie 108

Madagascar 75
Manchu people 144–5
Maulboyheenner 52
Mauritius 29–30, 75–6
Maybach engines 184
McIlrath, Hattie 107–28
Meakin, Annette 129–50
Missionaries 54
Mojave 232, 240–1
Moluccan Islands 29
Mongols 142
Montevideo 25
Moscow 135

Nanking, Treaty of 66
Napoleon 53–4
Nehru, Judge Motilal 165
Neptune 40
New Orleans 89–90
New York Cosmopolitan 91–2, 98–102
New York World newspaper 87–94, 97, 98, 101, 104
Nord Express 134

Oakley, Annie 109
Occidental and Oriental Steamship Company 96, 100
Opium wars 54, 66, 114
Origin of Species 51

Paris 15
Papeete 28, 65
Parker, Mary Jane 36–52
Parramatta 44
Patagonians 26
Pearl Harbour 199
Pearl River 67
Persepolis 124
Petropolis 61–2
Pfeiffer, Ida 53–76
Poivre, Pierre 30–1
Polynesia 27
Pontianak River 72, 74
Port Jackson (Sydney) 38, 41, 44–5, 48
Port Louis 31, 33
Puri people 63

Rawlinson, Henry 69
Rio de Janeiro 24, 59, 61, 64
Rochefort 20
Royal Collection 18
Royal College of Music 130
Rutan Aircraft Factory 232
Rutan, Dick 232–42, 248

Saint-Aulaye 35
Saint-Foy-la-Grande 34
Santo Tomas Internment Camp 199
Sarawak 72
Second Fleet 40
Seng chee 116
Shanghai 114–15, 199
Ships:
    Augusta Victoria 91, 93
    Boudeuse 19, 24
    Empress of Japan 147
    Etoile 19, 21–2, 24, 26
    HMS *Bounty* 47–8
    HMS *Gorgon* 37–9, 52
    John Renwick 64
    P&O *Britannia* 100
    P&O *Oriental* 94–6
    P&O *Victoria* 94

Sirius 86
SS *Great Western* 86
SS *Gripsholm* 199
SS *Oceanic* 98, 100
Siberia, Russia 130
Siberian Express 132–3, 135
Singapore 68, 72, 96, 100
Slaves 24, 40, 49, 60
Spratt's pet food 178
Sri Lanka (Ceylon) 94, 100, 170
Stalin, Joseph 210–11
Star City 216, 218, 226, 228
Statue of Christ 24
Straits of Magellan 26
Sugarloaf Mountain 24, 59
Sydney (Port Jackson) 41, 243–4, 247

Tahiti 27, 47, 65–6
Tarantass carriage 139
Tartars 138
Tenerife 39
Tereshkova, Valentina 209–28
Thomas Cook 92
Timor 48
Tolstoy, Leo 148, 212
Toulon-Sur-Arrout 12–13
Tunnerminnerwait 52

Valparaiso 64–5
Vanderbilt Cup Race 155
Vienna 53–6, 70–1, 75–6, 182
Vladivostok 132, 143, 146–7
Von Humboldt, Alexander 58
Von Metternich, Prince 69
Von Weigand, Karl 177, 181–7, 191–8
Von Zepperlin, Count 178
Vostok 6 spacecraft 218–20
Voyager aircraft 233–42

Yangtze river 115
Yeager, Jeana Lee 230–48
Yunnan Province 121

BY THE SAME AUTHOR

978 1 80399 154 2

'A real celebration of the women who defied tradition and followed their dreams into the sky. Readable and entertaining, this book is a worthy tribute to Britain's woman aviation pioneers.'

Sharon Nicholson FRAeS,
Chairwoman of the British
Women Pilots' Association

The destination for history
www.thehistorypress.co.uk